Return
Of The King

Return
Of The
King

ELVIS PRESLEY'S GREAT COMEBACK

Gillian G. Gaar

Return Of The King

ELVIS PRESLEY'S GREAT COMEBACK

Gillian G. Gaar

A GENUINE JAWBONE BOOK
First Edition 2010
Published in the UK and the USA by Jawbone Press
2a Union Court,
20–22 Union Road,
London SW4 6JP,
England
www.jawbonepress.com

ISBN 978-1-906002-28-2

DESIGN Paul Cooper Design
EDITOR John Morrish

Printed by Wai Man Book Binding (China) Ltd

1 2 3 4 5 14 13 12 11 10

Contents

ABOVE: **Before buying a ranch in nearby Mississippi in early 1968, Elvis frequently rode horses around Graceland.** RIGHT: **The film** *Live A Little, Love A Little*, **released in October 1968, was an attempt to 'modernize' Elvis's film image.** OPPOSITE: **The stunning opening sequence of the** *Elvis* **television special.**

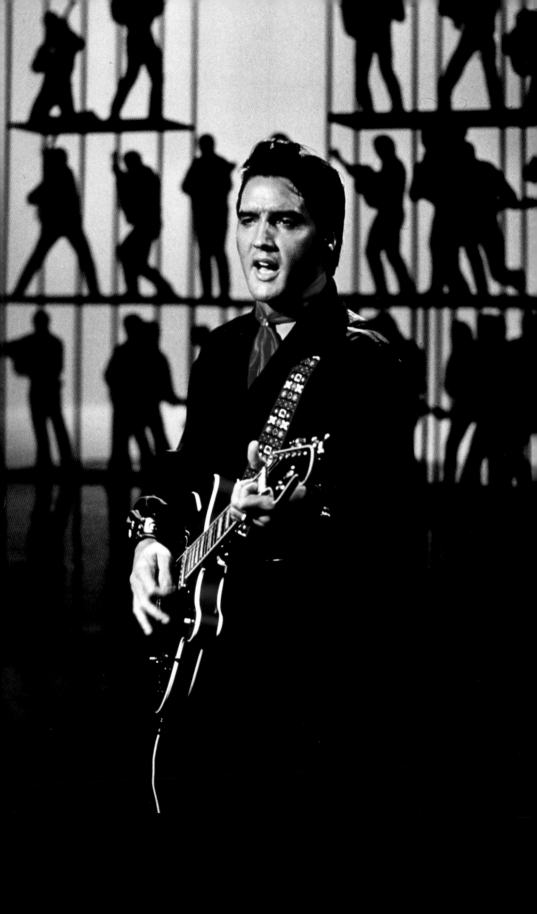

CLOCKWISE FROM LEFT: **Four images from the** *Elvis* **special: the 'stand-up' show, taped on June 29 1968; the 'bordello' sequence, with co-star Susan Henning, filmed on June 28; another view of the 'stand-up' performance; and the gospel sequence, also shot on the 28th.**
FOLLOWING SPREAD: **More from the 'stand-up' show.**

ABOVE: **On the set of** *Charro!*, **July 1968.** RIGHT: **A poster for** *Change Of Habit*, **Elvis's last dramatic film.** OPPOSITE: **Three shots from the press conference held at midnight on August 1 1969 to mark the start of Elvis's run of shows at the International Hotel, Las Vegas: Elvis with his father, Vernon Presley; and manager 'Colonel' Tom Parker in his 'Elvis International In Person' coat.**

MAIN PICTURE: **Elvis in performance at the International Hotel.** BELOW: **The marquee at the International.** RIGHT: **During filming of the documentary *Elvis: That's The Way It Is*, July 1970.**

LEFT: **In the dressing room with Sammy Davis Jr on the opening night of Elvis's third run in Las Vegas, August 10 1970.** ABOVE: **The President and the King, December 21 1970.** RIGHT: **The note Elvis sent to Nixon, giving instructions as to where he could be reached, under the pseudonym 'Jon Burrows.'**

WASHINGTON HOTEL) PHONE ME 85900
RM. 505-506.
UNDER THE NAME
OF JON BURROWS
PRIVATE
AND CONFIDENTIAL
Atten, President Nixon
via Sen George Murphy
from
Elvis Presley

"Do you believe in the afterlife?

Do you believe that there's more life coming?

I know generally the Southern way to think is that our personalities survive. That we continue on. You don't take your money and you don't take your fame, but who you are, the essence of who you are, lives on. If he believed that, maybe he'll get another chance to do something else. He lived his life and died his death just like he wanted to. He traded a normal life for 42 years of being Elvis, and I think he kinda knew what he was doing. And I think he loved being Elvis. Wouldn't you?"

WAYNE JACKSON *(The Memphis Horns)*

Prologue
Follow That Dream

On January 1 1967, a new contract went into effect between manager 'Colonel' Tom Parker, and his sole client, Elvis Presley. Parker (whose honorary title was bestowed on him in 1948 by Louisiana governor Jimmie Davis) was already receiving a 25 per cent commission on Presley's income from record and film deals; now, once the "basic payments" of those contracts had been satisfied, Parker would receive an additional 50 per cent cut of the royalties and profits, as well as 50 per cent on all side deals he could set up. It was an unashamed grab for a bigger piece of a profitable pie. But in truth, that pie had been steadily shrinking for some time.

Elvis's rise in the entertainment industry had been unprecedented. After a year and a half as a local, then regional, sensation in the American South (recording for Memphis-based Sun Records), he'd signed with RCA Records, releasing his first single for the label, 'Heartbreak Hotel,' in January 1956; by April, it had become his first million seller. Astounding success – and controversy – had followed, but Elvis's career had been put on hold when he was drafted and entered the army on March 24 1958. He wasn't completely forgotten during his two-year hitch – RCA continued issuing records, and *King Creole*, generally considered his best film, was released – but Elvis was understandably nervous about his career prospects when he was finally discharged from the service on March 5 1960. "When he came out of the army, he wasn't really sure that the public was going to take him back full with their arms wide open," says Gordon Stoker, a member of The Jordanaires, Elvis's longtime backing vocalists. "He was very leery."

But initially at least, all had gone well. Elvis's first post-army single, 'Stuck On You,' had been another million seller, and a string of successful singles followed; the next year and a half saw the release of hits like 'It's Now Or Never,' 'Are You Lonesome Tonight?,' '(Marie's The Name) His Latest Flame,' and 'Little Sister.' But there had also been a gradual career shift from music to movies as the decade progressed. Elvis had been anxious to establish himself as an actor, and his four pre-army films had laid the groundwork for what could have been a highly successful career. "He was good in the beginning," Julie Parrish, one of Elvis's co-stars in *Paradise, Hawaiian Style*, observed. "I think that he could've been a major star – the James Dean or Marlon Brando type."

He certainly exhibited the surliness – and the underlying vulnerability – of Dean and Brando in *Jailhouse Rock* and *King Creole*, the last two films he made before entering the service. But his first post-army film, the light comedy *G.I. Blues*, was a good deal more anodyne, casting Elvis as a soldier who bets his fellow GIs that he can 'score' with a nightclub dancer (played by Juliet Prowse). One scene features a limp re-recording of 'Blue Suede Shoes'; in another, Elvis is stuck babysitting a squalling infant. Truly, the one-time rebel had been tamed.

But the film was a success, and the soundtrack not only topped the charts, it sold twice as well as Elvis's first post-army album, *Elvis Is Back*, which was an excellent record that showcased both his versatility and his growing maturity as a vocalist. It was an ominous sign of the direction his career was about to take. Elvis's next two films gave him more dramatic roles, with minimal singing involved. In *Flaming Star*, he played the mixed-race son of a white father and Native American mother in the old West, at a time when friction between the two races is escalating, though the film's slow pace undercuts any sense of tension. *Wild In The Country* is a potboiler in the tradition of *Peyton Place*, with Elvis as a troubled young man trying to escape his small town environment, and romantic complications provided by a Good Girl (Millie Perkins), a Bad Girl (Tuesday Weld), and an Older Woman (Hope Lange).

Neither film did as well as *G.I. Blues*, and the success of Elvis's next movie, 1961's *Blue Hawaii*, his most successful film, set the template for the bulk of his cinematic career, its soundtrack staying at Number One for 20 weeks (all chart placings refer to the US charts, unless otherwise stated). His character is an ambitious young man, initially stymied in both his job prospects and his attempts to win the favors of his designated love interest – the kind of obstacles that are invariably overcome by the final reel. In *Blue Hawaii* his character's profession – an aspiring travel agent – was atypically genteel; in the future, he would generally be given a more 'manly' occupation, such as a boxer, race car driver, or pilot, who, naturally if somewhat improbably, also sings. Best of all, to Parker's way of thinking, the accompanying soundtracks provided the perfect cross-promotion; the films promoted the records, while the soundtracks promoted the films. By this logic, there was no need to release non-soundtrack recordings at all.

Unfortunately, it also put Elvis in a creative straitjacket. Though he'd been a movie fan since childhood, he was not especially enamored of musicals, tending to prefer action films or comedies (particularly the films of Peter Sellers, one of his favorite performers). Even on the set of *Blue Hawaii*, before the 'Elvis movie formula' had become formulaic, his unhappiness was obvious, as Anne Fulchino, an RCA publicist who'd first met Elvis when he signed to the label, recalled. "He was obviously uncomfortable with what he was doing, he was frustrated and disgusted – it was all in his face," she said. "The emotion that I respected most was that he was ashamed of it, which meant that he knew better – but you could see that he was trapped."

A major source of Elvis's dissatisfaction came from the poor quality of many of the film songs. Though not a complete musical wasteland – 'Can't Help Falling In Love,' from *Blue Hawaii*, became one of Elvis's signature songs, and 'Return To Sender,' from *Girls! Girls! Girls!* was a solid pop hit – most of the film songs were decidedly lackluster, their inanity readily seen in their titles: 'Song Of The Shrimp,' 'The Walls Have Ears,' '(There's) No Room To Rhumba In A Sports Car,' 'Shake That Tambourine.'

"He hated most of the movie songs," confirms Gordon Stoker. "He'd say, 'What can you do with a piece of crap like this?' Except he would talk a little plainer than that! And he'd be told, 'Well, you've got to do it.' And he always did the best job he could do." Tellingly, 21 of the 22 songs on the bootleg *Elvis' Greatest Shit!!* (released in 1980 on 'Dog Vomit Records') are film songs – "The Very Best Of The Very Worst," as the album's cover put it. Complicating the choice of material was that songwriters were expected to surrender part of their publishing to Hill & Range, the firm that administered Presley's own publishing companies, Elvis Presley Music, and Gladys Music (named after Elvis's mother, who died in 1958). It was not an uncommon demand, and in the 50s, when Elvis's records were big sellers, songwriters were more willing to make such a deal. But the Presley name on a record no longer carried a guarantee of commercial success.

The back-to-back shooting schedule for the movies – generally three a year – also ended up curtailing his live appearances. When he'd left the army, Elvis had been looking forward to touring extensively. "He wanted to see the world," recalls Scotty Moore, who'd played guitar for Elvis from his very first record on. "He really did. He wanted to go all over Europe and see the whole shebang!" Indeed, Elvis had told *Melody Maker* in 1959 that once he got out of the service, "One of the first things I want to do is play to a British audience and get to know some of the people who write me from England." But his live work turned out to be minimal: two performances in Memphis on February 25 1961 (which raised funds for various local charities as well as the Elvis Presley Youth Center in Tupelo, Mississippi, where Elvis was born), and one more exactly a month later, on March 25, at the Bloch Arena in Honolulu (a fundraiser for a memorial for the sailors who'd died on the USS *Arizona*, sunk by the Japanese on December 7 1941, and still submerged in Pearl Harbor).

The idea of cutting back on film work to allow Elvis time to tour in between movies was not seriously pursued, though Parker did try and set up a large-scale tour in 1962, hoping it would be funded by RCA. But the record company ultimately declined to put up the funds, the tour was scrapped, and the thought of future touring was not considered again. Scotty is of the opinion that letting Elvis continue working as a live performer would have actually aided his film work. "If [Parker] had let him do one of those movies, and then let him get out and do four or five shows, Elvis would have come back in on that next movie just raring to go," he says. "'Cause he was so good on stage; that was his arena. He was just born to be out there on stage. He didn't like the movie songs, with the exception of a few, and he wanted to get back in front of people. That was his forte. He loved being on stage."

Perhaps the lure of making a lot of money with minimal effort (the films could be seen by a much larger audience than Elvis could ever have reached through touring) was too good to pass up. But by the mid 60s, there were clear signs that the films and soundtracks were not the guaranteed moneymakers they had once been. Sales were steadily slipping; 1963's 'Bossa Nova Baby' from *Fun In Acapulco*, was the last movie single to reach the Top Ten. Elvis wouldn't have another Top Ten hit until 'Crying In The Chapel' – which was not only not a film song, but had originally been recorded in 1960 – peaked at Number Three in 1965.

Why didn't Elvis Presley insist on making better films or demand higher quality songs? "That is the $164,000 question!" says Scotty. "He could've done anything he wanted to, all he had to do was buck up to Parker. And he just would not do it." Gordon Stoker says The Jordanaires also encouraged Elvis to stand up for himself: "We once told him, 'If you don't want to do it, tell the Colonel you don't want to do it.' He said, 'No, I'd rather do it than argue with him.' It's just so sad that he didn't set his foot down."

But confrontation had never been Elvis's strong suit; if there was every any dirty work to be done, he left it to his manager, or his father, Vernon, to handle. And for all his later shortcomings, it was Parker's tireless promotional work in the early years that had made Elvis into an international sensation. Though Elvis's complaints about his manager would increase over the years, he would never jettison the man who had taken him to such unimagined heights; it was as if without Parker, he would lose his lucky talisman.

And as Jerry Schilling, who was part of Elvis's inner circle of buddies, dubbed 'The Memphis Mafia,' has pointed out, Elvis was locked into his career in a way outsiders couldn't necessarily understand. "I saw him protest the scripts; he tried to do something and was told, 'You do this, or you do nothing,'" he said. "I've had people say to me, 'But he was Elvis Presley, he could do what he wanted in his career.' And it wasn't just the Colonel. It was the Colonel, it was the record company – they were all together. Elvis did not have anyone to represent him like artists have today. I always thought that the Colonel would have been happier if Elvis had turned out to be Bing Crosby rather than a rock and roll star."

Instead, Elvis dealt with his unhappiness over his career in more passive-aggressive ways. In spite of his dislike of the songs in his films, he nonetheless worked to turn in a good performance. "He was absolutely perfect; he was well rehearsed, and he knew his part," recalls Don Robertson, who wrote songs for such films as *Blue Hawaii* and *Fun In Acapulco*, and played piano and organ on the soundtrack for *It Happened At The World's Fair*. "And he was very gracious to the musicians. Because a lot of the times something would go wrong and they would have to interrupt the recording and start over again. And it was very rarely him [that made a mistake]; it was one of the musicians that blew it or whatever. And he would just say, 'Well, let's take it again.' He was gracious and generous with the people as far as when I was present. He was pretty much a joy to work with."

But over time, his attitude subtly changed. Gordon Stoker had observed Elvis becoming "more moody" over the years, and now saw him developing a more lackadaisical approach to the film song sessions. "Elvis just really fooled around," he recalls. "The sessions were set at six o'clock, and he wouldn't get there until eight or nine. And then he'd sit around and talk and play, tell jokes, and things like that till midnight. That was just the way it was."

Elvis also began a retreat into drugs. Accounts differ as to when he began his recreational use of pharmaceuticals, but it's generally believed it didn't start until his army stint, when soldiers would routinely pop amphetamines so they could remain awake during their watch. Scotty Moore first noticed Elvis's use of pills when they were traveling to Miami to tape a Frank Sinatra TV special in March 1960: "I had never known him to do that before," he said. By the mid 60s, amphetamines and sedatives were a regular part of Elvis's – and his entourage's – life. "We lived on amphetamines," said Joe Esposito, who had met Elvis in the army and was part of his inner circle until the end of his life, a description seconded by Priscilla Beaulieu, Elvis's girlfriend and later his wife: "Eventually Elvis's consumption of pills seemed as normal to me as watching him eat a pound of bacon with his Spanish omelet."

As Elvis received his pills by prescription, he never saw himself as an illegal drug user. And in the entertainment industry, the use of prescribed drugs was often seen as just another aid to one's career; taking speed to lose weight, for example, or a sleeping pill to get sufficient rest before an early morning shoot. "It was the 60s and we didn't know what prescription drugs would do to you," said Julie Parrish of her own experiences with drugs. "I didn't really need diet pills, but you could get them easily – all you had to do to was ask your doctor. On *Paradise, Hawaiian Style*, I'd go out with the crew and people from the cast after shooting and we would drink – not that much, but enough. And I'd be kind of wired up by the time I went to bed and have to get up early, so I would take a sleeping pill. And then in the morning, if I was tired, I'd take one of those diet pills." It was an example of the kind of dangerous cycle of drug use that would eventually have serious repercussions on Elvis's health.

He'd also developed an interest in spiritual matters. On April 30 1964, he'd met Larry Geller, a hairdresser who'd been summoned to Elvis's Los Angeles home to style his hair. A simple question about Larry's other interests led to a discussion lasting four hours on the search for meaning in one's life. Elvis responded with great enthusiasm, telling a startled Geller, "Larry, I've finally found someone who understands what I'm going through, and someone I can talk to," and offering to hire him full-time.

The next day, Larry arrived armed with a battery of books, including *The Impersonal Life*, *Autobiography Of A Yogi*, *The Initiation Of The World*, and *Beyond The Himalayas*. *The Impersonal Life* would become a particular favorite, Elvis keeping a copy with him and handing out hundreds of copies to friends over the years. His search for an answer to "Why I was chosen to be Elvis Presley" led to his visiting the Self-Realization Fellowship in the Pacific Palisades regularly, and eventually meeting with the Fellowship's president, Sri Daya Mata, at the organization's headquarters in Mt Washington, outside LA, for further guidance. He even spoke of giving up his career entirely; Sri Daya Mata gently persuaded him his path lay elsewhere.

Whatever his private concerns, Elvis always managed to put on a good face for his public. Unlike other stars of his stature, he made it a point to stop and talk with the fans who were always hanging around outside the gates of his various homes in Los Angeles and Memphis, eventually becoming friends with some of them; deprived of the contact of a live audience, it was a way of staying in touch with his most ardent supporters. Sandi Miller was one fan-turned-friend who got to know Elvis during this period. Sandi had been an Elvis fan since seeing *Flaming Star* while growing up in Minneapolis, Minnesota. After seeing the film, she promptly informed her mother, "I'm gonna meet him one day," only to be told, "Honey, people like us don't meet people like him." "And I said, 'Nope! I'm gonna meet him. Period,'" she recalls. "I mean, there was never any doubt in my mind I'd meet him."

And a few years later, while visiting a friend in LA, she did meet Elvis outside his Bel Air home. She moved to California the following year, and when she next met Elvis outside his house, was surprised to find that he remembered her from their previous brief encounter. "When I first met him, he'd rolled down the window of his car, shook hands with everybody, smiled and went in," she says. "The whole thing took five seconds. And the next year when I came back and we went up to the house, he stopped his car, rolled down the window, pointed at me and goes, 'You're the one from Minnesota.' I mean, his memory was amazing. It was. I noticed that over the years, that he had a phenomenal memory."

Soon, Elvis's buddies invited Sandi and her friends to come inside the house, but the young women demurred. "It wasn't Elvis doing the asking, it was the boys," she explains. "They kept saying, 'Come on in,' and we were like, 'No. ...' I mean, they were like 28, 29; we were 17, 18. And we just kept saying, 'No, we can't do that, we don't really know you.' It's just not something we felt comfortable doing. And then one day Elvis drove up and he said, 'Listen, we're having a BBQ, come on in.' And my girlfriend said, 'I can't, my mother would absolutely kill me.' And he goes, 'Well, let's give her a call and get her permission.' Which is what happened. And from that point on, we just continued to be invited in. As long as you behaved yourself and you weren't a total lunatic, they continued to invite you; once you were friends they kind of kept you around."

Even his brief chats with fans outside his home revealed that Elvis no longer took his film career that seriously. "There really wasn't much to say about the movies," says Sandi. "People would say, 'What's the movie about you're doing now?' and he'd say, 'Oh, driving down the highway and out of nowhere a big orchestra comes up,' or 'Today I said to a dog ...' He'd poke fun at himself and he'd poke fun at the movies. They were not deep conversations by any means; it was basically conversation that was dictated by the fans. Which was a totally different thing from what went on in the home. In the home, that's his territory, and he would talk about current events, entertainers, whatever he was reading, or shows that he was interested in. He'd want to know about whoever was in the house, the various girls; where were they from, what did they do, he'd want to know about their families. He was like you'd be if you invited a bunch of people you really didn't know into your house. You'd find out a little bit about them and you'd let them know a little bit about you and what you're interested in. And he was no different; he did the same thing."

Finally, in the midst of all the soundtrack work, Elvis had a chance to return to the music he loved in May 1966, when his second religious album, *How Great Thou Art*, was recorded. "Elvis was always on to RCA to do gospel songs, and RCA kept telling him, 'We didn't spend all this money on your contract for you to go and do gospel songs,'" Gordon Stoker contends. "And he fought them the whole time, and they fought him all the time, and the Colonel, of course, didn't have any desire for him to do gospel songs at all." However, it was noted that Elvis's first religious album, *His Hand In Mine*, had been a steady seller since its initial release in 1960, when it reached Number 13 in the charts (Number Three UK). And 'Crying In The Chapel,' recorded during those same sessions, had reached the Top Five when it was finally released as a single, in addition to selling a million copies (his first million seller since 1962's 'Return To Sender'; it also topped the UK charts). And even if the new album didn't produce a hit, it was hoped that it would get Elvis excited about working again.

As indeed it did. In preparation for the sessions, Elvis went over songs with Red West, whom he'd known since high school in Memphis (Red had famously prevented Elvis from being beaten up by some fellow students who'd disliked his hairstyle, longer than the standard crew cut even then), and who was branching out as an actor and songwriter; and Charlie Hodge, a musician he'd met during his army days who was also part of the inner circle. Home recordings of the period showcase the variety of material roughed out: Eddy Arnold's 'After Loving You,' Patti Page's 'Tennessee Waltz,' 'Oh, How I Love Jesus,' and Bob Dylan's 'Blowin' In The Wind,' all of which were later released on the 1997 collection *Platinum: A Life In Music*. Elvis was also excited that along with The Jordanaires, the gospel group The Imperials had been booked for the sessions; the group had been founded by Jake Hess, formerly a member of The Statesmen, one of Elvis's favorite gospel groups.

Another important element of the sessions was that they introduced Elvis to a new producer: Felton Jarvis. Jarvis (born Charles Felton Jarvis) had produced Tommy Roe's Number One hit 'Sheila,' and had also worked with such artists as Gladys Knight & The Pips, Fats Domino, and Willie Nelson. He'd been an Elvis fan since seeing him in concert in 1955, and later recorded an Elvis tribute record ('Don't Knock Elvis'), before deciding his skills were better utilized behind a control board than behind a microphone. In 1962, he'd also worked with an Elvis imitator he named "Vince Everett" (after Elvis's character in *Jailhouse Rock*), who enjoyed a small hit with a cover of Elvis's 'Such A Night.'

Chet Atkins, the legendary guitarist who was also head of RCA's Nashville division, had worked on some of Elvis's sessions as a producer, and thought that Felton and Elvis might work well together. The two men hit it off immediately, and Elvis would continue to use Felton as his producer for the rest of his life. "He and Felton worked real good together," says Gordon. "Because everything that Elvis came up with Felton would say, 'Yeah man, that's good, that's great!' In other words, Felton joined in with all the guys that were hired to be one of Elvis's boys, Charlie Hodge and all the rest of them. He was just one of them. And I guess that's what Elvis liked about him."

But it was an attitude that also suggested that Felton would not be the kind of producer that would push Elvis to do better. "Elvis had to sing a song the way he felt like singing it at the moment he was recording it," Felton later explained of how he worked with the singer. "I couldn't tell him how or when to do a song." It was an inadvertently telling statement, one that overlooked – or disregarded – the fact that Elvis could have used more direction at times; he was always at his best when faced with a new challenge.

How Great Thou Art, released in February 1967, was not destined to jump-start Elvis's career during a year in which the biggest selling act were pop rockers The Monkees (whose *More Of The Monkees* sat on top of the *Billboard* album charts for 18 weeks). Some non-religious material had also been recorded at the *How Great Thou Art* sessions, for singles and to fill out the *Spinout* soundtrack. Of these, the most interesting was a haunting version of Bob Dylan's 'Tomorrow Is A Long Time,' which

Dylan himself hadn't recorded; Elvis had heard the song on the 1965 album *Odetta Sings Dylan*. One wonders what the public response would have been had the first single released from the May 1966 sessions been this song instead of the number that was chosen, 'Love Letters.' While 'Love Letters' was a pleasant enough ballad (the single would reach Number 19 US, Number Six UK), the news that Elvis Presley had recorded a song by one of the most acclaimed songwriters of the 60s might have gone a long way in restoring some of his credibility. Instead, one of Elvis's finest performances languished as filler on a soundtrack (unconvincingly described in a press release as "Elvis at the top of his form") that stalled at sales of 300,000.

Though *Spinout* had Elvis's character unusually avoiding any romantic commitments, remaining a freewheeling bachelor at the film's end, things were about to take a very different turn off-screen. A month after *Spinout* opened, Elvis proposed to his longtime girlfriend, Priscilla Beaulieu. The two had met in September 1959, while Elvis was stationed in Germany; Priscilla, the 14-year-old stepdaughter of an Air Force captain, had been introduced to Elvis by a mutual friend. In March 1963, Elvis managed to persuade her family to let Priscilla come live in Memphis, where she finished high school; though 'officially' staying with Vernon Presley and his wife Dee, in reality she immediately moved into Elvis's Graceland mansion around the corner from his father's home on her arrival. It was a potentially scandalous situation that the media somehow never picked up on – or perhaps they simply turned a blind eye. Elvis Presley, after all, epitomized the American Dream, the classic success story of bringing one's self out of impoverished circumstances through sheer hard work and persistence, the ultimate case of a local boy making good.

But was he still a viable entertainer? He was making a move to become more settled in his personal life, but it seemed as if his career had become more uncomfortably 'settled' as well. Record sales and movie revenues were falling; Elvis's own interest in his career was waning too. Something had to give.

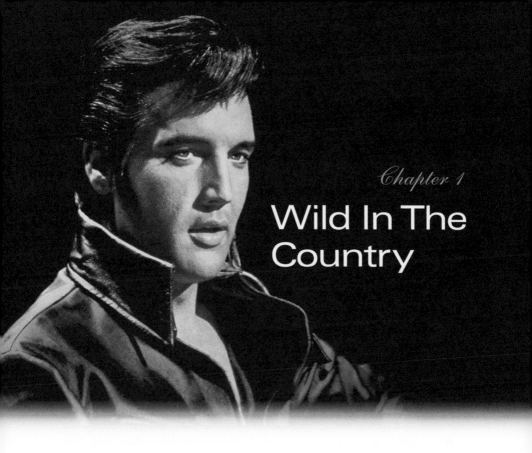

Chapter 1

Wild In The Country

As 1967 began, Elvis Presley had one thing on his mind, and it wasn't the state of his career. It was horses.

The previous month, he'd bought Priscilla a horse as a Christmas present. He also bought one for Jerry Schilling's fiancée, Sandy, so Priscilla would have someone to ride with. He then decided the rest of the gang needed horses, as did their girlfriends or wives, as did Elvis himself. "As with anything he enjoyed, he wanted for everyone else to join the fun," Priscilla explained. By the end of January, he'd purchased nearly 20 horses.

Elvis's newfound interest in horses quickly became an all-consuming passion. "It was impossible for him to say 'This is just right,'" said Jerry Schilling. "He must have felt that if having ten horses was a good thing, having 20 would be even better, and having 30 would be even better than that." "What Elvis did to the horse market in northern Mississippi was unbelievable," observed Dr E.O. Franklin, who worked as a veterinarian at Graceland. "We would go out and look at a horse that was a $300 horse, but when the people found it was maybe for Elvis it became a $3,000 horse!" The barn at Graceland was renovated to house the animals (and with Elvis's horse named Rising Sun, the barn was jokingly dubbed "The House of the Rising Sun"). Some smaller buildings on the property were bulldozed to create a larger riding area. And all the horses – and their riders – needed to be outfitted with proper equipment and attire.

The fans who constantly hung around Graceland's front gate shot numerous pictures of Elvis and his friends riding their horses; to their great delight, he'd occasionally ride over to chat with them and sign autographs, often receiving a Butterfinger candy bar in return (a favorite treat). But Graceland's grounds could only comfortably accommodate so many horses. Elvis found a solution in early February, when he and Priscilla drove past a ranch outside of Walls, Mississippi, just over the Tennessee state line, and 10 miles from Graceland. The 160-acre property, named Twinkletown Farm, was a working cattle ranch, and had another feature that captured Elvis's eye: a 65-foot white cross towering over a small lake (Sonny West, Red West's cousin, claimed this was actually a landmark for a local airport). On learning the property was for sale, Elvis quickly acquired the ranch for $437,000, and renamed it Circle G (later Flying Circle G), the 'G' for Graceland.

Priscilla was initially excited about the purchase, as the ranch's accommodation, a small farm house, was too small for Elvis's substantial entourage, and she imagined the place could become a private escape for her and her future husband. But Elvis had other ideas, and his spending spree continued, as he bought mobile homes, trailers, pickup trucks, tractors, and other equipment ("He bought 22 trucks in one day," claimed Lamar Fike, another of his friends), and began constructing an eight-foot fence around the property to provide a modicum of privacy. Once everyone moved in, days were spent riding horses and otherwise relaxing outside. Elvis's enthusiasm never waned in those early weeks; he'd rise early to check on the livestock, and, eschewing meals, rode around with a loaf of bread under his arm to snack on. For Ray Walker of the Jordanaires, who came out for a visit, it was the best he'd ever seen Elvis look: "He was tanned, and his eyes – they just shone like diamonds."

When his father bemoaned the amount of money this new hobby was costing (expenses for February alone totaled nearly $100,000), Elvis merely replied, "I'm having fun, Daddy, for the first time in ages." He was having so much fun, in fact, that for the first time in his career he showed a marked reluctance to get back to work – something that was now all the more necessary, given his recent expenditures. The plaintive 'Indescribably Blue,' released in January, had stalled at sales of 300,000, reaching Number 33 (Number 21 UK). *How Great Thou Art*, released in February, sold just 200,000, though it was not expected to be a big seller but the kind of catalogue item that sold well over time, and it charted respectably enough at Number 18 (Number 11 UK); the next year, it would also became Elvis's first Grammy winner, securing the award for Best Sacred Performance. Like it or not, Elvis had to bring more money in.

The first order of business was work on his upcoming film, *Clambake*. The story had Elvis, playing the wealthy son of an oilman, swapping places with a water-skiing instructor at a Florida resort, also finding time to win a boat race and the hand of Shelley Fabares (a favorite co-star of Presley's, making her third appearance in an Elvis film) along the way. Production had been scheduled to begin February 21, but with Elvis disinclined to leave the ranch, the starting date was pushed back, and a recording session at RCA's Nashville studios was scheduled instead.

Elvis's lack of interest in the session was obvious from the start. The songs recorded February 21, 'The Girl I Never Loved,' 'How Can You Lose What You Never Had,' and 'A House That Has Everything,' were pleasant, but lightweight – the standard to which the movie songs had sunk. "Of the early songs in the movies, there was always two or three that was pretty good," says Scotty Moore, who played guitar on the session. "Then Parker seemed to think, 'Okay, it don't matter, Elvis could stub his toe and they're gonna buy it.' So that's when they started getting writers that would just turn out such crap, and it was crap. You know it, I know it, and everybody knows it. But as long as Elvis was on the screen, that'd be fine. That's when I started going out and playing poker a lot of the times [during the sessions] with the other henchmen that was hanging around." Even 'You Don't Know Me,' by one of Elvis's favorite artists, Eddy Arnold (Parker's first client), proved hard to nail down, though Elvis's performance was at least more soulful than on the other songs.

Elvis was suitably dispirited by the proceedings to not even bother showing up the next night, having flown back to his ranch, leaving the musicians to lay down the backing tracks without him. He returned on February 23, kitted out in full cowboy regalia, including chaps, to record his vocal parts. The material was no better, and included 'Clambake,' the film's title song, 'Confidence,' which would be performed to a gaggle of children, and 'Hey, Hey, Hey,' a song extolling the virtues of a hardening agent called "goop." It was a far cry from what the film's poster would later promote as "That *wild* Presley beat." While flying back to Memphis afterwards, Elvis instructed the pilot to fly over Circle G, so that he could admire his ranch from the air.

If Parker was irritated at the initial delays on the film, he was nearly apoplectic when informed that Elvis would miss the newly rescheduled starting date for *Clambake*, March 3, as well. He insisted Elvis provide a doctor's certificate backing up his claim that he was ill. When Elvis's regular doctor was unavailable, the girlfriend of George Klein (a Memphis DJ who'd known Elvis since high school) recommended the physician she worked for, Dr George Nichopoulos. 'Dr Nick,' as Elvis nicknamed him, duly visited Elvis at the ranch, treating him for saddle sores. He was immediately struck by the insularity of Elvis's world, later recalling: "That night he seemed kind of depressed and lonely; he just wanted to talk. Even with everybody that was out there, to me he just sort of remained a lonely person. It seemed like they didn't have new things to talk about; everything was old hat."

Elvis finally left for LA on March 5, meeting with *Clambake*'s producers and director the following day, as well as reporting for costume fittings; despite his outdoor lifestyle, he'd gained substantial weight, meaning his entire wardrobe for the film had to be refitted. He also recorded further vocal overdubs for the soundtrack that evening at Annex Studios. But work came to a sudden halt a few days later, when on the morning of Thursday, March 9, Elvis emerged from his bedroom saying he'd fallen in his bathroom the previous evening and hit his head on the edge of the bathtub. Doctors were summoned and it was soon determined that while Elvis had not seriously injured himself, he did need rest to fully recuperate.

Parker used this opening to regain control of both his wayward client and his entourage. Rounding up Elvis's guys, he declared that it was time to make some changes. Some people would have to be let go, to cut back on expenses. Joe Esposito was designated as the new foreman for the group, and everyone was told to take their problems to him, not Elvis. Finally, everyone should make it their business to look after Elvis better; he should be focusing on his work, not wasting his time pondering the meaning of life. Henceforth, no one was allowed to bring Elvis any spiritually oriented books, and Larry Geller was never left alone with Elvis again. "Suddenly it was open season on the Swami," Geller concluded, "and the guys made no effort to be discreet or cute about the name-calling." He left Elvis's employ soon after (though the two would become friends again during the 70s). In fact, no one in the entourage ended up being fired; Parker's speech had more to do with reasserting his authority than getting rid of Elvis's friends. More alarming to some was how Elvis sat by his manager's side, saying nothing, only nodding in mute agreement. "I think he'd reached a point where he just didn't feel like putting up much of a fight anymore," said George Klein.

Filming for *Clambake* finally began on March 22. Coincidentally,

Elvis's film *Easy Come, Easy Go* opened the same day, to such poor business that it initially failed to break even (the *New York Times* called it "a tired little color clinker that must have been shot during lunch hour") . The accompanying 'soundtrack' – a six song EP – failed to chart in the US and only sold 30,000 copies (in the UK, 'You Gotta Stop' was released as a single, reaching Number 38). *Double Trouble* was rushed out a mere two weeks later, to equally tepid response. Its soundtrack reached Number 47 US (Number 34 UK), while the single 'Long Legged Girl (With The Short Dress On)' only made it as high as Number 63 US (Number 49 UK), receiving a decidedly mixed review from *Billboard* as a "strong rhythm entry with traces of his earlier songs."

Perhaps recognizing how antiquated Elvis's movies had become, each one made clumsy attempts to update the star's image. In *Easy Come, Easy Go*, Elvis, playing a former Naval frogman in pursuit of sunken treasure, finally meets the counterculture when he partakes in a yoga class taught by none other than Elsa Lanchester. In the strangest duet of his film career, Elvis and the one-time Bride of Frankenstein trade lines in 'Yoga Is As Yoga Does' (in the most painful line, "serious" is rhymed with "posterious"). *Double Trouble* begins more promisingly, with Elvis first seen performing at a nightclub in Swinging London. Unfortunately, the 'action' soon moves to Belgium, where, in between dealing with diamond smugglers and the usual romantic complications, Elvis is reduced to singing 'Old MacDonald' to one of his love interests, as the two ride in the back of a truck, surrounded by cages full of chickens. *Variety* summed up Elvis's performance by noting, "[he] gives a pretty fair account of himself, despite what's handed him."

As soon as filming on *Clambake* was completed, plans for Elvis's wedding were put into effect. That the event was stage-managed by Parker was evident in the choice of locale – not the family-style gathering one might have expected in Memphis, but the hotel suite of one of Parker's cronies in Las Vegas, with a ceremony as rushed as those held in the city's many wedding chapels. The wedding party left Palm Springs at 2am on May 1, with Elvis and Priscilla using Frank Sinatra's private jet for the occasion. By 3:30am they'd secured a marriage license at the Clark County Courthouse. Everyone then proceeded to the Aladdin Hotel, owned by Parker's friend, Milton Prell, where the wedding was held in Prell's second floor suite, at 11:45am, with Nevada Supreme Court Justice Judge David Zenoff performing the ceremony. On meeting Elvis and Priscilla beforehand, he assured the nervous couple, "I'll have you in and out of here in two minutes." The actual ceremony ran a bit longer; just under 10 minutes.

Unfortunately, what should have been a happy day was marred by inner turmoil. It was only after everyone had arrived in Vegas that members of the entourage learned they wouldn't be allowed in the suite on the pretext that there wasn't enough room, though they were all welcome at the reception afterwards; aside from family, the only members of the inner circle to attend the ceremony would be Joe Esposito and Marty Lacker, who were co-best men. This caused considerable bad feeling amongst the group; Red West refused to even attend the reception, and flew back to LA in a huff. Priscilla later regretted that everything had been so rushed, admitting, "I wish I'd had the strength then to say, 'Wait a minute, this is *our* wedding.'" But as soon as vows were exchanged ("It seemed that as soon as the ceremony began, it was over," she noted), the couple was whisked off to a press conference, and then a buffet breakfast, which featured such down-home items as fried chicken alongside eggs Minette, oysters Rockefeller, and poached candied salmon.

The couple spent their honeymoon in Palm Springs before returning to Memphis. On May 29, they held a second reception at Graceland to soothe the feelings of those who hadn't been able to attend the wedding, even re-donning their wedding outfits for the occasion. Elvis had a few weeks off before preproduction was scheduled to start on his next film, and the trip back to California was a leisurely one, with the group traveling on a customized bus, and even wives and girlfriends allowed to come along for the ride. Just before the trip, Priscilla had learned she was pregnant, something she had mixed feelings about, as she'd hoped to have time alone with her husband before assuming the responsibilities of raising a family. She even briefly considered an abortion, Elvis telling her he'd support whatever she chose to do. But she quickly realized it was a decision they would both regret, and her pregnancy was announced publicly, Elvis proudly passing out cigars on the set of his next film.

The film was _Speedway_. Back in March, Parker, who rarely made any suggestions regarding the content of Elvis's movies, had been concerned enough about the falling movie revenues to write to MGM recommending that it was time for some variation in the Elvis movie formula, expressing the hope that the studio could come up with "good, strong, rugged stories." _Speedway_ wouldn't fit that bill (Elvis plays – for the third time – a race car driver, who lands in hot water when his business partner fails to pay their taxes), but it was the last of such pictures to be made; Elvis's subsequent movies strove, albeit unsuccessfully, to have a more contemporary feel. His _Speedway_ co-star, and love interest, was Nancy Sinatra (playing an IRS agent), whose singing career had taken off the previous year with her chart topping 'These Boots Are Made For Walkin''; she'd recently hit the top again in a duet with her father, 'Somethin' Stupid.' As a result, she was allowed a solo spot in _Speedway_, the slinky 'Your Groovy Self,' written by Lee Hazlewood, who'd also written 'Boots' ('Your Groovy Self' would also be the only song ever featured on a Presley soundtrack that was not performed by Elvis).

Elvis's songs were the usual batch of uninspired material, recorded over two nights on June 20 and 21 at MGM Studios in Hollywood. The title track was the kind of bright pop that typified most of the theme songs from Elvis's movies. 'There Ain't Nothing Like A Song' had previously been considered for the _Spinout_ soundtrack, an indication of how interchangeable the movie songs were. Though it was at least more rousing than 'He's Your Uncle Not Your Dad,' a chipper song about the necessity of paying one's taxes (the 'Uncle' in the title referred to Uncle Sam). Both 'Your Time Hasn't Come Yet Baby' and 'Five Sleepy Heads' were designed to be sung to children; the latter song was cut from the film but appeared as a 'bonus' number on the soundtrack. 'Who Are You?' was a pretty ballad with a light bossa nova swing.

'Suppose' was a ballad that Elvis took more of an interest in; it had originally been submitted for the *Easy Come, Easy Go* soundtrack. It didn't make the cut, but Elvis had taken a liking to it and recorded a home demo of it, which he gave to producer Felton Jarvis, who had in turn overdubbed further instruments on the track at a session in March (this version was eventually released in 1993 on *From Nashville To Memphis: The Essential 60s Masters I*). Elvis used the *Speedway* sessions as an opportunity to record the song again, and though it was ultimately cut from the film, it nonetheless appeared on the soundtrack. 'Let Yourself Go' was another track with more than the usual amount of substance, a bluesy, sexy number about seduction that would soon be used in a more dramatic setting.

Work on *Speedway* was completed by August 21, and a non-soundtrack session had been scheduled for the following day at RCA's studios on Sunset Boulevard in Hollywood. Since the *Easy Come, Easy Go* EP had flopped, it was decided future soundtracks had to be full-length albums, even if it meant padding out the LP with non-soundtrack material. Elvis had suggested a number of songs he'd like to try, including 'From A Jack To A King,' 'Guitar Man,' 'After Loving You,' and 'The Wonder Of You.' But the session was canceled before it began, when Richard Davis, one of Elvis's gang, accidentally killed a pedestrian while driving one of Elvis's cars. Parker urged Elvis to leave town to avoid any potential controversy, so Elvis, Priscilla, and a few friends decamped to Las Vegas for a few days, then flew on to Memphis. But a number of the songs that had been considered for recording would resurface at future sessions.

The session was rescheduled for September 10 and 11 at RCA's Nashville studios, and would be Elvis's first non-soundtrack session in over a year. Elvis had wanted to tackle Jerry Reed's 'Guitar Man' ever since hearing it on the radio the previous summer (1967 had also seen the release of Reed's tribute song to Elvis, 'The Tupelo Mississippi Flash'). Its country-rock blend was well suited to Elvis; even its storyline seemed a distillation of his own career ("It's a make-believe story but it sort touches what you go through as a guitar player," Reed explained). And when the session musicians couldn't match Reed's own distinctive finger-picking style, the call went out to find him (he was eventually located fishing on the Cumberland River, outside of Nashville), and he was invited to join the session.

"As soon as we hit the intro, you could see Elvis's eyes light up – he knew we had it," Reed later recalled. Elvis's enjoyment is obvious even as he stumbles over the lyrics in the early takes, and when Felton Jarvis encourages him to "Sing the living stuff out of it, El!" he loosens up to the point that he starts riffing on Ray Charles' 'What'd I Say' during the fade out (this take, with a newly recorded instrumental backing, would first appear on the 1981 release *Guitar Man*; the original take later appeared on *From Nashville To Memphis*). It served up a refreshing, altogether modern sound that had been missing from Elvis's recordings since the *Elvis Is Back!* sessions in 1960.

The next track, Jimmy Reed's 'Big Boss Man,' was just as memorable, its macho strut underscored by Boots Randolph's sax part. But it then became apparent that the publishing had never been cleared for 'Guitar Man,' and with the song already recorded, Jerry was in no mood to surrender his copyright. Freddy Bienstock, Hill & Range's representative at the session, told him that if a deal couldn't be made the song would not be released, but Reed steadfastly held his ground. "I'll put it to you this way," he told Bienstock. "You don't need the money, and Elvis don't need the money, and I'm making more money than I can spend right now – so why don't we just forget we ever recorded this damn song?"

Though a deal would eventually be worked out, Reed's stance put a damper on the rest of the session (though Reed had left the studio after his exchange with Bienstock). 'Mine' was a ballad originally considered for *Paradise, Hawaiian Style*, but would end up as filler on the

Speedway soundtrack; 'Singing Tree,' another ballad, which was first attempted at the September 10 session but not finished until the next night, was used to pad out *Clambake*. 'Just Call Me Lonesome,' a country weeper, also turned up on *Clambake*. There was nothing wrong with the performances, but they missed the bright sparkle evident in 'Guitar Man' and 'Big Boss Man.' The obvious conclusion was that they were not songs in which Elvis had any interest. But Elvis's interests were not the primary concern; the publishing deals were.

When the sessions continued the next night, guitarists Harold Bradley and Chip Young caught Elvis's attention when they began playing 'Hi-Heel Sneakers,' previously a hit for Tommy Tucker. This was material he could get into, and he jumped right in, turning in a suitably gritty vocal, with Charlie McCoy's harmonica wailing on top (though Bradley was sternly warned by Felton to not pitch any other songs). 'You Don't Know Me' had previously been recorded during the February *Clambake* sessions (it later appeared on an expanded version of the soundtrack released in 1994), but hadn't been used in the film. The new version, with its restrained musical backing (taken at a slightly slower tempo), had a far more mature sound, as well as a stronger, more heartfelt delivery from Elvis.

Then came two songs destined to make up both sides of next year's Easter single, 'We Call On Him' and 'You'll Never Walk Alone.' The latter song was a particular favorite of Elvis's, which he sang frequently at home, and he was moved to accompany himself on piano. His performance has great dramatic flair, Elvis throwing himself wholeheartedly into the number, displaying an intensity undoubtedly seen by his friends during home jam sessions, but which had been too rarely evident in his recent studio work. The session finished when work on 'Singing Tree' was finally completed.

With a batch of material noticeably stronger than the soundtrack offerings having been assembled, 'Big Boss Man' was rushed out as a single at the end of the month, even though RCA had just released a single in August ('There's Always Me,' pulled from the 1961 album

Something For Everyone). 'Big Boss Man' charted substantially higher than 'There's Always Me' – Number 38 versus Number 56 – but it wasn't the breakthrough hit everyone had hoped for (neither song charted in the UK). And 'Guitar Man' initially languished on the *Clambake* soundtrack, which was released in October, a month prior to the film's release. Of the album, *Billboard* wrote, "Elvis' latest movie track places the singer miles away from his early rock days," while the *Los Angeles Times* was equally dismissive of the film: "Elvis' songs are as forgettable as ever, and the whole picture has a garish, cluttered look."

By then, Elvis was already at work on his next film, *Stay Away, Joe*. The film marked a big step away from the usual Elvis movie formula, striving to be along the lines of the more "rugged" stories Parker had requested the previous spring. Based on the 1953 novel by Dan Cushman, it cast Elvis as Joe Lightcloud, a Native American who's the kind of loveable rogue who always has some hustle going on, in this case taking advantage of a government scheme to provide work for the Indian community by taking on a head of cattle to raise; Elvis even described his character to the *Los Angeles Herald Examiner* as "part Hud, part Alfie. He's a man, not a boy." The film's co-stars included Burgess Meredith, best known at the time for his role as The Penguin on the TV series *Batman*, and veteran wisecracking character actress Joan Blondell (who, though in her sixties, played one of Elvis's love interests).

The film was shot on location in Sedona, Arizona, and Elvis invited Sandi Miller and her friends to drive over and visit him. "It wasn't so much being on the set," she explains. "He just said, 'This is where I'm gonna be,' and we said, 'Well, maybe we'll come down.' And he goes, 'Okay! Come on down.' He didn't say 'Don't come,' so we went. It was different, because it wasn't like a movie set is in LA, where it's off limits or something. This is out in the middle of nowhere, and there were a lot of the townspeople standing around watching the filming. You just stay out of camera range. He was real good about stuff like that, he didn't care."

Elvis was especially pleased to be filming outside of Hollywood.

"He liked the fact that it was on location instead of all on a set," says Sandi. "He actually got to go somewhere. Just like he loved doing the Hawaii-based ones because it gave him a reason to go to Hawaii. He was in a good mood while he was filming. He looked good, and he had a lot of fun. He was enjoying himself." But despite the contemporary feel, the film's antics verged on slapstick, with Lightcloud and his buddies spending most of their time engaging in endless wrestling matches when they're not busy drinking. It reflected a condescending attitude toward the minority group being portrayed, as readily seen in the film's promotional materials; one movie poster said of its star: "He's an 'In' Indian who prefers necking to scalping!" Even Sandi, who liked the film, describes it as "absolutely dorky."

In another change, the film only featured four songs (including the title song, which, confusingly, was called 'Stay Away,' while the number 'Stay Away, Joe' was performed during one of the film's many party sequences). But it would take three sessions to record them all. The first session was held October 1 in Nashville, and went fairly smoothly. 'Stay Away, Joe' was an upbeat, jokey number that worked well in its party setting, while 'All I Needed Was The Rain' was a bluesy number that was better than the usual generic Elvis film songs, though as each song ran under two minutes, they come across more as afterthoughts in the movie. But the final song of the evening was quite possibly the nadir of all of Elvis's film songs, the infamous 'Dominic.' When Lightcloud's stud bull is eaten during a particularly raucous party, a new bull, Dominic, is secured for the purpose. But when Dominic proves reluctant to mate with the expectant herd, Lightcloud is moved to cajole his bull to get moving in a song that happily also runs under two minutes. In a rare moment of defiance, Elvis actually asked his producer not to release the song on record, and aside from its film appearance, it remained safely in the vaults until 1994, when it finally surfaced on one of the *Elvis Double Features* soundtrack reissues (perhaps appropriately, its first unofficial release came on the *Elvis' Greatest Shit!!* bootleg).

The next sessions were held on January 15 and 16 1968, in Nashville, with Jerry Reed again present as an additional guitarist. Elvis seemed in an unusually aggressive mood to those in attendance; whereas before he'd taken care not to swear in front of The Jordanaires, on this occasion "things got jokingly rough; there was some language going on," Gordon Stoker recalled. He was in part frustrated by the lack of decent material offered to him, spending some time throwing numerous acetate demos against the wall; "It was sad to watch Elvis wrestle his way through the less-than-impressive movie material that needed to be done," Jerry Schilling observed. They eventually fell back on Chuck Berry's 'Too Much Monkey Business,' which wouldn't be a movie song, nor was it a likely candidate for a single. In contrast to the bluesy swing of Berry's original, Elvis's version moved at a faster clip, recast in a country-rock vein that was perfect for him, with Berry's clever word-play also appealing to his own off-beat sense of humor (he even injected a little contemporary flavor; instead of going to "Yokohama" to fight, Elvis substitutes the word "Vietnam"). He had a much harder time with another potential film song, 'Goin' Home,' a paean to the wide-open Western spaces where the movie was set. Elvis couldn't get through the song without cracking up, with the guys all joining in, resulting in the recording dragging on through 30 takes.

The next night also got off to a slow start, with 'Stay Away,' the song that would actually play over the title credits of *Stay Away, Joe*. Set to the melody of 'Greensleeves,' the initial takes were slow and somewhat plodding. Boosting the tempo gave the song a welcome dose of energy, though it didn't make Elvis warm to the number any better; he took four hours to nail it down. The sessions then stalled again, when no other good songs could be found, finally prompting an exasperated Elvis to exclaim, "Doesn't anyone have some goddamn material worth recording?" Finally, Jerry Reed, who had pointedly not been asked to provide any material, was prevailed upon to see if he could come up with something. He responded by playing Elvis his own 'U.S. Male.' The jokey number, with its Southern references and tongue-in-cheek tone, was right for Elvis, but his concentration wavered on the early takes, and he began singing off-color material. After yet another take, when he flubbed the lyrics, he jokingly castigated himself, "Aw, you fucked up US male!" "If you do two more like that, Elvis, then we'll have a complete 'party' album," Felton Jarvis said in response, before gently reminding him, when the laughter had died down, "We need two more sides." Felton wouldn't get those two sides, but they did finally lay down an acceptable version of 'U.S. Male.'

Because there would be no soundtrack for *Stay Away, Joe*, the songs were spread out over a variety of releases: 'U.S. Male'/'Stay Away' on a single, 'Goin' Home' (ultimately cut from the film) as a filler track on the *Speedway* soundtrack, 'Too Much Monkey Business' and 'All I Needed Was The Rain' on the budget album *Flaming Star*, and 'Stay Away, Joe' on another budget collection, *Let's Be Friends*.

In addition to the poor material he was forced to work with, Elvis's mood may have reflected a broader discontent. His work in 1967 had produced no big selling recordings, or high grossing films; indeed, the poor performance of *Easy Come, Easy Go* made it the first Elvis movie that had ever flopped. Toward the end of the year, when Priscilla was in her seventh month of pregnancy, he'd stunned his wife by suggesting they needed a trial separation, telling her, "It's not you. It's just that I'm going through some things." Without asking what those "things" might be, Priscilla agreed, but Elvis never brought up the subject again. Nor did Circle G hold any allure for him. Vernon had begun selling off the ranch's many vehicles and mobile homes in August, and more equipment was sold at auction in November. (The ranch itself would be a little harder to unload. It was sold in 1969, but when the buyers defaulted, ownership reverted to Elvis; a new buyer wasn't found until 1973.)

The birth of Elvis's daughter, Lisa Marie, on February 1 1968, helped shake him out of his malaise; "She's a little miracle," he proudly proclaimed to his dentist. Meanwhile, RCA continued its steady stream of releases. 'Guitar Man' was finally released as a single in January

1968, but had only gone as high as Number 43 US (Number 19 UK). 'U.S. Male,' released in February, reached Number 28 US (Number 15 UK), his highest chart placing since the 1966 single 'Love Letters,' and selling substantially better than his recent singles. The greatest hits collection _Elvis' Gold Records Vol. 4_, also released in February, outperformed most of his recent soundtracks as well, both in sales and on the charts, reaching Number 33 US, even as _Billboard_ observed, "To get enough 'gold' to label this LP, the company had to do some searching." 'You'll Never Walk Alone' was released in March; though only reaching Number 96 US (Number 44 UK), it would secure a Grammy nomination for Best Sacred Performance.

But there was no momentum built on this modest bump, as Elvis began work on his next film on March 4 (the same month _Stay Away, Joe_ opened to the usual indifference; _Variety_ said it "caters to out-dated prejudice"). Another self-consciously 'modern' story had been fashioned for Elvis, based on the novel _Kiss My Firm But Pliant Lips_; the film would eventually be retitled _Live A Little, Love A Little_. Elvis plays a hip photographer who juggles two jobs, at an ad agency and _Classic Cat_ magazine, a soft-core/cheesecake publication. He also attracts a free-spirited artist (played by Michele Carey), who effectively imprisons Elvis in her house with the help of her Great Dane, Albert (the dog, whose real name was Brutus, was actually owned by Elvis). There were two other unusual elements in the film: a painful attempt at creating a 'psychedelic' experience via a dream sequence, and, while Elvis and his love interest spend most of the film sleeping in the same bed with a sturdy wooden divider, by the end of the film the plank of wood is gone – without the benefit of wedlock. Elvis's father Vernon also made a cameo appearance in the film.

Despite the changes in the movie formula, it was still believed that an Elvis film should have some music, however little, and four songs were recorded in two sessions on March 7 and 11 at Western Recorders in Hollywood. The session was overseen by Billy Strange, who served as arranger and conductor; he had been set to play the same role at the

August 1967 session that had been canceled. And instead of utilizing the same Nashville-based crew that usually appeared on the soundtracks, Strange drew from LA's crop of studio musicians. The result was a more modern sound, fleshed out by a rich orchestral backing, even if the songs themselves were lacking. But Elvis himself was in good spirits. "I can picture him in my mind, I can picture us in the room," says Chuck Berghofer, who played string bass on the session (with Larry Knechtel doubling on electric bass). "I can remember the vibe and the feeling. I felt comfortable around him. He was humorous, everything was laughing and fun. It wasn't serious."

'Wonderful World,' which played during the film's title sequence, was pleasant enough easy listening, though Elvis's bland delivery reveals his lack of engagement (the song was originally recorded by Cliff Richard, whose version came in third in the UK heat for the 1968 Eurovision Song Contest). 'Edge Of Reality,' the song used during the dream sequence, is only of interest because of how strange it is, a striking mismatch of performer and song. He sounds more in tune on 'Almost In Love,' a ballad with a light Latin feel. But the underrated gem of the session was 'A Little Less Conversation.' After a snappy drum intro, the bassline sets up the funkiest groove that had yet appeared on an Elvis record. The excitement builds as the strings and horns enter, and Elvis handles the complicated lyrics with ease.

The song was co-written by Strange and a young songwriter named Mac Davis, who would soon contribute more substantially to Elvis's career. Born Scott Davis (a name he used professionally until launching his own solo career), Mac had grown up in Lubbock, Texas, then moved to Atlanta, where he played in local bands and also served as regional manager for Vee-Jay Records. By the late 60s, he was living in Los Angeles, working for Metric Music, the publishing arm of Liberty Records. Billy Strange gave the aspiring songwriter the script for *Live A Little*, and Davis thought 'A Little Less Conversation,' a song he'd originally written with Aretha Franklin in mind, might work in a party sequence. "In all honesty 'A Little Less Conversation' was not my favorite recording of Elvis's," he later confessed. "I kind of thought it was sloughed off because it was done for a movie." But Parker was impressed with the singer-songwriter, and on meeting him asked to rub his head. Davis was taken aback, but as Elvis's entourage nodded in agreement, he consented. "He put his hand on my head, like Oral Roberts, and he said, 'You're going to be a star. You tell everybody the Colonel touched your head,'" he later remembered.

May brought the release of both 'Your Time Hasn't Come Yet Baby,' from *Speedway*, and the full soundtrack itself. Neither performed well, peaking at Number 71 and Number 82, respectively (the single reached Number 22 in the UK; the album didn't chart). *Speedway* opened the following month, barely breaking even. The *New York Times* wrote it off as "Just another Presley movie – which makes no great use at all of one of the most talented, important and durable performers of our time." It concluded, "Music, youth, and customs were much changed by Elvis Presley 12 years ago; from the 26 movies he has made since he sang 'Heartbreak Hotel' you would never guess it." But it's likely that Elvis didn't even notice the lack of interest in his latest film. For by then, he was involved in a new project, one that was about to turn his career completely around.

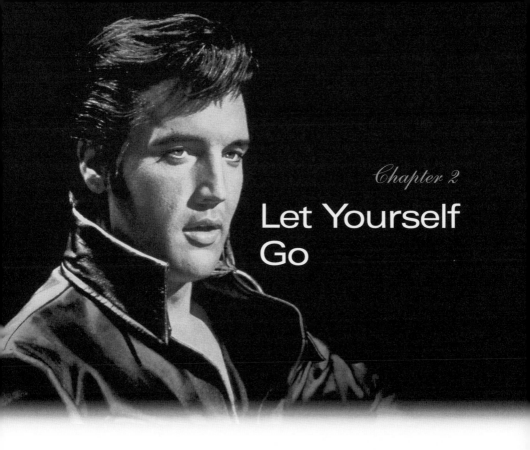

Let Yourself Go

At 9pm on Tuesday, December 3 1968, the debut broadcast of the NBC TV special *Elvis* began. The first shot was a tight close-up on Elvis's face as he sang the opening lines of 'Trouble' from his 1958 film *King Creole*, his favorite out of all his movies. The look on Elvis's face is menacing, the slicked-back pompadour of his recent films is gone; instead a few locks of hair hang with perfectly studied casualness over his forehead. By the time he reaches the chorus, the camera has pulled back enough to capture him from the waist up, sleekly attired in a well-tailored pair of black pants and a shiny black shirt rakishly open to halfway down his chest, his wrists encased in sturdy black leather cuff-style bracelets. The somber look is offset by a crimson red scarf around his neck, matched by the red Hagstrom V-2 guitar, with its red-patterned strap, that hangs on him with its neck pointing down.

At the end of the chorus, he stands stock-still while the camera pulls back further to reveal he's standing in front of a huge set of scaffolding, each rectangular space filled with a silhouetted replica of himself, each with its own guitar, each striking a series of different poses as the music switches from dark rhythm & blues to a bright country-rock – at least as country-rock as you can be when you're using an orchestra. Elvis is determinedly strumming his own guitar now, and right before the verse begins, a bemused smile crosses his face, a momentary look of jaunty, playful confidence that shows how fully in command he really is, and he launches into 'Guitar Man.' The song had always been a good match for Elvis, but he sings it now with a renewed intensity, a fierceness even, that his previous studio version had lacked. The screen behind the scaffolding turns red now, as Elvis sings of the itinerant guitarist, searching for a place to fit in but only encountering rejection.

And just when you think it can't get any more exciting, it does. After an instrumental break, Elvis concludes the song, singing flat-out through the last verse that invites the listener to drop in and catch the guitar man at the latest club where he's playing, in Mobile, Alabama. He's singing seemingly alone in the dark, until the camera pulls back once again to show that he's actually standing between the 'L' and 'V' in a set of giant letters that spell out his name, E-L-V-I-S, in brilliant red lights. The horns wail as the song comes an end, and there's a slow fade-out as Elvis scratches out a rhythmic beat on his guitar.

It was one of the most remarkable moments of Elvis's career. If you'd closed your eyes when Elvis went into the army and not opened them again until the airing of the special, it would have seemed an entirely natural progression; it would have been easy to imagine that the movie years hadn't happened at all. Just the opening three-and-a-half-minute sequence of what has come to be called the 'Comeback Special' represented not just a moment of rebirth for Elvis, but also one of redemption.

But the special didn't begin with the thought that it would play a major role in resurrecting Elvis's career. Instead, the show had its genesis when Colonel Parker ran into an unexpected roadblock in securing his standard $1,000,000 fee for an Elvis movie; no one was interested in meeting his price. Humbled, he worked out a compromise solution with NBC, negotiating a deal whereby the network would finance both a television special and a feature film (1969's *Change Of Habit*) for $1,250,000, thereby still getting a $1,000,000 payment for his client.

On January 12 1968, Tom Sarnoff, NBC's West Coast vice president, publicly announced the special (a small item, "Elvis Presley Signs For First TV Special," ran in the January 18 edition of the *New York Times*). It would be Elvis's first television appearance since 1960, when he'd been a guest star on *The Frank Sinatra Timex Show: Welcome Home Elvis*; Elvis had sung both sides of his current single ('Stuck On You'/'Fame And Fortune,' and duetted with his host, tackling Ol' Blue Eyes's hit 'Witchcraft' while Frankie gamely took on 'Love Me Tender.' It had received solid ratings, and Elvis had offers for other TV work, but they were all turned down (though Parker had toyed over the years with the idea of a closed-circuit broadcast of a live performance; a similar idea would finally come to fruition in 1973).

Parker worked on the assumption that the TV show would follow along the lines of the Elvis Christmas special he sent out to radio stations each year, featuring Elvis singing various carols, interspersed with quotes that would allow the DJ to conduct an 'interview' with Presley, and a brief spoken holiday message from the star at the end. Bob Finkel, who was to be the show's executive producer, thought otherwise, as did the show's primary sponsor, the Singer Sewing Company; at a meeting in May, Singer representative Alfred DiScipio suggested the special explore "the story of Presley as the initiator of a style of music which has become an integral part of our contemporary culture." Elvis himself, in meetings with Finkel, expressed his own desire that the show not be a retread of the fare presented in his movies; "He wants everyone to know what he can really do," the producer noted in a memo.

The key decision, though no one realized it at the time, was the hiring of Steve Binder as the special's director. Binder, a Los Angeles native, had been working in television for a decade, having started in the mailroom for ABC affiliate station KABC ("I heard that if you get a job in the mailroom at a network you can meet pretty girls," he explains). He quickly moved up the ranks, becoming a director for such programs as *The Soupy Sales Show* and *The Steve Allen Westinghouse Show* (Jerry Hopkins, who wrote the first major biography on Elvis, was one of the program's talent coordinators). In 1964, he directed *The T.A.M.I. Show* ("Teenage Music International"), one of the first rock concert films, which most notably featured James Brown and The Rolling Stones. He then directed the rock variety series *Hullabaloo* for NBC, which was meant to rival ABC's similarly-styled programme *Shindig!*

"If you've seen any of the *Hullabaloos* today, you'd say, 'That was a rock'n'roll show? Give me a break!'" says Steve. "With George Hamilton hosting it and so on. But for its time it was trendsetting." The show also introduced go-go dancers to the mainstream; *Hullabaloo*'s young women dancing in cages had been inspired by the similar dancers seen in the LA club Whisky A Go Go. Steve also introduced a note of social commentary into the program, placing models on the set during the musical numbers to suggest an underlying voyeurism. "I wanted the models in there not just as eye candy and window dressing, but also to represent adults, observing what the kids were doing," he explains.

Most recently, Steve had made his name as a maverick while working on a television special with British singer Petula Clark, simply entitled *Petula*. The show's sponsors had already expressed their unhappiness with guest star Harry Belafonte, and the issue came to a head when, during the taping of Clark's anti-war song 'On The Path Of Glory,' she took Belafonte by the arm, a casual gesture that nonetheless provoked controversy at a time when people of different races might appear on television side by side, but certainly couldn't touch. Steve faced down the network and the sponsors and refused to have the sequence removed. "I was kind of unhappy that everybody's attention went to the moment of 'the touch' instead of really paying attention to the show," he says. "As a result, I think a lot of people walked away with the impression it was just a publicity gimmick or something. The sequence certainly led to breaking the color line in prime time variety television. But I think audiences embellished the story at the end and started putting out rumors that they were practically fornicating on air! Which had nothing to do with the truth."

Steve's business partner at the time was Dayton Burr 'Bones' Howe. Bones was born in Minneapolis, but grew up in Sarasota, Florida, where his career in music began as a drummer in local bands. He continued playing in bands while studying at Georgia Tech in Atlanta, and was able to meet the numerous musicians passing through town on tours. While serving as an impromptu tour guide for drummer Shelly Manne, Bones mentioned he was also interested in electronics, and Manne suggested he combine his interests and move to LA to become a recording engineer. "And it was like a light went on," Bones recalls. "I went, 'Okay, that's what I'm going to do.'"

His first studio job in Los Angeles was at Radio Recorders, and he soon found himself working on Elvis's LA sessions in the 50s. Bones had actually seen Elvis perform back in Sarasota, in a February 21 1956 date at the Florida Theater when Elvis shared the bill with a Western film. "He was a country singer and I liked jazz, so I hated him!" says Bones. "It was just a country show as far as I was concerned, and I wasn't particularly interested in the music." He later saw Elvis's name on a theater marquee in Atlanta while walking with some friends; "I can remember somebody saying 'Elvis Presley – what a stupid name that is.'"

Nonetheless, when he finally worked with him, Bones was impressed with how Elvis ran his sessions. "Elvis would listen to an acetate and if he didn't like it, he'd make a cut-throat thing with his finger across his throat – 'Cut that off!' And I'd just keep playing them until he found one he liked, and then he would pat the top of his head, like 'Once more from the top.' Then the band would work out the arrangement. But Elvis chose the takes and chose the tunes." He later worked with Elvis during the _G.I. Blues_ sessions, and noticed a distinct change in his personality: "He seemed less loose than he was. He was still clowning around like he always did, but he seemed a little more buttoned up. I mean, for Elvis."

Steve and Bones had formed a production company called Binder/Howe Productions; Bones had been producing the acts The Fifth Dimension and The Association, and Steve was trying to get a film project with producer Walter Wanger off the ground when Bob Finkel called. "I think Finkel wisely realized the Elvis special was sort of going down the tubes because he couldn't get Elvis to do anything to move it along," says Steve. Finkel had also explained, "I don't relate to Elvis. He calls me 'Mr. Finkel.' I need to find somebody he can talk to who can convince him to do the special."

At first, Steve was not interested. "My initial instinct was to turn it down, to be honest with you," he recalls. "I truthfully was never an Elvis fan. I was more into the West Coast sound with The Byrds and Crosby Stills Nash & Young and that whole world. When I first started watching Elvis, it was more for amusement, to see what all the fuss was about."

But after discussing it, the two partners decided it would be worthwhile to at least meet with the producer, given his stature at NBC. "We thought, 'If we stiff him, maybe he'll never call us again,'" says Bones. "In show business, you never say no until you're too busy to say yes. So we said okay, we'll go out and talk to him." Bones also felt Steve would be a great match for Elvis, telling him, "Steve, you've gotta do it. You and Elvis are going to turn out to be great friends. You'll love working with him and vice versa. Don't turn him down."

After meeting with Finkel, the two agreed to meet with Parker, and a date was set for May 17. It would be the pair's introduction to the manipulative games that comprised Parker's way of doing business, beginning with a request that they provide a bag of Danishes for the 7am meeting. A bag of pastries was duly provided, though it languished on the table throughout the entire meeting, during which "We never were offered anything, including coffee or our Danishes!" says Steve.

CHAPTER 2 LET YOURSELF GO

After being led through the maze of Parker's offices on the MGM Studios lot, noting the Elvis memorabilia plastered over the walls, Steve and Bones were ushered into a large kitchen for the meeting. "It was like a big country kitchen, with a big round table in the middle of the room," says Bones. "There might have been a pot bellied stove! It was really down-home." Everyone sat down at the table, covered with an oilcloth tablecloth, then carefully sized each other up – like at the beginning of a poker game, Steve felt.

"The Colonel dominated the conversation," Steve says. "It was all about him and how smart he was and how clever he was. The first thing I remember him telling us was that all of his contracts were one page long, and Elvis came to work at a certain time and left at a certain time and you owned him during that time frame. You could get him to do basically anything you wanted." It was this kind of decision making, in Steve's view, that had led to the sorry state Elvis's career had fallen into. Without demanding any kind of script or song approval (beyond securing the publishing rights for the songs), Parker had effectively been squandering his client's talent.

Steve was equally unimpressed with Parker's idea for the direction the special should take. Parker handed him a box ("Which I still have," he notes) with Elvis's picture on the top, containing a reel of tape and an accompanying script for the Christmas radio show that had aired the previous year, telling him, "Here. I want you to have this, because this is going to be the special."

"I had absolutely no intentions of doing a Christmas special, especially with Elvis," says Steve. "I knew a Christmas special would be a disaster. And I wasn't about to turn Elvis into a wimp and have him do what anybody else could do. I was young enough and arrogant enough to say, 'I'm gonna do what I want to do. What's the worst they can do to me? Fire me.' And I think the Colonel in the back of his head would've loved to fire me all the way through the production. But as it went on, his gut reaction or his instinct said, 'Something special's happening here. I'd better not get in the middle of it.'"

Before seeing them off, Parker inducted both men into the "Snowman's Club," his own private club that celebrated the art of 'snowing,' and, perhaps indulging in a snow-job of his own, assured them they'd have a "million dollar experience" working on the special (an experience, needless to say, whose financial payoff would be substantially less for Binder and Howe). Later that day, they met with Elvis at the Binder/Howe offices at 8833 Sunset Boulevard. "Elvis walked in, and our introduction was 'Hi Steve,' 'Hi Elvis,'" Steve recalls. "So it was never formal. And we just went into my office in back. I found him incredibly personable and outgoing."

The discussion quickly took on a frankness that Elvis had not encountered for some time. When Elvis asked the director how he'd evaluate the current state of his career, Steve's response was blunt and to the point. "What career?" he said, prompting an appreciative laugh from Elvis. He then went on to reiterate what Elvis himself already knew and had been complaining about to his entourage, if not his manager; he hadn't had a big hit record, or film, in years, and was on the verge of becoming irrelevant. But this show offered him a chance to change that. "If you do this special, the next morning you're either going to be the biggest hit in the country or the biggest disaster," Steve told him. "Television gives you instant results. America will know whether they like you or they don't like you, and if it's the latter, you'll be known as somebody who everybody respected in the 50s, but your career will be over." It was, Steve admitted, a gamble.

"I think that very first meeting we took set the tone for everything," Steve says. "Because I wasn't trying to get a job, so I was brutally honest with him and I told him that as far as I was concerned, he was no longer a hit rock'n'roll star. He was living off his past exploits and the new generation growing up only knew of him as a has-been. And I think those kind of conversations hit home. He even said later on that he totally trusted me because I was giving him straight answers, whereas I'm sure he was surrounded by other people just stroking him all the way."

Another key point of the conversation came when Steve mentioned that The Association had been offered the song 'MacArthur Park,' but turned down the opportunity to be the first to record it because they couldn't secure the publishing (actor Richard Harris went on to have a Top Five hit with the song). Would Elvis have recorded it himself, Steve wondered? "And the reason I asked him, I just wanted to see if this was a guy who was living in the glory of his past or if he was really looking at the future," Steve explains. "And without hesitation he said, 'I'd record it in a second.'" It was an answer that confirmed that while publishing might have been Parker's predominant concern it was not Elvis's – even if he couldn't always win that argument with his manager.

Of greater concern to Elvis, Steve realized, was that he wasn't comfortable with the idea of performing on TV. Despite the success his television appearances had brought him in the 50s, experiences like his July 1 1956 performance on *The Steve Allen Show*, where he'd been made to wear a tuxedo and sing 'Hound Dog' to a poor basset hound, had left a bad taste. "My turf is in a recording studio, not on a television stage," he told Steve, perhaps tellingly not mentioning his film work. "Well," Steve replied, "why don't you make a record, and I'll put pictures to it?" It was an exchange that fully sold Elvis on the project. As Elvis told Steve later, "You know, it was that first meeting when you told me to go make a record and you'd put the pictures to it that really relaxed me. And I knew I was heading in the right direction with you."

Elvis and Priscilla left for a vacation in Hawaii the next day, and Steve and his team got to work crafting the special. "I've never believed in the one man theory," he says. "In film and television, to me it's a collaborative effort. You need to have a team around you who gets all the credit – the producer, the director, the star – but there are tons of people who've made major contributions along the way, whether they're special effects or even holding the cue cards or running the teleprompters. So I like to get them all in a room together and say, forget what our titles are, let's just start throwing ideas around."

Two members of the team were writers Chris Bearde and Allan Blye. Chris, born in the UK, grew up in Australia, where he began his career reading poetry with a jazz band in local clubs, eventually moving into comedy and TV as both a writer and performer. He eventually emigrated to Canada where he worked for the Canadian Broadcasting Corporation, working on the comedy shows *Nightcap* and *Network* in addition to music specials featuring acts ranging from Jefferson Airplane to Dionne Warwick. While working at CBC Chris met Allan Blye, a Canadian who'd established himself as a singer (replacing fellow Canadian Robert Goulet on the TV programme *G.E. Showtime*) and had also appeared as "Captain Blye" on the children's television show *Mister Rogers' Neighborhood*. Chris encouraged Allan's budding writing skills and soon he was working for CBC as a writer as well. Both men also had their sights on America, and made a pact that whoever got a break stateside first would give the other a hand.

By 1967, they'd both cracked the US market, Allan landing a job on *The Smothers Brothers Comedy Hour* and Chris working for *Laugh-In*, winning an Emmy for his writing after being in the country barely three months. ("It was quite an amazing thing," he says, "because I was in the country only 13 weeks, and there I was standing on the stage with Frank Sinatra on one side of me and Sally Field on the other, holding this big Emmy in my hand – it was the most incredible Hollywood story.") Allan had worked on the *Petula* special, and when he was called about working on the Elvis show suggested Chris also be hired.

"My immediate reaction was of course I want to do it, because I just want to meet Elvis!" says Chris. "I didn't know what the deal was, but I wanted to meet Elvis." And from the start, the writers were determined to stake out their own territory. "I was standing in the hallway when Elvis came down with this entourage," Chris recalls of the writers' first meeting with Presley. "He looked like a caged panther. He was electric, he was totally electric. And then I saw a little sparkle in his eyes. I figured, mmm, okay, I'm just going to be Mr Little Quiet In The Background here for a while. But I was going to take a bit of a chance when I got to say hi to him, to see if Elvis was in a place where we could communicate from, that was a very different place from where he had been. And if they were going to do some goody-goody little show then I would've stepped back and just taken the money and been Mr In The Background Writer Person.

"I got introduced last: 'This is Chris Bearde,'" he continues. "And I said, 'It's great to meet you Elvis.' And I looked at the Colonel and said, 'Colonel, I really like what you've done with Elvis. And I also like your chicken.' There was this long silence. And I thought 'Shit, what's going to happen, did I say the wrong thing, what the hell did I do wrong here?' And then Elvis just burst out laughing. And of course when Elvis laughs the entourage laughs, and when the entourage laughs everybody else laughs, and it was a big win for me. I saw that this guy had a great sense of humor, and that was to me the ultimate. Because being the comedy and music person, I wanted to get a place for myself, as being somebody who could say things to Elvis and he would listen. On behalf of Allan and myself, I was kind of saying, 'Hey, let's get in here and have a say here, and not just be two little lackey boys standing in the background from Canada.' And that worked great for us."

The two were further encouraged by Elvis's own candor. Asked what he wanted to do in the special at another meeting, Elvis declared, "Well, I'll tell you one thing I don't want it to be – I don't want to be a goody goody cocksucking singing mechanic anymore." "Those were his exact words," says Chris. "I'm not going to forget those words! So we immediately pounced on that and said, 'No, what we want to do is we want you to sing. We want you to sing "Hound Dog." We want you to shake it and break it and do your thing.' When we got to close the door and it was just the creative people and Elvis, I could see how he absolutely loved that. He just loved it, that we were away from all the stuff from his past and this was the new Young Turk group. Which we all were at that stage. So basically, that's how the show got started."

What was needed for the show was some unifying element. "With music artists, like Elvis and Petula, it was really a case of getting all their material and going through it, poring through it, and seeing what connects to what," Steve says. "And usually there is a theme connected to it. When I approached specials I wanted an A theme, which is, Does it have a beginning and does it have an ending? It's not just music and sets and scenery and costumes. There has to be a story. Because people get involved in stories."

The writers had already visited Tower Records (next door to the building where the Binder/Howe offices were) to buy all of Elvis's available recordings to listen to, searching for connections. "I knew everything that we bought, it was just like listening to it again," Chris explains. "But it was great because we got to keep all the records!" And what Chris calls "probably the key story to the whole thing" came on the night of June 4. Since returning from Hawaii, Elvis had been coming by the Binder/Howe offices regularly, going over ideas in informal rehearsals for the show. On June 4, a television in the office was tuned in to a broadcast of Senator Robert Kennedy's victory speech at LA's Ambassador Hotel; the Democratic presidential hopeful had just won California's state primary. Minutes later, Kennedy was shot (he eventually died on June 6), leaving everyone in the room stunned.

Kennedy's assassination provoked a cathartic reaction in Elvis, especially coming just two months after civil rights leader Dr Martin Luther King Jr had been murdered in Elvis's hometown of Memphis. "From the moment that was on, for the rest of the night, we sat in that room and Elvis started to tell us his life story," says Chris, "and he played the guitar for all that time himself. And we sat there enthralled. He told us all these stories about his life in Memphis, and his mom and his dad, he told the story of how he got started, and the people that used to try and hit him because they wanted to hit Elvis Presley. And he sang all these songs. And that's when Steve and all of us said, 'This is what the show's gotta be. It's gotta be you doing all this.'"

'Guitar Man' had already been identified as the show's theme song. "The main theme was this guitar man leaving his roots and going out to seek fame and fortune," says Steve. "And then finding out, after he had all this success, that the happiest he ever was, was just being that old guitar player. Going full circle in a sense. [The essence of the storyline was drawn from Maurice Maeterlinck's play *The Blue Bird*, about finding happiness within one's self, rather that searching the world for it.] I think the job of producing or directing is not to ask people, 'Okay, you create the show.' I think you've got to give them a focus and a direction, and then let them fill in the holes. Elvis was symbolically a musician, a guitar man; that's plain and simple, basic."

For the writers, 'Guitar Man' provided a strong conceptual link to the two sides of Elvis they wanted to present, "both the real story of Elvis sitting on the stage, and sort of a fantasy Elvis story where we can get these big production numbers in as well," Chris explains. "And that's how the two styles of the show came about." 'Guitar Man' needed a some lyrical tweaks to fit the storyline, including a new last verse, and Allan Blye approached Jerry Reed to get his consent to make the changes. "I didn't know Jerry Reed, and he certainly didn't know me," he says. "I told him I was calling about 'Guitar Man' and I wanted to change a few words to use it on a television show. And he was very reluctant; he interrupted me saying, 'Why would you want to change my lyric?' I said, 'It's a fabulous lyric. I just want to adjust a couple things so that they ring more true for Elvis.' And he said, 'Elvis?' 'Yeah, yeah, Elvis Presley, we're doing an Elvis Presley special.' Which I'd forgot to say to start with! And that was it. He said, 'You got it!'"

For the opening, Allan suggested starting the show with a close-up of Elvis's face, and Chris had immediately responded by singing the opening lines of 'Trouble.' "It just was magic," says Allan. "The whole thing just came together." The scaffolding was inspired by the set used when Elvis sings the title song in *Jailhouse Rock*, what Allan describes as "the pillbox look." Allan also 'dressed' the set in effect, by saying to Steve, "Wouldn't it be great to have 100 Elvises behind him?" "I took it to Bob Finkel never thinking I'd get it through," says Steve. "And the interesting thing with that is, to this day people who spend money in film and television usually think that it's quantity, not quality that they're paying for. So the first question was, 'How many minutes are you going to use them on the screen?' And I said, 'Probably no more than one.' Which even made it a tougher sale to NBC. But had we had 100 Elvises two or three times in the show, it wouldn't have meant anything. But the fact that it was just that opening moment, people to this day talk about it, or try to imitate it or emulate it." The letters that spelled out 'E-L-V-I-S' were inspired by the letters that spelled 'J-U-D-Y' at the beginning of *The Judy Garland Show*.

The opening number also introduced the color scheme for the programme, the dominant colors being red, black, and white; Elvis himself would begin the show wearing a black outfit, and end it in a white outfit. His clothes were designed by Bill Belew, another veteran of the *Petula* special, who had previously had little interest in Elvis. "I was one of the few people I think that never saw any of his films," he said. "And I didn't really hear much about him or know much about him until Steve said that we were going to do a special with Elvis." Bill – or "Billy," as Elvis called him – had a free hand in creating his designs. "Steve was great in that respect," he said. "He trusted everybody that worked on his special to do what they did the best." Belew's outfits for the special were especially effective because of their simplicity; in the opening sequence, Elvis cut a stark figure in black pants and an open-necked shirt, with just a touch of color coming from the red scarf around his neck. "The scarf came about because I didn't want Elvis to wear a necktie for what I was doing," Belew explained. "I just didn't feel that that was the look I wanted him to have at that time. And also I was experimenting with things, and he happened to grab on to that idea. At that time we were always wearing scarves, so I adapted that into the outfits that I did for him."

Along with a concert segment, it was planned that there be other segments exploring the musical genres Elvis represented and/or had an interest in, so a gospel sequence was a logical inclusion. "The gospel segment was twofold," Steve explains. "One was to take his gospel albums and find a way to weave songs together in a medley. And secondly, I've always loved dancing and dancers on television, and I wanted to find a way to show them off. And that was the perfect segment to do it in."

The gospel medley segment begins with a brief dance sequence performed by Claude Thompson, one of the show's choreographers (and another *Petula* veteran) to the spiritual 'Sometimes I Feel Like A Motherless Child.' Thompson then walks off screen through a group of women dressed in white and men dressed in black into a sort of 'mod' church set, with Elvis, wearing a tailored burgundy suit to make him stand out against the dancers, on a stage above his 'congregation.' As he sings 'Where Could I Go But To The Lord,' he's joined on stage by his backing singers, The Blossoms (dressed in white), a trio who had provided backing vocals on numerous girl group records (as well as singing lead on 'He's A Rebel,' which was nonetheless credited to The Crystals), and had appeared on *Shindig!* During the number, Elvis and The Blossoms walk down the steps to the main floor, leaving room for the dancers to perform as the song segues into 'Up Above My Head.' But the most exciting moment comes when the medley suddenly snaps into 'Saved.' The Jerry Leiber/Mike Stoller song was nearly a parody of a gospel number (as the songwriting team's 'Love Me,' recorded by Elvis in 1957, also poked fun at old-time country), but Elvis's enthusiastic, heartfelt delivery makes it electrifying.

The racial mixing in the segment also highlighted the element of integration present in the entire show. "I'd just come from this amazing controversy with Petula and Belafonte, so I was a little shell-shocked at the time," Binder says. "When I put the Elvis Presley special together, I had a black choreographer [Claude Thompson], I had a Puerto Rican choreographer [Jaime Rogers, who played one of the Sharks in the film version of *West Side Story*], I had The Blossoms on camera accompanying Elvis throughout most of the special [the trio was

African-American], and the entire core of musicians, extras, dancers, were totally integrated among all the races. And not one comment was made in terms of race on the entire production. I found that really significant, that everybody accepted them as colorless and were blinded to any kind of controversy over prejudice or racism or anything. Everybody just said 'Great.'"

The show's other big production number was designed to highlight the 'fantasy Elvis.' In a scenario that might have come from one of his films – and which was definitely meant as a send up of them – Elvis is seen rising from humble roots to fame and fortune. "Elvis knew what a satire the production number was," says Chris. "He understood that it was our way of saying 'This is Elvis in satire.' And you can take it that way or you needn't take it that way. But if you know that you're dealing with a comedy writer who's writing it, myself, you can understand that's what we were doing. And you can also understand that maybe Elvis totally understood that and totally loved it and totally had a tongue-in-cheek attitude about it the whole way through."

The opening has Elvis, clad in a working man's denims, walking along a stylized neon highway singing of being lost in 'Nothingville' (where life is a rat race "at a snail's pace") before setting off in search of better things, with 'Guitar Man' becoming a linking song throughout the sequence.

His first stop is a bordello, where 'Let Yourself Go' provides suitably sexy accompaniment ("Oh God, he was in seventh heaven with all the girls crawling all over him and everything," says Chris). When his fun is interrupted by the arrival of the law, he winds up at a carnival where he's urged to move on by a threatening gangster type, singing 'Big Boss Man' in response. He attempts to rescue the gangster's woman, tossing thugs over his shoulder while singing 'It Hurts Me' without breaking stride. He then begins his musical ascent, providing the music for a belly dancer as he sings Leiber & Stoller's 'Little Egypt.' He next sings 'Trouble,' first in the belly dancing club, then in a succession of better clubs, with a change of costume for each (gold jacket and black pants, the black outfit from the opening sequence, a black velvet suit, and a leather suit). The sequence closes with 'Guitar Man' as Elvis takes off down the highway once again.

Elvis responded positively to each idea brought forward for the show. "I used to joke with him," says Steve, "saying 'I'm scared we're gonna bomb because I'm getting no negatives from you at all.' Anything I said, 'Let's do,' he said, 'Great, let's do it.' And with most stars I worked with, there's always a confrontation somewhere along the line where they're either testing your belief in something or your strength or they're kind of questioning, 'Why are you having me do this?'"

Bill Belew encountered the same acquiescent reaction. "I found Elvis to be a very sweet person," he said. "And we got along really really well. I thought I was going to have reactions different than what happened, but he, for some unknown reason, placed his trust in me. When he saw the sketches and my ideas of what I wanted to do, he never said a word about anything." There was one notable exception. In the 'fantasy Elvis' production number, when Elvis sings in the club with the belly dancer, Belew had designed a suit that emulated the Nudie Cohn-designed gold lamé suit Elvis had worn on the cover of the 1959 greatest hits collection *50,000,000 Elvis Fans Can't Be Wrong*. Despite his own penchant for sartorial excesses, this was one time when the compliant star put his foot down, saying, "Billy, I have to be honest with you. I always hated that suit and I will not wear it." Belew never knew what bothered Elvis about the suit, only speculating that by refusing to wear it "it was a way of rebelling against the Colonel" (the book *Elvis Fashion* notes that Elvis thought the suit "looked more carnival than cool"). Binder urged Belew to find a compromise, and it was settled that Elvis would simply wear the jacket paired with plain black trousers.

It had been a long time since anyone outside of Elvis's immediate circle had challenged him about the insularity of his world. During rehearsals one day, Steve caught Elvis looking out of the window at the activity on busy Sunset Boulevard below. Steve asked what Elvis thought might happen if he went outside on his own. Elvis countered by asking Steve what he thought would happen. After thinking for a minute, Steve said he didn't really think anything would happen, and thought that was the end of it.

But a few days later, when Elvis arrived for rehearsals, he invited Steve to step outside and see what exactly would happen. Nothing did. Cars and pedestrians passed by without giving them a second glance. Elvis even began waving at passing cars in an attempt to attract attention, with equally little success. Eventually, he suggested they all go back inside.

Allan Blye provoked a stronger reaction when he questioned the all-enveloping nature of Elvis's entourage. "Chris and I would be in the office with Elvis, just Elvis and Charlie Hodge, and sometimes Steve," he recalls. "And we'd just be having a great old time, and then Elvis would say, 'I've got to go to the bathroom.' And he'd stand up and you'd hear five guys in the room next door stand up, and he'd walk out the door and they'd surround him and walk him to the bathroom. You know, it was like the infantry."

Allan noted that "a couple of them really had a job – like Joe Esposito was really kind of the road manager. But some of the other guys, I couldn't figure out what they did." One afternoon he broached the subject, asking Elvis, "What does so-and-so do?" "Oh, he's around," said Elvis. "And what does this other guy do?" Allan persisted. "He's around." "What is 'around'?" Allan asked. "What does it mean? 'Around'?" "Around means around!" Elvis snapped. "It was the only time I saw Elvis lose his sense of comedy for ten seconds," Allan recalls. "I said 'OK,' and we went back to doing this laughing and having a good time."

Two weeks later, on a Saturday night, Allan was surprised to hear his doorbell ring around 9pm, and even more surprised to open the door and find Elvis standing on his doorstep. "What are you doing?" Allan exclaimed. "I came to see you," Elvis replied, grinning. "And where is everybody?" Allan asked. "There's nobody here," said Elvis. "It's just me." "And I got the message," Allan says. "And my wife was beside herself!" Allan quickly rounded up his neighbors to come over. "They thought maybe I had a burglar in the house," he says. "And they walked in the kitchen and there's Elvis Presley with a little bandana around his neck! And I'd got my little half-sized guitar out, and he sat and played and we just had a fun evening. We stayed up pretty late, and then we had to get him home; I knew that Joe would be in a panic if he realized he was gone."

But while Elvis was on board with the show, there were a few hiccups in other areas. Steve just tried to stay focused. "I was doing the best job I knew how with blinders on," he says. "I just didn't think about the politics or what was going on behind the scenes. I was just plunging ahead doing what I thought was the best thing I could possibly do to make the special as good as I could make it."

One area that was of concern to both Steve and Bones was the possibility of a soundtrack album. There was no mention of one in the contract with Binder/Howe Productions, and Bones had, as a producer with a growing track record of hit songs, begun making enquiries about it. "I got in trouble," he admits. "I made trouble through my whole career!"

"The Colonel didn't want to acknowledge that Bones and I were bona fide record producers and we should be given a royalty," explains Steve. "That became a big issue, and as a result, since we were both represented at the time by the William Morris Agency, you knew who the agent was gonna side with! So we were kind of in a weak position to stand up for that. But we threatened not to do the show unless they would promise that if there was an album released we would get a royalty. And they agreed to that. The Colonel called me personally to tell me there would never be a soundtrack of the show so there was nothing to worry about." What neither of them knew at that point was that Parker had already worked out a deal with NBC to turn over tapes of the special to RCA for a possible soundtrack.

Putting the music together for the show proved to be its own headache. Elvis had asked that Billy Strange be the show's conductor and musical arranger, and Steve had agreed, tapping Billy Goldenberg to be the show's musical director; Strange had recently served as arranger and musical conductor for the *Live A Little, Love A Little* soundtrack sessions, while Goldenberg had worked with Steve on *Hullabaloo* and *Petula*. But Strange failed to deliver any arrangements, leaving Goldenberg stymied. Realizing something had to be done, Steve decided to fire Strange and make Goldenberg the show's arranger, only to face Parker's displeasure; Elvis would surely quit the show if his arranger of choice, Billy Strange, wasn't used, Steve was told. But when Steve explained the situation to Elvis, he simply agreed without further comment.

Goldenberg was a bit unsure about how well he could relate to Elvis and his work, rock'n'roll not being his forte, and the knowledge that he would be introducing orchestral instruments into the arrangements was met with some derision among Elvis's associates. But dealing directly with Elvis himself proved to be a different matter entirely. Billy arrived for rehearsals one day to find Elvis at the piano playing Beethoven's 'Moonlight Sonata'; he sat down next to him and the two began playing the piece together. It was a moment that broke the ice between them. As always, when working with someone who respected his talent and presented him with a new challenge, Elvis responded with enthusiasm, and when he first rehearsed with the orchestra it was a moment that Goldenberg described as "thrilling ... he was on such a high, he was so involved and excited and emotionally charged."

Recording sessions were held June 20-24 at Western Recorders in Burbank. NBC had protested the choice of location, citing expenses and questioning why recording couldn't be done at the station's own studios, using the same musicians that worked on Bob Hope's specials. While Steve and Bones had no objections to using some of NBC's musicians, they pointed out they were working on a rock'n'roll show, and wanted to draw on the vast pool of experienced session players LA had to offer. (The roster would eventually include many of the musicians from the legendary 'Wrecking Crew' of studio musicians: guitarists Tommy Tedesco, Mike Deasy, and Al Casey, bassists Chuck Berghofer and Larry Knechtel, pianist Don Randi, and drummer Hal Blaine. The Blossoms also provided backing vocals.) Though the show would feature live vocals from Elvis (singing to a backing track) when possible, studio recordings were made of Elvis's vocals as well, chiefly for use in the production numbers. In the opening sequence, for example, Elvis's vocal for 'Trouble' was live, while he lip-synced to 'Guitar Man' (he also played Al Casey's red Hagstrom guitar during the number). Elvis also wanted to lip-sync during the gospel number, due to his moving throughout the sequence, which Steve reluctantly agreed to; he felt the syncing didn't match up in the end.

The sessions went smoothly. 'Nothingville,' 'Let Yourself Go,' 'Big Boss Man,' and 'It Hurts Me' were recorded on June 20; 'Guitar Man,' 'Trouble,' 'Little Egypt' (all from the 'Guitar Man' production number), and 'Where Could I Go But To The Lord' on June 21; and 'Trouble' and 'Guitar Man' (both for the show's opening), 'Up Above My Head,' and 'Saved' on June 22. (The sessions also saw the recording of numerous instrumental linking sequences, as well as the numbers that required female vocals, the first verse of 'Let Yourself Go' and 'Sometimes I Feel Like A Motherless Child.')

In their new settings, the songs revealed their hidden strengths; only 'Trouble' had been previously associated with an acclaimed project (the film *King Creole*). 'Guitar Man' and 'Big Boss Man' were overlooked singles. 'It Hurts Me' had languished as the B-side of the 1964 single 'Kissin' Cousins.' Leiber & Stoller's sassy 'Little Egypt' had appeared in the 1964 film *Roustabout*; 'Let Yourself Go' had just appeared in *Speedway*. In every instance, the new performances of the songs were stronger in the special than in their original versions, with a rawer, gutsier vocal delivery on Elvis's part.

Elvis had previously recorded 'Where Could I Go But To The Lord' as well, on *How Great Thou Art*. All the gospel numbers displayed a fervor not present on Elvis's previous religious recordings; the closest he'd come to revealing that fire was when he sang the medley 'Down By The Riverside'/'When The Saints Go Marching In' in the 1966 film *Frankie and Johnny*. 'Nothingville' (written by Billy Strange and Mac Davis), 'Up Above My Head,' and 'Saved' were new. Steve also heard another sound during the sessions that he made use of during the special; on hearing Tommy Tedesco and Mike Deasy scratching out a funky rhythm on their guitars during a jam, he decided he had to use it somewhere, and it was placed at the conclusion of the 'Trouble'/'Guitar Man' opening sequence, as Elvis stands strumming his guitar between the E-L-V-I-S letters.

The climax to the sessions came, fittingly, on the last day of recording with the orchestra, when the show's closing number was recorded. The issue of what exactly that song would be had been a matter of contention for some time. Parker had been adamant in telling "Bindle" (his nickname for Steve Binder) that the show had to close with a Christmas song, or something in a similar vein (one suggestion was 'I Believe,' a huge hit for Frankie Laine in 1953), as the special was supposed to be a Christmas show, and it looked like no holiday music would be featured in any of the other segments. Binder was just as determined to steer clear of any hint of schmaltz, especially as he'd developed a new respect for his star while working with him over the past weeks. "I really felt, here's this guy coming from a Southern state which was kind of known for its racism, who seemed pretty void of any prejudice whatsoever," he says. "The Colonel kept insisting that we end the show with 'I Believe,' and I kept racking my brain as to how I'm going to get anybody to know who the real Elvis Presley is."

Steve explained what he was looking for to Billy Goldenberg and W. Earl Brown, the show's choral director (officially credited for "Special Lyrics and Vocal Arrangements," he was also the composer of 'Up Above My Head'). "You've been around Elvis now for weeks," Steve told them. "We know what he stands for, what his philosophy is. Put it in words. Go write me a song that says what we know him to be." A few days later, he was awoken at home by an early morning phone call from Brown, who told him, "Steve, I think we got it."

Steve rushed in to the NBC studios, and was presented with a lead sheet for a song called 'If I Can Dream,' credited to both Brown and Goldenberg. The two quickly 'auditioned' the song, Earl singing and Billy playing the piano, and Steve was convinced he had found his closing number. When Elvis arrived, Steve called him in, and had Earl and Billy play him the song, while Parker waited impatiently outside, fuming. After one run-through, Elvis asked to hear the song again. And again. And again. "They played it three or four times," Steve recalls. "And Elvis thought a little bit, and he looked at me, and he said 'I'll do it.' In the meantime, Parker and Diskin [Tom Diskin, one of Parker's assistants] and all the RCA guys are in the next room, and they could hear what was going on in there. And the Colonel I understand was saying 'Well, over my dead body is he going to sing "If I Can Dream"!'

"And once Elvis said, 'I'm gonna do it,' I walked into the other room and said, 'He's gonna do it,'" Steve continues. "And immediately RCA wanted the publishing. And Colonel Parker just sat there totally frustrated because he wasn't about to challenge Elvis in front of all these people. And the best part of the whole story is, after Elvis said, 'I'll do it,' Billy went over Earl's shoulder, took a pencil with an eraser and erased his name off of the song, and he said, 'This is Earl's song, it's not mine. I had nothing to do with it.' Which probably cost Billy Goldenberg hundreds of thousands of dollars in royalties. But the staff that worked on that show, in my opinion, and I've stayed friends with almost all of them, were real special artists, who cared about the integrity of the product more than how much they were being paid. It's a rare thing to say these days."

Brown, who died in 2008, has contested Binder's version of how the song was written, claiming in interviews he had been told that a melody would be presented for him to write lyrics to. Then, when nothing materialized, he decided to write the song entirely, thinking that if Elvis didn't use it, Aretha Franklin might record it.

But Binder stands by his story. "I talked to Earl about his writing 'If I Can Dream' a few times before his death," he says. "His version is completely fictional. The only person he communicated with or took direction from was me during the entire production. He admitted his memory was vague at the time he talked or wrote about it years later. My memory is very clear on this, and how I described it is exactly how it happened. The lead sheet definitely had Billy Goldenberg's name on it when the two came in early to NBC to play it for me. While he was erasing his name, Billy told me in front of Earl that Earl really wrote the song by himself after I told them both to go home and write a song that expressed Elvis's feelings about the world around him in 1968 that would replace the traditional and 'expected' closing Christmas song at the end of the special."

In any case, 'If I Can Dream' accomplished everything Steve had wanted it to. The dramatic showstopper begins quietly, slowly building throughout to a majestic, sweeping conclusion. The lyrics are a plea for tolerance, a wish for an all-encompassing universal brotherhood, a timely sentiment in a year which had seen not only the murders of King and Kennedy, but also increased divisiveness in the country about civil rights issues at home and the Vietnam war abroad. In another performer's hands, the song could simply have become a conventional ballad. But Elvis's searing delivery made it an impassioned plea that seemed to come from the very depths of his soul. Darlene Love, who considered her role as a backing vocalist on the track (as one of The Blossoms) one of the highlights of her career, said, "Anyone who hears 'If I Can Dream' and still calls rock and roll the Devil's music is committing blasphemy." "Elvis sings this song like a gospel singer," said Joe Moscheo, a member of The Imperials, the gospel group that appeared on the _How Great Thou Art_ album. "He seems completely carried away by the message, almost like someone in a trance."

Elvis's movements in the studio when the song was recorded on June 23 matched the high drama of his vocal. "He did it complete with knee drops, in front of the strings," says Bones. "The violin players couldn't believe what they were seeing. They were sawing away looking at this guy, dropping down on his knees. It was just brilliant what he did; he was doing all that stuff that he does on stage. And the guys in the band, the guys in the rhythm section, I guess they'd seen all that before. But the string players were really astonished."

But Elvis wasn't completely satisfied, and asked if he could record his vocals again after the musicians had left. "It was this huge studio, and the chairs were still set up and all the musicians were gone," says Steve. "And right before he sang, I said, 'Turn off all the lights in the studio.' And so in the dark Elvis sang 'If I Can Dream.' And it was one of those unbelievable moments where nobody gets to see it except a handful of people who are sitting in the control room, looking out the glass at the big vast studio. And there's Elvis, literally on the ground in a fetal position with this hand mic, singing the song." Elvis stayed at the studio another hour, listening to the song repeatedly, clearly pleased and perhaps surprised at the magnitude of his work. The following day, the sessions concluded, with Elvis recording vocals for 'Memories,' a nostalgic Mac Davis/Billy Strange composition (though recorded live for the show, it was this studio version that would appear on the soundtrack album), and 'A Little Less Conversation,' recording a new vocal to the backing track used in *Live A Little, Love A Little*; this version of the song was eventually cut from the show, but would have a surprising rebirth 34 years later.

By now, Elvis's excitement about the show was increasingly obvious to those around him. "Priscilla [later] told us he was so happy during that period," Bones says. "He came home every day just bouncing, she said. He was so happy. He was having such a good time." When rehearsals moved to NBC's Burbank studios on June 17, he even moved into his dressing room suite (formerly used by Dean Martin), so invigorated by the show that he simply didn't want to leave the studio. It was a move that would also, unexpectedly, provide the inspiration for the show's most exciting sequence.

"As soon as we finished the day's work on stage, he would go into his dressing room with his guys," Steve recalls. "He would basically unwind from a hard day's work and spend hours in there just jamming with the guys and having fun; rather than watch television in the dressing room or whatever, they would play music for hours." It was while watching these jam sessions that Steve suddenly got the idea that this could be the way to showcase the real Elvis to the audience. A performance segment had already been planned for the show, but the loose feel of what Steve witnessed in the dressing room had a much greater authenticity.

"I didn't want to recreate it," Steve explains. " I wanted to _do_ it. And I kept going to the Colonel insisting I be able to bring a professional camera in there and audio equipment and record it. And the Colonel was adamant about no cameras, no audio, no still pictures even. And finally I think I just wore him down, where he said one day at my umpteenth attempt at getting him to give permission, 'Well, if you want to recreate it, you can do it out on stage. But I'm not going to promise you can even use it.' But I jumped on it, and that's how the improv happened."

For Steve, the improv sequence would be the emotional heart of the show. "The whole special was to let Elvis do his thing, and the improv, which to me was the most important part of all the show, was sort of getting the peek in the window of Who is Elvis Presley? Was he the figment of Colonel Parker's PR machine? Or did he really have this indefinable thing called talent? And I think if anybody's doubted why Elvis Presley became such an icon, I think that improv segment shows why he did. But it could've even been better. In a sense the Colonel screwed himself by not letting me bring those cameras in the dressing room. I can accept anything from anybody as long as they give me a rationale as to why they make decisions. With the Colonel it was always just an ego trip of power. It was never about anything artistic, it wasn't even about money. It was really about control. The Colonel was a total control freak, and he didn't want anybody to challenge him or his power. And so as great as the improv was with Elvis on stage, it was still superficial compared to the real thing that I got to see behind the scenes in the dressing room."

Instead of jamming with his buddies, it was decided that Elvis's old bandmates, Scotty Moore and DJ Fontana, should be brought in (Elvis's original bass player, Bill Black, had died in 1965). "He just out of the blue called and said they were doing a quote-unquote Christmas show," says Scotty. "And so DJ and I went out there expecting to just stand up and play like we had on *Ed Sullivan* and all the other TV shows." They were surprised to find something quite different waiting for them, a kind of performance Scotty describes as "the first *Unplugged*."

Two days of informal rehearsals were held on June 24 and 25; widely bootlegged, the sets were finally officially released in 2008 in the boxed set *The Complete '68 Comeback Special*. Allan Blye and Chris Bearde had a written a rough script for the segment (which, among other wry asides about his career, cleaned up Elvis's description of the roles he'd played as "I'm usually the 'goody goody' singing mechanic who always gets the girl"), but Steve wanted him to speak more off the cuff. "In between every song, tell like one or two things," he told Elvis during the rehearsal on the 25th. "Otherwise the whole section ends up a lot of tunes locked together … Is it comfortable for you to just fall into the story?" "I might need something to go on," said Elvis. "Just as a reminder." Notes could be provided, he was assured; and if he ran out of something to say, he could always go back to singing. The directions for the rest of the band were equally circumspect; "The director told us to do whatever you want to do, just don't cuss!" Scotty recalls.

Bill Belew had already designed an outfit for the show's other planned concert sequence, which would have Elvis performing in front of an audience before a live orchestra. Steve had asked for something "outstanding" for Elvis to wear, and after considering various ideas, Bill observed, "Steve, the only thing that I can remember about Elvis is that I have seen him in a leather jacket, but I have never seen him in total leather. What if I do a leather outfit?" "That would be great!" Steve replied. Bill then had his tailor make a black leather suit patterned after the denim jeans and jacket outfit Elvis wore in the 'Guitar Man' production number. Like the gold lamé suit of the 50s and the jumpsuits of the 70s, it would become one of his most iconic outfits, a visual signifier of 'Elvis' as much as his name. (Ironically, the outfit was almost destroyed when swatches of the Elvis's clothes were included in the 1971 boxed set *Worldwide 50 Gold Award Hits, Vol. 2*; it was saved at the suggestion of Elvis's Circle G ranch hand Mike McGregor, who was also a leather craftsman.)

Despite giving his grudging approval, Parker was still not happy with the idea of the improv sequence, and according to Binder, made a deliberate attempt to sabotage the shows. Parker demanded that he be given all the tickets to the two improv shows to give out himself. "He implied that he was going to fly a 747 out of Memphis with blonde blue-eyed girls with bouffant hairdos and said, 'You'll have a real Elvis audience out there!'" says Steve. "So I bit. I took the bait. And I went to Finkel and NBC and the sponsors and begged them to let me give all the tickets to Colonel Parker. And they agreed. And so I gave him all the tickets.

"But he had no intentions of giving out those tickets," Steve continues. "And I was naïve; I should have known. When I was driving out of the gate the night before we were supposed to tape the improv, the guard asked me if I needed any tickets. And there was a whole stack of them sitting on the guard table. And I said, 'Where'd you get those?' And he said, 'Oh, some bald headed guy in the morning told me to give them out.' And so I realized the Colonel had really gone out of his way to sabotage me." The next day, he says, was spent trying to round up an audience, spreading the word through radio announcements, calling family and friends, and even asking the patrons at the local Bob's Big Boy restaurant if they'd like free tickets to see Elvis.

But some of those who attended the shows recall that they were able to get tickets in advance. Judy Palmer, an Elvis fan club president from Spokane, Washington, heard about the show while visiting

Memphis with friends the previous winter and wrote NBC for tickets (she attended the 6pm show on June 27 and the 8pm show on June 29). Sandi Miller had also written NBC for tickets after the show was announced in *TV Guide*. "All you had to do was write to NBC studios and send a self-addressed stamped envelope; I think they limited you to six tickets," she says. "So we sent in for our six tickets. And then the next time we were up at Elvis's house, he had a handful of tickets and he was just handing them out to whoever was there that night. There were some other girls that went up the next night, and they got some too. He was scared to death nobody was going to show up. Every day he'd ask people 'Are you coming?' He'd ask everybody."

Evidently, Parker hadn't been able to commandeer all the tickets. Darice Murray-McKay is yet another fan who got her tickets to the improv show in advance. Darice had been an Elvis fan since she was five years old and her mother had woken her up to watch Elvis's performance on *The Steve Allen Show*, saying "You need to see this!" She'd followed his career ever since, even getting an okay from her priest to watch his movies, something that a "good Catholic girl" shouldn't be seeing. "He said, 'Oh, go ahead, it's not going to hurt anything. Don't worry about it. You don't have to confess it, you don't have to feel bad. Just go!' I thought that was so cool, you know," she says. She also admits to being "absolutely crushed" when Elvis married Priscilla.

Darice had just graduated from high school and was living in San Diego when her mother saw an ad in the local paper offering a bus tour to LA to see the Elvis shows on Thursday, June 27. They bought two tickets, only to be told three days before the show that the bus company was cancelling the trip. Darice was disappointed, but not dissuaded, and promptly called the NBC's Burbank studios.

"The truth of the matter is, this was an industry show, for people who were coming to visit LA, and people on a studio tour, just like any other show that they had an audience for," she says. "A lot of the tickets were gone because people write months in advance saying, 'I want a tour of Burbank Studios; I'm going to be there such-and-such a week,' just like you get on the Jay Leno show [*The Tonight Show*]. You don't really know who's going to be on. When I called, they told me, 'There are no tickets, we're totally booked for all of the filmings, there's nothing.' I'm kind of an assertive personality, and I said, 'No, I don't think that's right. These people had 40 tickets for this bus tour, and they canceled yesterday which means that they handed you 40 tickets back. So you have 40 tickets.' I gave them all the information and they put me on hold. And they came back on the line and they said, 'We'll have a ticket at will call [at the box office] for you.'"

Darice took a Greyhound bus to LA and made her way to Burbank, making friends with two teenage boys standing in line behind her who were also from San Diego. "I was totally aware of how historic this was," she says. "I had gone to LA to see numerous people; by this time I'd seen The Beatles, I'd seen the Stones four or five times, Dave Clark Five, Jefferson Airplane, Quicksilver Messenger Service. I went to Monterey Pop. But the one person that was the core of my musical experience I couldn't see in person. It was like this unfulfilled hunger to finally see him."

On entering the studio, Darice and her new friends were surprised at the set up. The audience was seated around a small square stage, bordered by ropes, giving the impression of a boxing ring, a feeling enhanced by the bleachers rising behind the floor seats. "No one had any idea of the intimacy of this venue," she says. "Everyone thought that we were going to go somewhere like the Ed Sullivan Theater and he would perform on stage. So once we got in there the feeling was, 'What's happening? We're going to be in this tiny room with this legend.' And everyone was pleasantly excited."

"This was a concept that wasn't out there yet," says Sandi. "This was something totally new, to throw a bunch of fans in a little room with a performer, throw him up on a little stage and say 'Have at it.' You know? I mean, that hadn't been done before."

Darice and her companions sat near the top of the bleachers, only for Darice to be pulled out and seated closer to the stage, so that Elvis would be surrounded by friendly female faces. "The two guys I'm with are just furious because here they are, diehard Elvis fans, and all the girls are getting down there and they're stuck up at the top of the bleachers watching this show!" she says.

Meanwhile, backstage, the star was becoming increasingly nervous. Building up to day of the performance, Sandi had noted his growing unease in his chats with the fans outside his home. "Oh, he constantly was nervous!" she says. "He was nervous about what if nobody came, he was nervous about what if they didn't like him, what if the show's no good, what if, what if." A final rehearsal at 3pm on the day of the show hadn't relaxed him. "Do you think they'll like us?" he'd asked DJ Fontana, whose response – "Elvis, all you've gotta do is go out there and do what you've always done and you'll find out in about three or four songs!" – wasn't exactly comforting. "He was afraid, and we was afraid," DJ admitted. "We didn't know what was going to happen – they might boo us off the stage!"

Even so, Steve was taken aback when he was called to see Elvis in the make-up room minutes before show time and was told, "Steve, I can't do it." "What do you mean, you can't do it?" Steve said in astonishment. "My mind is a blank," Elvis protested. "I don't remember anything I sang or said, and you want me to go out there and improvise."

"Elvis, I'm not even going to ask you, I'm going to *tell* you – you've got to go out there," Steve replied. "I don't care if you go out and say 'Hello' and 'Goodbye,' and come on backstage, you're going out there. I'm not going to *not* let you go out there."

"So I sort of forced him out," says Steve. "It was just a case of he had stage fright. But I wasn't sure when I went back out to the control room; I'd given him this talk, but I wasn't sure he was going to come out."

The audience, of course, had no idea of the backstage turmoil, though their own anticipation was also building: "The feeling there was just electric," says Darice. The audience was then warned to not get overly excited during the taping. "It was kind of, 'Elvis is going to be coming out. Everyone needs to stay in their seats. Remember we're filming so this is important,'" Darice recalls. "It was the equivalent of 'We don't want 100 million screams of "We love you Elvis!"' But I think everyone was just so in awe of the situation that they didn't do anything like that."

At around 6pm, Elvis's band came out to the stage. In addition to Scotty and DJ (playing an empty guitar case instead of his drum kit), Charlie Hodge, the best musician in Elvis's inner circle, had been tapped to play guitar, with Alan Fortas, another member of the gang, sitting in on additional percussion (slapping the back of a guitar laid across his lap). At the last minute, Elvis also asked Lance Legault, his film stand-in, to play tambourine; because there was no room for him on the small stage, Legault crouched nearby on the steps leading to the stage. The men all wore burgundy suits, except for Legault, who was all in black. Because everyone on stage was seated in a chair, these two performances are known as the 'sit-down' shows.

After the band has settled in, Elvis arrives, casually strolling out, glistening in his black leather suit, stopping to put his hands on his hips and survey the crowd (who can't keep from screaming a little bit), with an amused grin on his face. Perhaps to give Steve a momentary scare, after he sits down he leans forward into the mic, says "Good night!" and acts like he's going to get up and leave. But he then sits back down, straps his guitar on, and says, "So, what do I do now, folks?"

To Darice, Elvis's nervousness was obvious, and heightened by the intimacy of the setting. "This is a captive group in a very small, small space where you can't really make large, large gestures," she observes. "This is not being on stage, this is someone's living room." Though speaking quietly, and often looking down, Elvis nonetheless manages to make a few jokes during his opening remarks, as when he explains, "This is supposed to be like an informal section of the show where we faint or do whatever we want to do – especially me!" Then he introduces Scotty as the guitarist he had "when I first started out in

1912." The guys joke back and urge him along so there aren't too many pauses, and he finally introduces the first number, 'That's All Right' (from his very first single, on Sun Records), with a simple "... and it went like this."

From that point on, he never looked back. "He sang eight bars and he knew he had 'em," Bones recalls. "You can just see him change ... you can just tell by the look on his face, he gets that quirky smile." Carried along by the applause that bursts out when he starts to sing, by the end of the number Elvis is practically bouncing out of his seat. Instead of the high, keening vocal of the original, his voice has an appealing roughness, and the song, taken at a faster pace, has a newfound urgency. It was one thing to vamp through songs surrounded by his buddies, who invariably provided unquestioning support, but sitting down in front of an audience again proved to be the kind of invigorating experience Elvis had been missing for some time. "Boy, my boy!" he exclaims at the end, a catchphrase from W.C. Fields' movies that's quickly picked up by Charlie Hodge.

"The second that he got in front of those people his little antennae went on – Ding! – like that and he was away to the races," observes Chris Bearde. "He was stunning. He came out, and it was the perfect conducive atmosphere; he had everything absolutely covered and he didn't have to do anything except just be himself. And he trusted all of us totally, and boy did it pay off. He was in seventh heaven. His confidence came back immediately. It wasn't like it grew or anything; he just sat down and whack, he was into it."

"He was very nervous," Sandi Miller agrees. "Aside from the fact that he kept saying he was nervous, it was quite evident. But once he got going, I think he did just wonderfully. If the reaction was good, then he relaxed and he felt comfortable. His shows very much depended on his audience – that became especially true in Vegas. If you had a good audience, you got a good show. If you had a not so good audience, it showed in him."

The rest of the set sticks largely to Elvis's 50s repertoire. "And then we did, uh ...," he says by way of introducing the second song, 'Heartbreak Hotel,' his first national hit. He makes the first of several attempts to stand up, prompting excited squeals and applause from the audience, laughs at his own inability to remember all the words, then continues with barely a pause into a soulful 'Love Me'; "That's dirty, dirty!" he says at one point. Following the number, Elvis switches his acoustic guitar for Scotty's snazzier Gibson Super 400; most pictures of him from the sit-down shows show him holding Scotty's guitar, not his own. He then goes into Jimmy Reed's 'Baby What You Want Me To Do,' a bluesy stomper Elvis frequently played during jam sessions at home; here it provides a kind of bedrock for the session, a number Elvis can drop in and out of easily, knowing that Charlie will be right there with him, providing the harmony.

By now, his apprehension long gone, Elvis is comfortable enough to tackle the dialogue he feared he might not be able to handle. "Give me that piece of paper, man, and let me see what I'm supposed to do next," he says, asking for the notes that had been provided for him to base his anecdotes on. "It says here, 'Elvis will talk about first record,'" he says in a dry, overly exaggerated monotone, provoking more jokes from his band. He tries to get serious for a moment, talking about the current music scene and enjoying groups like "The Beatles and The Beards and whoever." (Chris Bearde felt this ad lib – "I first thought he meant The Byrds" – was Elvis's way of "giving me a personal thank you ... that was his way of saying, 'Thanks, Chris.'") Then he explains his view that gospel is at the root of all rock'n'roll. But he quickly becomes self-conscious ("I don't know what I'm talkin' about, really; I'm just mumbling, man. They tell me to talk, so I'm talkin'."), and jumps right back into a song, 'Blue Suede Shoes.'

After the number, he segues neatly back into 'Baby What You Want Me To Do,' only to break off by having his lips go into his trademark sneer while he cracks, "Wait a minute, there's something wrong with my lip!" After the laughter and applause has died down, he waits with perfect timing to deliver the punchline: "I got news for you baby, I did

29 pictures like that!" He then pokes fun at how his gyrations provoked outrage from the authorities, leading to one performance where he couldn't move. "The only thing I could move was my little finger, like that," he explains, wiggling his pinky as he breaks into the first verse of 'Hound Dog,' and the audience laughs and applauds again. "It was like we were an audience that had shown him that we really cared, so he could be at ease with us," says Darice. "It was like sitting around with a bunch of people that he knew; he could make jokes, and he could make mistakes, and he could flub the words, and it wasn't all that important because we're all in this thing together. It was very intimate."

Relaxed as he now is, Elvis has little trouble launching into a full-bodied rendition of 'Lawdy Miss Clawdy,' followed by a sweet 'Are You Lonesome Tonight?,' both performances revealing how much more expressive a singer he's become over the years (though he's unable to keep from mugging through the first line of the spoken monologue that comes in the middle of 'Lonesome'; unwilling to spoil the moment, he quickly drops the monologue and goes back into the song). Then comes a brief snatch of 'When My Blue Moon Turns To Gold Again,' before he remembers he has to put a Christmas song in the show somewhere, and goes into 'Blue Christmas.' Then it's back to the Sun era with 'Trying To Get To You,' Elvis heightening the tension by going up an octave every other verse, before howling out the last line.

It's a performance that sets the stage for what's clearly the emotional core of the show for Elvis, 'One Night.' When the song was first released by Elvis as a single, in 1958, the lyrics had been cleaned up; one night "of sin" had become one night "with you," and here Elvis slightly mixes up the lyrics of the original and the rewritten version. His vocal is incendiary, positively scalding, and even when a momentary interruption occurs – he's moving around so much, his guitar becomes unplugged – he snaps right back in, wringing every last drop of emotion from the number, pounding both feet on the stage throughout, attacking the guitar with equal gusto. A return to 'Baby What You Want Me To Do' provides a cooling off period of sorts, but

Elvis can't let 'One Night' go. When no guitar strap can found for Scotty's guitar to enable Elvis to stand up and play, Charlie starts improvising "No strap for you ..." to the tune of 'It's Now Or Never.' Elvis picks it up, then goes right back into 'One Night' proper, standing at last and putting one leg on his chair to balance his guitar on his knee as the mic is held up for him to sing into.

It's the show's most cathartic moment, with Elvis reveling in a display of unbridled passion, what Billy Goldenberg called his ability to be "tuned into the darkness, to the wild, untamed, animalistic things." For longtime fans like Darice, it showed how the Elvis of the 50s could be reinvented for a new generation. "This isn't nostalgic, this is real, this is someone vital who can go out and do a show and make people so very involved," she says. "He's got it and he can still do it, and it's kind of like we're looking forward to the future where he's going to be able to go out and do these songs in that grand scheme. I think his versions were different enough from the recorded one to say, 'I'm not stuck in a rut. I can do these old songs, but I can trim them down and I can do something new with them.'"

After such a performance, it would've have been anticlimactic to continue with the band, so 'Memories,' which Elvis sang to a prerecorded backing track, provides a perfect closing. It was planned that Steve would cue up the track when he felt the set had run its course, but in fact Elvis had announced there was only one more song just prior to singing 'One Night' for the second time, so 'Memories' feels like more of an encore. As the track comes on, Elvis sits on the top step of the stage, while the two young women seated right next to him tried to appear nonchalant about their sudden proximity to the star. "It was just like there was a static electricity around him," says Darice. "Everyone was just energized, but we weren't moving because we were afraid if we moved, they would shut the cameras down. But it was just absolutely electrifying." At the end, Elvis returns to the stage for the final applause, then exits as simply as he'd arrived.

There was just over an hour until the next sit-down performance at

8pm. As Steve was preparing for the second show, Bill Belew came running up, exclaiming, "You're never going to believe this!" Elvis's own excitement during the show had been raised to such heights he'd actually ejaculated. "That was true!" says Steve. "I learned a great lesson then; never make one costume of anything. And that was aside from the heat of the lamps and the sweat and the adrenaline, excitement, etcetera – I mean, that leather suit was dripping wet. Compounded with Bill Belew saying, 'How am I going to get this out in time for the next taping?'" A crew of wardrobe people with hairdryers was quickly mustered, and the suit was cleaned up and dried off by the next performance.

Some of the audience, like Sandi Miller, was able to stay over for the second show. Elvis was noticeably more relaxed from the beginning, exclaiming "Boy, my boy!" as he gets on stage, adding "It's been a long time, Jack, I'm telling you," as he settles in his seat ("About 15 minutes!" Charlie Hodge cracks). He then repeats the same joke from the previous show, announcing "Good night!" and standing up as if to leave, before settling back down again, an indication that some of the spirit of the improv is already hardening into tailored set pieces.

Though the setlist was largely the same, the running order for the show varied. Elvis launches right into 'Heartbreak Hotel' with no introduction, pausing part of the way through as he jokes that he's out of breath. When he begins again, he's much looser compared to the performance in the first show, ad libbing, wiggling and mugging to bring on screams from the audience, coughing and laughing as he again forgets the lyrics. "Man, that's the worst job I've ever done on that song!" he says afterwards. Perhaps to get back in the groove, he then goes right into 'Baby What You Want Me To Do.'

As he reads from his notes, he again makes some of the same jokes (e.g. in reference to the presumed raciness of his performing style in "touching hands with body – touching body with hands, excuse me!"). "I got a question," Charlie says at one point as the conversation begins to meander. "What is it?" Elvis says. "What you want to sing?" Charlie replies, prompting Elvis to introduce 'That's All Right.' 'Are You Lonesome Tonight?' follows, with Elvis making jokey ad libs in the first line, but mostly playing it straight the rest of the way through, and skipping the spoken word recitation (though he does look down at his lap at one point, saying "Man, these leather pants are hot, I'm telling you!").

After switching guitars with Scotty again, he then returns to the 'Baby What You Want Me To Do' riff that he seemed to love playing more than anything else. With a better mic stand now in use, he's able to stand up, again propping the guitar on his knee as he sings 'Blue Suede Shoes,' then improvises a few lines from 'MacArthur Park' in a high falsetto before going into 'One Night,' which, coming earlier in the set, robs this second show of its most effective climax. Being able to stand also diffuses some of the energy, as Elvis is able to move a bit more freely, though it's still a wonderfully compelling performance, with audience members breaking into occasional shrieks throughout.

Sitting back down, Elvis goes into a heartfelt 'Love Me.' This audience is a good deal more expressive than the first, screaming even when Elvis is thrown a handkerchief to mop his brow, and a small scuffle breaks out when he tosses it back into the front row. Clearly finding his music-of-today/rock'n'roll-and-gospel speech a distraction, he rushes through it in less than a minute, wrapping up with "That's about it, baby; that's all I've got to say," then goes into 'Trying To Get To You,' immediately followed by an equally searing 'Lawdy Miss Clawdy.'

After casually tossing another hankie in the audience to more screams, Charlie playfully plucks some lint from Elvis's face to hand to another woman in the front row, who delightedly wraps it up and places it in her purse. "Never ceases to amaze me, baby, I'll tell ya!" Elvis responds. Moving on to the Christmas songs, he gets through 'Santa Claus Is Back In Town,' despite having forgotten most of the words, then segues right into a more sincerely delivered 'Blue Christmas.'

At what might have been a perfect place to go into 'Baby What You Want me To Do' again, Elvis instead jumps into a rollicking 'Tiger Man' (co-written by Joe Hill Lewis and Elvis's first producer, Sam Phillips, using the pseudonym "Sam Burns"), singing just two verses of the song, but barreling through them repeatedly with the force of a locomotive. "Ain't no end to this song, baby!" he notes at one point, but he manages to bring the number to a conclusion anyway. He gets through a longer version of 'When My Blue Moon Turns To Gold Again,' nicely harmonizing with Charlie at the end, and Steve then cues up 'Memories' to end the show.

The first show had been the stronger performance; as Chris Bearde notes, "The first was more real. It was electric, and it had that moment of renewed power in it." And in the broadcast version of the programme, more songs would be drawn from the 6pm show than the 8pm show. Nonetheless, both shows were a rejuvenating experience for Elvis, providing him with a dramatic illustration of how his audience still loved him simply for who he was. "This guy just sat on the stage and told the history of his life," says Chris Bearde. "And he was totally relaxed and totally at ease, and could get up when he wanted to, and sing when he wanted to. Steve gave him the freedom to be exactly what he wanted to be."

Just as importantly, the shows had demonstrated to Elvis that his music could still readily translate to contemporary audiences. An inveterate music fan himself, as the displays of his record collection at Graceland reveal (and even these represent only a fraction of the albums he actually owned), Elvis was well aware of the music being made by other performers, and was just as keenly – painfully – aware of how his own music in the 60s had so often fallen short, not just in comparison to the work of others but also to his own recordings in the 50s. Now he saw that his hits were not merely 'golden oldies,' but still vital, exciting pieces of rock'n'roll that could come alive in performance.

This was just as true of the other live shows shot for the special, on Saturday, June 29, again at 6pm and 8 pm. The set was again a small square, though not quite the 'boxing ring' set up for the sit-down shows; this stage was made up of white illuminated squares, and bordered in red. Elvis, wearing the same leather suit, would also be alone, without his band; an orchestra, conducted by Billy Goldenberg, was off to the side, out of camera range. As Elvis stood for the entire time through both sets, the performances are known as the 'stand-up' shows.

Among those in the audience was Chris Landon, accompanying his father, Grelun. Chris had first met Elvis when he was five years old and his father worked for Hill & Range. Grelun had taken Chris on a trip to Memphis in 1956, and Elvis had entertained the youngster by playing darts with him. "When I looked up at Elvis, he was like 25 feet tall," he recalls. When Grelun lost his job at Hill & Range, Parker got RCA to hire him as a publicist, and Chris avidly followed Elvis's career while growing up, though he was disappointed by Elvis's "Schlock movies … I just kept wishing he could break loose. I'm sure he did too."

Now, father and son sat in the audience, not sure what was about to happen. "In the face of everything else that was happening at the time, with the Jefferson Airplane and The Doors and all that, here's this guy making a comeback after he sold out," says Chris. "And bringing back genuine music that he genuinely could feel and emote and get out to the audience. It was pretty overwhelming. He was putting his entire ego out there and if that hadn't succeeded, I don't know, he might have exploded. I'm seeing it from the inside, with my dad being anxious about it too. You know, is this thing gonna work? That was a big deal."

Bob Finkel makes the introductions, as he had done for the other shows: "Welcome to NBC and the Elvis Presley Special! And here's Elvis Presley!" The audience is much more expressive than the sit-down audiences were as Elvis strolls out, ascends the stage, and walks around nodding and smiling at the crowd before putting on his guitar, clearing his throat, and saying, "Well, I gotta do this sooner or later, so I might as well do it now, baby." He then cues the band, who go into 'Heartbreak Hotel.' But a glitch ruins what starts out as a strong performance; the sound goes out. If this had happened during the first sit-down show, he might well have been flustered. But Elvis is fully in command now, and when the sound comes back on, he's singing 'One Night,' which he brings to a close, announces, "Now we can start the show," and re-cues the band for 'Heartbreak Hotel.'

Billy Goldenberg's arrangements worked well in the shows, and foreshadowed Elvis's work with an orchestra in his future shows. In contrast to the more restrained orchestra heard in his first TV appearances on *Stage Show* in the 50s, this collection of musicians was brighter and sharper, and also included a brace of rock musicians, which gave the music a harder edge (and a bluesey touch via Tommy Morgan's harmonica). Elvis is fully assured, brimming with confidence from the start, undoubtedly helped by the fact that the set sticks almost exclusively to his biggest hits, ensuring a good response from the audience.

The opening turns out to be a medley; after 'Heartbreak Hotel,' he removes his guitar and works with a hand mic for the rest of the segment, first going into 'Hound Dog,' which has him dropping to his knees for the first time, then segueing into 'All Shook Up,' his carefully combed-back hair already flopping over his forehead. "It's been a long time, baby!" he says at the medley's end, clearly pleased with his work.

'Can't Help Falling In Love' comes next, the audience breaking into applause before the song is even completed. Then it's back to rock'n'roll with 'Jailhouse Rock,' Elvis moving his body to accentuate the percussive beats of the song, showing off his leather suit to its full advantage, spreading his legs and contorting his body backward, swiveling his hips, thrusting his arm up as he drops on one knee. "Boy, my boy!" he exclaims before taking something of a breather with 'Don't Be Cruel.' He takes up the guitar again for 'Blue Suede Shoes,' but seems to use it more as a prop, only playing about half the song; as a performer, he's far more effective (and comfortable) without the guitar. 'Love Me Tender' gives him another chance to catch his breath, with The Blossoms providing delicate backing vocals. Afterwards, he pulls the 'handkerchief' routine again, taking one from a woman in the audience to mop his brow, only to be offered several more by eager audience members.

Sandi Miller remembers the high energy of the performance, with Elvis "just roaming that stage, just pacing, pacing, pacing – somebody bring that boy a chair!" She also appreciated how he acknowledged the fans he knew in the audience. "He'd go around, he'd wink at somebody he knew, or he'd sit down and sing to them," she says. "Nobody else was going to know that he actually knew these people, but I think that made it special for everybody. And of course, we knew that these girls were people he knew, so that made it special for us. It was nice to watch him connect with those people. And I don't even know that you'd notice it unless you knew what to look for."

The next song is shot for use in the 'Guitar Man' production number, and is meant to bring the sequence to something of a surreal close. The section where Elvis is shown performing 'Trouble' in increasingly higher-class clubs ends with him singing the song in his own stand-up show. The song then segues into the newly written final verse of 'Guitar Man,' in which he notes that the journey he thought he'd completed by becoming a star isn't really over yet, and that he'll never be more than what he is – a "swingin' little guitar man." He then walks off down the same neon-lit highway where he began his journey in the first scene.

But there were problems nailing this section. On the first run through, Elvis doesn't go into the 'Guitar Man' verse properly. It's left to be worked on during the second show, and, taking a break, Elvis picks up his guitar and goes into his reliable standard, 'Baby What You Want Me To Do.' The band leaps in to jam along, and Elvis strolls around the stage with apparent casualness before he begins to sing.

He then mimes to a recording of 'If I Can Dream.' Though it ultimately wasn't used in the show (Steve says he had Elvis do the number as a rehearsal for the final version that would be taped the following day), Elvis used many of the same movements he'd use in the version that was aired, waving his left arm back and forth during the latter half of the song, holding it up on the line "in the dark," and ending the number with both arms outstretched. "Oh my God, it was like everybody was holding their breath," says Sandi of the performance. "I mean, you just held your breath because it was so intense." Immediately after the song ends, he leaves the stage, pausing and turning as he goes through the crowd to acknowledge the applause.

As with the sit-down shows, the first of the two stand-up shows is the stronger performance. Once again, in the second show, there's a problem with 'Heartbreak Hotel,' when Elvis misses his cue, and once again, his carefully combed-back hair is flopping over his forehead by the end of the opening medley. He's noticeably looser, changing song lyrics, coming in slightly early on 'Hound Dog,' but easily carrying on, making an exaggerated grunt before 'All Shook Up,' toying with the crowd as he unexpectedly drops to his knees in front of the first row of young women, who squeal excitedly each time. It's as if, having proved himself in the first shows, he can now send himself up the second time around, effectively parodying his own performance style.

The same songs are performed in the same order, though he makes more jokes throughout. Before 'Don't Be Cruel' he brandishes the mic stand like a spear and shouts "Moby Dick!" He gives a slight chuckle as he starts to sing 'Love Me Tender,' and plays around with words; you've made my life "a wreck," he says, before shaking his head and substituting "complete" with another laugh. There's again some difficulty with the 'Trouble'/'Guitar Man' pick-up. "Okay, are you ready?" Steve Binder asks, when they've finished discussing the sequence. As if anticipating the problems he'll have, Elvis says, "No, but we'll try it anyway." "Let's get it, it's rock'n'roll," Steve replies encouragingly.

The first attempt is spoiled as Elvis is still having his costume arranged. He doesn't have the mic ready for the second take. He laughs during the third take, joking, "I got my lip hung up on the microphone!" That gives him an excuse to curl his lip and pull out the

"I did 29 pictures like that, baby" joke again. The fourth take appears fine, but Elvis says, "Better do another one, I got hung up on the guitar here," referring to the moment at the end where he puts on his guitar while leaving the stage; the audience's applause in response suggests they wouldn't mind seeing Elvis do the sequence several more times. While waiting for the number to begin again, a woman calls out, "Elvis, tell us about your daughter." "Well, she's little," he says, holding his hands apart to indicate, then goes into some more jokey improvs, singing bits of 'Tiptoe Through the Tulips' and 'MacArthur Park' again. The fifth take is finally the keeper.

During the pause before 'If I Can Dream' is cued up, Elvis again chats with the audience, explaining how he finds it difficult to be 'on' instantaneously. "With no more time than I've got in this part, it's hard to get really into it," he says, and when the audience protests its disbelief, he insists, "No, it really is." As if to prove him wrong, the audience gives him a standing ovation after he mimes to 'If I Can Dream.' Unlike the previous show, he stands still for much of this performance, then simply says "Thank you. Good night, thank you very much. Good night," before walking off stage.

If Elvis had any doubts about his ability as a performer, or how an audience would respond to him after so many years of not performing live, the sit-down and stand-up shows had eliminated those doubts for good. Indeed, in the future he would draw such sustenance from his live work that he would continue to perform in concert until a month and a half before his death. And he was excited to talk about how the shows had gone when he next ran into the fans outside his home, one of whom had brought a stuffed tiger as a gift, in reference to the song 'Tiger Man.'

"How was I?" he asked them. "Did you think it was good? Did you think it'll go over good? Do you think other people will like it, people that aren't fans? What was your favorite part? What didn't you like?"

"Good God, it was like a little kid going to prom or something," says Sandi. "We told him, listen, it was such a good show, there was such electricity in the air, even if somebody wasn't a fan they would enjoy it. I remember my roommate told him, 'People that aren't fans, they're going to watch it because you're cute!' And he got all beet red."

The fans then asked Elvis what he thought of the show. "I'm happy with it, I think it's good," he said, "but I just don't know what people will think. I want people to like it." "It's so weird, because here he is, he's Elvis Presley and he's like, 'But I want people to like it,'" says Sandi. "We told him, 'Don't worry they'll like it…or we'll kill 'em!'"

It had been a busy week for Elvis. A press conference for the special had been held on June 25. Taping for the show's other segments began on June 27 and ran through June 30. In middle of all the activity, a birthday party for Colonel Parker was held on the set on June 26, when Presley's manager turned 59. As a surprise, Chris and Allan had rejigged the words of 'It Hurts Me' with lyrics that satirized Parker's frequent complaints about the show, from the rising budget to the lack of any Christmas songs. Elvis crooned the song to Parker with perfect mock sincerity, to the cast and crew's amusement. The original lyric sheet was later auctioned off by the Presley estate.

"It was a bit of a lark, it was a throwaway thing," says Chris. "Honestly, when we did it, we didn't think it would become this cause célèbre over all these centuries." Not that Parker appreciated the joke. "No," Chris agrees. "The Colonel did not have a sense of humor. He didn't. He didn't understand what we were doing. He was just very wary of us and he didn't understand what we were doing at all, quite frankly. But it didn't matter. But the smartness of the Colonel was he wasn't going to get in the way because he saw how happy Elvis was and how totally together the show was. And so his animal smarts, his little carny smarts, told him, 'Don't fuck around with this. Let it go the way it's going.'"

The taping of the show's other segments began on June 27 with 'Big Boss Man' and 'It Hurts Me.' In an interesting mix of the sacred and the profane, the gospel sequence and 'Let Yourself Go' were taped on June 28. June 30 saw the taping of the rest of the 'Guitar Man' production number ('Nothingville,' and the different club sequences as Elvis is shown rising to fame) and the show's opening and closing segments.

'If I Can Dream,' also taped on June 30, would provide the show with its most emotionally powerful moment, and brought the special to a dramatic conclusion. Elvis stood in front of the E-L-V-I-S letters, resplendent in a white suit – a color chosen by Bill Belew to represent "the basic idea of white for purity," as well as providing a contrast to the all-black outfit worn in the show's opening – offset with a crimson neck scarf. He would sing a live vocal to a backing track.

On the first take, he comes in too early, and the taping is halted. Over the course of the next two takes, his performance is increasingly refined. At the beginning of the second take he plays with the microphone cord too much; on the third take he simply holds the mic in front of him, then lifts it to his mouth to sing. But the singing at the end of the third take isn't quite as strong, and he forgets to speak into the mic at the song's conclusion to say good night.

On the fourth take, everything comes together perfectly. Elvis's head is looking down in contemplation as the song starts, but the intensity soon begins to rise, with Elvis slightly crouching down by the end of the first verse, his right hand reaching out, as he begs to know why his dream of brotherhood can't come true. He knows exactly when to move, and exactly how much; when he sings of the pain in the world, his body bends over nearly double as if in grief, but when he sings of redemption and flight he arches back, right palm facing up. In the final verse, as he sings of the beckoning candle burning out there in the darkness, he reaches out with his right hand, as if he could touch it; during the final lines, with his feet firmly planted, he swings his right arm from side to side, building a momentum that nearly lifts him off the ground. After he finishes singing, on the song's final chord, he stretches both arms up to the heavens where he holds them for a moment before they drop to his sides. "Thank you," he says in a voice that's both a bit rough and out of breath, "Good night."

There was little time to contemplate what he had achieved on the special. After a week's break, Elvis headed off to the set of his next film, *Charro!*, while Steve began putting the show together. He first tried to make the show longer than had initially been called for. "Originally, I edited the show down to 90 minutes," he says. "I tried to sell Singer and NBC to open up another half hour. No. They thought I was nuts."

His next headache was due to the so-called 'bordello' sequence, when Elvis sings 'Let Yourself Go.' The brass bed on the set had led one NBC executive to proclaim "It looks like a bordello!" leading to concerns that the sequence might be too risqué. Steve was asked to make the women's costumes less revealing, and he agreed, though asking for a guarantee that as long as he made the changes the sequence wouldn't be cut. "And after they re-examined the production number in rehearsal, they said, 'Okay, you have a green light, do it,'" he says. "But they lied to me. After it was over, they said, 'You've got to take it out of the show.' And I refused to.

"So in their inimitable network way, instead of anybody having the balls to make the decision there, they brought in some guy from General Electric [which owns NBC] to be the final arbiter," Steve continues. "So I went down to the editing room to meet this guy, and he's in brown shoes and a suit and tie. And I thought to myself, I'm in trouble. So I meet him, and he's sitting there laughing and watching *The Dean Martin Show* on another machine. And there's Dean Martin, Phil Harris and some 6'5" blonde bombshell in cleavage a lot more risqué than any of the girls that were in the Elvis show. And they're basically doing a dirty joke without the punchline for this little sketch they're doing. And General Electric is laughing his head off, thinking it's the funniest thing he ever saw. So I thought, 'Hey, maybe there's hope.' And he comes over and he says, 'Okay, let me look at what I've got to see.' And I played the sequence for him and the second it's over, he's totally predetermined everything: 'No, unacceptable, take it out of the show.'"

While undeniably steamy, the sequence is actually more campy than sensual. The women, clad in tight pink, midriff-revealing outfits, writhe around Elvis seductively at first (and in a series of quick cuts, one is seen popping a cherry into her bright red-lipsticked mouth while another runs a knife teasingly across her lips). But at other moments they're seen scrapping with each other, during an instrumental break they suddenly start to dance flapper-style to a 20s vaudeville melody, and in the last verse they're shown sitting around, reading magazines, looking bored. Ironically, Steve had been trying to show how Elvis's character was drawn to purity even in the midst of corruption. "What I was trying to say is that here were ladies of the night, and here's this innocent, it's her first day in the bordello, and she's the one Elvis is attracted to, not any of the other ones," he says. "And then before anything consummates, they're raided by the police, and he's off and running. So it was trying to show his innocence." The sequence was nonetheless cut from its initial screening (as was the 'It Hurts Me' sequence), though it was restored in subsequent screenings and video/DVD releases.

No sooner had that crisis been resolved than another raised its head. "I got a call that I had to go up to the front office because Colonel Parker was refusing to have the show broadcast," Steve recalls. "And so I reported to the program director's office. And everyone was there from Finkel, to Sarnoff, the president of NBC, and so forth. And there was the Colonel. You could cut the air with a knife."

"We have a problem, Steve," one of the executives began, "and it seems you're the only one who can solve it." "What's the problem?" Steve asked. "We've just looked at your tape of the show, and it's been called to our attention that there's no Christmas song. And the Colonel is insisting that there be a Christmas song in the show or he's not going to let us air it." "But we haven't recorded any Christmas songs," Steve replied. "And the Colonel knew that when we made the show."

Everyone was momentarily stumped. "They were scared to death of me by then, period," says Steve. "'Cause I'd also fought over the editing of the bordello; I'd fought that battle and lost. And everybody's looking at me to solve the problem. Then it dawned on me that in the improv Elvis had sung a verse and a half of 'Blue Christmas.' So I said, 'Well, there's one Christmas song we did do, but somebody's voice while Elvis is singing is saying "Sing it dirty, sing it dirty!" There's no way to take that out of the track.' So there was this hesitation in the room. And the Colonel said, 'Well, I want it in anyway.' So I said, 'Fine.' Which I loved. And so that's what I did. And that's how the Colonel got his one Christmas song in the show, with 'Sing it dirty, sing it dirty.'"

The show's final edit ran as follows: The 'Trouble'/'Guitar Man' opening; 'Lawdy Miss Clawdy' from the second sit-down show; 'Baby What You Want Me To Do' from the first sit-down show; the 'Heartbreak Hotel'/'Hound Dog'/'All Shook Up' medley, and 'Can't Help Falling In Love' from the first stand-up show; 'Jailhouse Rock' and 'Love Me Tender' from the second stand-up show; 'Are You Lonesome Tonight?' from the first sit-down show; the gospel production number; 'Baby What You Want Me To Do,' 'Blue Christmas,' 'One Night,' and 'Memories' from the first sit-down show; the 'Guitar Man' production number, and 'If I Can Dream.'

Once the edit was completed, Steve invited Elvis to a private screening. "We saw it with everybody in the room with us, his group and so forth," says Steve. "And nobody said anything, everybody was kind of waiting for Elvis. Elvis didn't really react very much. And when it was over, at any kind of screening like that, I assure you, every director in the world starts feeling sick to their stomach, like, 'This is a disaster!' And then Elvis asked everybody to leave; he wanted to watch it again with just me. And so everybody left the room. Then he roared. He loved it. It was like he was watching another person performing on that television screen; he was sitting there constantly applauding himself and telling me how great it was. I think we saw it twice in a row, by ourselves. So I knew he loved it."

To Elvis, it must have seemed like his career was being given a new lease on life; clearly, his talent, his skills as a performer, had been there all along, shamefully untapped by the mediocre songs and films he'd been pushed into making over the past decade. As he'd known for some time, it was the properties he'd been offered that were lacking, not him. So excited was he about the possibilities of a suddenly bright future, he exclaimed, "Steve, I'll never sing a song again that I don't believe in, I'll never make a movie again that I don't believe in." So it must've been something of a comedown when Steve responded, "I hear you Elvis, but I'm not sure you'll be strong enough when the time comes."

Though Steve genuinely liked and respected Elvis, he had doubts about his ability to follow through on his decision to have more of a say in the direction of his career. "I'd seen so many instances, at least in confrontations with the Colonel, where he had backed down so many times," he says. "But every time he had the nerve to say 'I'll do it' in front of the Colonel, the Colonel did not challenge him. And that's what I kept stressing to Elvis – you've got to take control of your life and stand up to him. Because he just was very weak when it came to standing up and making decisions for himself. Whatever that bond was, in the back of his head he kind of said, 'The original deal I made with the Colonel, he'd make the decisions and I would just do what he tells me to do.' It was such a strong strong bond that it was very difficult for Elvis to break that. And I think at that point in time, I was kind of a window of fresh air for him, where all of a sudden he started thinking outside the box."

A post-screening party had been planned at Bill Belew's home; Steve had invited Elvis to attend only to be told, "No, I could never do that." Now, still riding high after finally seeing the special, and perhaps wanting to make a point to his director, he suddenly told him, "Okay, I'm going to do it." "What are you going to do?" asked Steve, surprised. "I'm going with you to Bill Belew's house to have pizza and beer," said Elvis. "Which was like a major decision in his life," says Steve. The two then drove out to Belew's Hollywood apartment, only to find no one was there when they arrived.

"It was unbelievable, I couldn't believe it," says Steve. "And I could see the look on Elvis's face of complete disappointment and rejection. So we went downstairs to his car; it had a car phone in it. And we called Bill and nobody answered the phone. So Elvis said, 'Well, it wasn't meant to be,' and he gave me his phone number to call him. And he took off. And it wasn't a minute later when Bill Belew and Gene McAvoy [the show's art director] and a whole group of people arrived with pizza and beer; they'd been to the pizza place getting the food. So it was really tragic that he didn't experience that."

It was the last time Steve Binder would see Elvis. Though he called the number Elvis had given him, and was told by Billy Goldenberg (who served as music director and wrote the score for Presley's last feature film, *Change Of Habit*) that Elvis had asked about him, he was never able to get through to him again. "Elvis was completely shut off from any communication with me," Steve says. "I was persona non grata in the Elvis world after that."

Steve was more annoyed about the Binder/Howe team receiving no credit, or royalties, on the soundtrack album, when it became apparent there was going to be such a release after all. "We just didn't have the wherewithal to fight William Morris and Colonel Parker and lawyers and all that stuff," he explains. "As soon as we did the special, I got a check in the mail for $1,500, which was a complete and total buyout of our rights as music producers for the album, with a letter from the Colonel telling us how lucky we were. And I took the letter and the check and I sent it back to him saying, 'Thank you, but no thanks.' As a result, we got no money and no royalties, ever! I don't even get residuals for the show. Nothing. Zero." Producer Bob Finkel got a bit more out of Parker. The two had been playing practical jokes on each other throughout the making of the special, and Finkel had extracted a promise from Parker that he'd give Finkel his cane, if Finkel could top him in a stunt. After the taping was concluded, Parker returned to his Palm Springs home one night to find the E-L-V-I-S letters set up on his front lawn, complete with a generator to keep them burning bright.

Finkel duly received Parker's cane and hung it on his wall as a souvenir.

The other cast and crew members saw the special at a private screening held at a local club. "That's the first time I saw it all put together," said Bill Belew. "I have to honestly say I thought it was just another job. I hoped that it would be a great success, but I really didn't know. And we all adored it. We really just adored it. We just thought it was absolutely great."

The first song released from the special passed unnoticed; the version of 'Tiger Man' performed at the second sit-down show was tucked away on the hodge-podge collection *Singer Presents Elvis Singing Flaming Star And Others*, released in October. The record gathered together a strange assortment of songs from sessions going back to 1960, including some previously unreleased tracks, the January 1968 version of 'Too Much Monkey Business' among them, and was initially only available in Singer Sewing Centers. (Retitled *Elvis Sings Flaming Star*, the album was released by RCA the following year.)

Then came the release of 'If I Can Dream,' in early November, followed by the release of the *Elvis* soundtrack album a few weeks later, the cover featuring a shot of Elvis singing 'If I Can Dream' (as a sign of his renewed attention to his career, Elvis had actually asked that some changes be made to the final master before the album's release). 'If I Can Dream' reached Number 12 (Number 11 UK), something of a disappointment in light of how strong a performance it was, as *Billboard* noted: "Potent and timely lyric message with exceptional production." But it was still Elvis's highest charting single since 'I'm Yours' in 1965 and sold over 800,000 copies, his best selling single in years. *Elvis* reached Number Eight, his first Top Ten album since 1965's *Harum Scarum* (Number Two UK), and sold over 500,000 copies, his first gold record since 1963's *Elvis' Golden Records Vol. 3*. (According to Steve Binder, he and Bones Howe were credited as the producers of the special's singles in the charts of *Billboard*, *Cash Box*, and *Record World*, but their names were quickly removed on Parker's orders).

When the special itself aired, it received mixed reviews; along with the praise ("There is something magical about watching a man who has lost himself find his way back home," Jon Landau wrote in *Eye* magazine), there were still detractors (the *Los Angeles Times* griped about Presley's sweaty appearance). Darice Murray-McKay was among those who thought Elvis looked "a little bit stilted" during the production numbers, "A little bit like Barbara Stanwick, in one of those scenes where she's actually counting the steps; they're making them do something that isn't natural. He hadn't gotten in the karate moves yet, which was the only thing he could do on stage that was flamboyant that was his. I didn't like the production numbers, because they were so over-produced; I was into jams and the music that he'd done for us, the intimacy. I just didn't like the dress-up kind of things; it was like he was playing a role. The opening and closing sequences, I did like them. You have to remember, this is television, you only saw it once then."

Even so, she recognized that the special showcased a performer on the verge of recapturing his power. "If Elvis was going to succeed in coming back and taking the crowd back again and doing shows, he had to do something like this," she says. "I thought he succeeded so well in captivating the audience and showing us that he could be gritty and do the old songs, and bring in new songs, and he could move with the times. I thought it was a turning point in his career, and I thought he succeeded. He rose to the challenge."

"It was wonderful," says Chris Landon. "It justified me liking Elvis. Because everybody else at that time was smoking dope, listening to The Doors, and it was just Elvis, how cool is Elvis? Well, now he's cool!"

It was the kind of resurrection his audience had been longing for. Pamela Des Barres (future author of *I'm With The Band*), had been an "absolute fanatic" for Elvis since buying the 'Don't Be Cruel' single at a garage sale. She'd carefully marked off the days he was in the service on a special calendar, and followed him through his "bad movie phase." "I felt sorry for him," she says. "I knew he was doing things that were beneath him. But I really had faith in him that he would get through those dog days. And he did. I was just beside myself watching the show.

Yes! I knew it. I knew it. And wow, he chose the right outfit; Elvis seemed really at home in that leather outfit. He seemed really to relax into that in a way that just let him cut loose. That was the highlight of the show, where he sat there with the boys and played; that was obviously the highlight of the show for me and everyone else. He was bigger, brighter, bolder, brassier, wilder than ever when he came back."

Nor could anyone argue with the ratings; *Elvis* was NBC's biggest hit of the season (when the show aired again in August 1969, an ad noted that more women between 18 and 49 had watched *Elvis* than any other TV special in 1968), and immediately after the show aired, offers for more appearances came pouring in. Steve Binder had been correct; overnight, Elvis knew exactly where he stood with the public. The show went on to win a Peabody award for producer Bob Finkel, but, to Steve's chagrin, never even received an Emmy nomination because no one had thought to submit it. "I was so naïve in those days," he says. "I'd heard the word 'ratings,' I'd heard how sponsors evaluate success or failure, but none of that meant anything to me. I was only into doing the special, period. I just didn't think about the results."

Even the costumes had made an immediate impression. Suzanna Leigh, Elvis's co-star in *Paradise, Hawaiian Style*, later told Bill Belew that after the special aired the producer of the film she was then working on, *Subterfuge*, came to the set and announced, "I want the wardrobe thrown out immediately! I want Suzanne in brown leather and Joan Collins [the film's co-star] in black leather! I saw a special last night, it was so hot, I don't care what you do, get these people in leather!" "You have no idea the effect you and Elvis had on the public at that time," Leigh told Belew. "Literally all of London, everybody was throwing away their denim and was running around trying to buy all the black leather that they could."

Before too long, the actual title of the show, *Elvis*, was forgotten; when the program is spoken of, it's generally referred to as the 'Comeback Special.' And Elvis had indeed come back: back into the charts, back into the ratings, back into the public eye, back into contemporary relevance. Had Elvis not risen to the occasion, all his past complaints about the material he'd been given to work with would have been meaningless. That he proved to be as dazzling a performer as when he'd first burst onto the music scene in the 50s was a testament to the fact that his innate talent had never left him. "Yeah, I think he was pleased," says Sandi Miller. "I think he was very pleased with himself and he was very pleased with the reaction. I think he knew he had done something that was going to really survive. Which was a nice change for him after all those dumb movies."

"You can put all the sets in the world up there and you can make the greatest music in the world," says Chris Bearde. "But if you don't have the person that the show's about understanding what it is, and not just giving you the performance that you want, but a performance beyond belief – it was the man that made the show, not the show that made the man. That's a good one, ain't it? Because it is. It is. Whatever we did was just supplemental to the fact that Elvis wanted so bad to get back up there and show everybody 'This is me folks, this is me. Not the goody-goody mechanic. This is me. This is *Elvis*. This is me. This is the sum total of what I am.' And that's why it's lasted through the years as the ultimate Elvis statement. It was his statement. And it still is today. And thank God he was able to get to the point where everybody allowed him to make it."

"The films and ballads and record hits may have made him into a super-star," Robert Shelton wrote in his review of the special that ran in the December 4 1968 edition of the *New York Times*. "Mr. Presley could make himself an artist again, by bringing it all back home, in the white and black South, where it all began." And though Elvis didn't know it yet himself, in just over a month's time, that's exactly what he would do – get back to where he once belonged.

Chapter 3

A Little Less Conversation

For the latter half of 1968, prior to the airing of the Comeback Special, Elvis's career was in something of a holding pattern. There was no way of knowing what kind of an impact the special would have on Elvis's career, so for the moment it was back to business as usual.

In July 1968, filming began on *Charro!*, a movie that strove to emulate the success of the 'spaghetti Westerns,' such as Clint Eastwood's film *A Fistful Of Dollars*. Elvis plays a reformed outlaw forced to work with his former gang when they frame him for theft and murder. In order to achieve a sufficiently scruffy appearance, Elvis grew a beard, with the rest of entourage following suit.

"They had a contest among them to see who could grow the best beard the quickest," says Sandi Miller. "And Elvis lost. He lost big time. His beard came in in these little patches. It was bad. They had to fill it in. I've got pictures of him that I took of him at his house before they were filming and after they were filming. And he just has a pathetic little beard."

Underscoring the fact that *Charro!* was a serious picture, it was the only film to feature just one song – the title tune – though the filmmakers had considered having Elvis perform the song 'Let's Forget About The Stars' in a scene where his good buddy, the local sheriff, dies. Thankfully, good sense prevailed. "They ultimately decided that it would be kind of hokey," says Lenore Bond, who was married to James Almanzar, who played the sheriff, "and they took that out of the picture."

Though the chance to play a straight dramatic role should've pleased Elvis, the script was flat and uninspiring, and he found the film to be as dissatisfying as the others. (As the *New York Times* would observe, "[Presley] seems determined not to push himself in a role that could have used a stronger personality to fill the lapses in the story and the wide open spaces in the dialogue.") Nonetheless, he was in a good mood while working on the picture; during breaks in the filming, James Almanzar played guitar on the set, and Elvis and his friends would join him in singalongs. Co-star Ina Balin also found Elvis "A lovely, warm, bright, nice person … I really do believe he could, one day, be a very fine actor if given the chance and the proper direction."

Some filming was done on location, in Apache Junction, Arizona, where Bond met Elvis when she visited her husband. "One night my husband and I had gone out," she recalls. "And it was probably midnight when we came back to the hotel. We were coming across the pool area, and there was a figure sitting way in the shadows. When he saw people walking toward him he jumped up and started to leave. Then he saw it was Jim and he came over, and it was Elvis. It was really the only time he could get out of his room or be out where he wouldn't be absolutely hounded by people. It was very exciting to meet Elvis, but I also thought it was very sad to see him be so nervous about having people hounding him. He just had no privacy and I felt sad for him."

However much he might felt the need to escape being "hounded," Elvis and his entourage nonetheless got high marks from the local paper, *The Superior Sun*, which noted: "Residents are enjoying Presley, Colonel Parker and their group not only because they are celebrities, but also because they are nice people." He also took the time to socialize with Sandi Miller and her friends when they drove out for a visit, teasing them by saying the area was haunted.

Work on *Charro!* was completed by the end of August. September saw the release of 'A Little Less Conversation' to promote the upcoming film *Live A Little, Love A Little*; but the single only reached Number 69 (it failed to chart in the UK) and sold barely 100,000 copies. The film itself did no better, the *Motion Picture Herald* writing: "Audiences may grow a little weary of psychological studies of frigidity." There was more bad news for Elvis on a personal note with the death of Memphis DJ Dewey Phillips on September 28 at age 42; Dewey had been instrumental in launching Elvis's career, being the first DJ to play Elvis's first single, 'That's All Right,' on the radio back in 1954. Elvis made a rare public appearance to attend the funeral and speak with Dewey's widow, Dorothy.

Two recording sessions were held in October, for both Elvis's last film and his next one. On October 15, he reported to Samuel Goldwyn Studio in Hollywood where he cut two numbers. 'Charro!' was suitably brooding, but otherwise unmemorable, as even its composer, Mac Davis, admitted. 'Let's Forget About The Stars' was a mid-tempo ballad that clearly failed to stir any interest on Elvis's part (it was later released on the 1970 budget album *Let's Be Friends*).

The next session, held October 23 at United Artist Recorders in Hollywood, was for a film then entitled *Chautauqua*, in reference to the traveling entertainment/education festivals held in turn-of-the-century America; because it was thought the term was too antiquated, the film was eventually retitled *The Trouble With Girls (And How To Get Into It)*. Elvis heads up a Chautauqua troupe, getting caught up in a murder mystery, as well as dealing with a confrontational female union organizer; though Elvis is ostensibly the film's star, the movie is more of an ensemble piece, giving him less screen time than usual. That he still wished to vindicate himself on the screen was evidenced by a comment he made to one of his co-stars: "I'd like to make one good film before I leave. I know this town's laughing at me."

The Trouble With Girls was one of the few Elvis films not to feature a title song, with marching band music playing over the opening credits instead. Both 'The Whiffenpoof Song' and 'Violet' were period pieces than ran less than a minute ('Violet' was set to the melody of 'Aura Lee,' the same melody used for the title song of Elvis's first film, *Love Me Tender*). 'Almost' is a simple ballad that barely gets a chance to make its mark, running just under two minutes. 'Signs Of The Zodiac' is the kind of zany, lyric-heavy number that one could imagine in a Broadway musical; unfortunately, the best lines are given to Elvis's co-star (Marlyn Mason). Two songs were above par; 'Clean Up Your Own Backyard,' a jaunty number attacking hypocrisy, co-written by Billy Strange (who also wrote the film's score) and Mac Davis, and 'Swing Down, Sweet Chariot,' a lively version of the gospel number that Elvis had previously recorded in 1960 for the *His Hand In Mine* album. Shooting for *The Trouble With Girls* began on October 29, and was completed by December 18.

By then, the *Elvis* special had aired, and suddenly the future was something Elvis could look forward to again. He had already been thinking that his next real recording session needed to be different – something he'd actually enjoy doing, his soundtrack work being little more than an unwelcome distraction by this point. While working on the special, he had invited Scotty Moore and DJ Fontana to his house one evening to have dinner, afterwards asking them into another room where they could speak privately. "He said 'Would you guys like to do a European tour?'" says Scotty. "We said, 'Well, sure. Just tell us.' And he asked me, 'Do you still have your studio? [Music City Recorders in Nashville, where Scotty worked] What's the chances of getting in there and just locking it up for a couple of weeks?' I said, 'Sure, no problem. Just give me a little advance notice.' But none of that ever happened. I don't have any idea what he had in mind of going in the studio, if he had some ideas he wanted to try out or what. But that all got squashed by management."

His plans to work with Scotty and DJ may have fallen through, but Elvis was still not eager to return to RCA's Nashville studio when Felton Jarvis came to Graceland in early January 1969 to discuss the details for his next recording session. While discussing the matter with Jarvis and his friends, it was suggested that he consider a studio that had recently been making quite a name for itself right there in Memphis – American Sound Studios. Though small, and located in a less than salubrious neighborhood in North Memphis, American was in the midst of a record run that would see 122 records recorded at the studio hit the pop or R&B charts through 1972. ("Magazines like _Billboard_ and _Cash Box_, they all had a different chart, and we was in every one of 'em one week except Classical," Bobby Emmons, one of American's studio musicians, notes with pride.) A number of Elvis's inner circle already had ties to American. Red West worked with the studio as a songwriter and singer; George Klein, who'd started a small record label, had his artists record there; and Marty Lacker, who had started the Pepper Tanner Company (which produced commercial jingles and operated a label called Pepper Records), recorded his acts at American (he would later become the studio's manager).

The studio's main producing force was Lincoln 'Chips' Moman. Moman, a native of LaGrange, Georgia, already had a considerable resume before American opened its doors. He'd hitchhiked to Memphis in his teens and ended up playing guitar with Sun Records artist Warren Smith, then toured with Dorsey & Jimmy Burnette and wound up in LA, where he worked as a session musician at Gold Star Studios (where Eddie Cochran had recorded 'Summertime Blues' and The Beach Boys would later record 'Good Vibrations'). It was while working at Gold Star that he discovered how much he loved studio work: "That was what I was into more than anything else. Making the record itself … I'm into songs, and I'm into sound." After getting in a car accident while touring with Gene Vincent, he returned to Memphis, where he helped set up the Stax record label, producing the label's first hit, Carla Thomas's single 'Gee Whiz.'

He eventually fell out with the label's owners, filing a lawsuit against them. With the proceeds from the out-of-court settlement, he set up American in 1964, in partnership with Seymour Rosenberg, the lawyer who'd handled the lawsuit against Stax (Wayne McGinniss became another partner; both he and Rosenberg would later be bought out by Dan Crews). Moman had found the Memphis location for Stax studios in a former movie house on McLemore Avenue; now he chose a former grocery store at 827 Thomas Street (the same block where Rosenberg's father owned an auto parts store) as the location for American. The name 'American' was chosen so it would come early in the telephone book.

The Ovations were the first act to have a hit recorded at American, when their single 'It's Wonderful To Be In Love' reached Number 22 in *Billboard*'s R&B chart. The Gentrys' 'Keep On Dancing' was next, reaching Number Four on the pop charts, and after that the hits kept coming (even the studio's secretary, Sandy Posey, had a hit with 'Born A Woman'). Artists like The Box Tops, Merrilee Rush, Wilson Pickett, Solomon Burke, Dionne Warwick, and Dusty Springfield, among others, all made pilgrimages to the studio to draw on the talents of Moman (who was also a songwriter, co-writing Aretha Franklin's 'Do Right Woman,' among others) and his in-house musicians, soon dubbed The 827 Thomas Street Band.

The band was made up of long-time veterans of the Memphis music scene. Guitarist Reggie Young's first band was Memphis rockabilly outfit Eddie Bond & The Stompers (who had a regional hit with 'Rockin' Daddy'). He later joined The Bill Black Combo (the band formed by Elvis's original bass player in 1959), then became a staff musician at the Hi Records studio in Memphis. "It sounds more important than it was," he says. "It didn't have any salary at all. And when we recorded something over there, it was union scale; if we only did one song and they cleared it, we only got paid $15. It was the only game in town, I guess is the only reason we played it."

At one point, there was a discussion about the fee being cut back to

$10 a side. It didn't happen, "but I never forgot that," says Reggie. "And I said, the next time I get an opportunity I'm getting out of here." The opportunity came soon enough. Reggie also played other sessions around town, including at American, and he, Chips, and bassist Tommy Cogbill would occasionally get work out of town together. "We'd go to New York and work for Jerry Wexler at Atlantic Records," he explains. "We'd go up there for $100 a day, working for artists like Solomon Burke, and also come to Nashville and work. And then the three of us decided, let's don't travel anymore, let's just stay here. That was Moman's idea; if we don't go anywhere, we'll just try to get everybody to come here at his studio. Of course he would benefit from that. And we would too; we wouldn't have to be traveling."

The strategy quickly began to pay off. "I remember I'd been to Nashville and recorded with an R&B artist named Joe Tex, and we cut a song called 'Show Me,'" Reggie says. "It was a hit. And the next sessions they set up, they wanted me to come to Nashville. And I told them I couldn't do it, the only place I was going to be working was Memphis, and if they wanted to use us, we'd put a rhythm section together and they could come over to Memphis. And that's what they did. And so we sort of bound ourselves together. We wouldn't work for anybody else; if anybody wanted us they had to come here. One for all, all for one, that kind of thing."

Reggie then brought in keyboardist Bobby Emmons, who was also a staff musician at Hi (and, like Reggie and Chips, had played in The Bill Black Combo). "And Tommy got [drummer] Gene Chrisman to come over from Sun Studio," says Reggie. "So that was the nucleus of our rhythm section: Tommy Cogbill, Gene Chrisman, Bobby Emmons, and myself. And Chips was the engineer. And we got so busy that we needed another keyboard player, so that's when we talked Bobby Wood into coming over; he was also at Sun Studio. And then Tommy started producing shortly after that, and we needed another bass player, so we got Mike Leech. We all knew each other, because we all played on different sessions around town, and we played in little club bands.

Anyway, Mike was our friend, so he threw in with us also. And Tommy kind of stepped back and produced a lot of stuff."

"Tommy kind of ascended to the producer's chair and I kind of ascended to the bass chair," Mike Leech explains. "However, Tommy would play on something every now and then, if he felt he could come up with something kind of cool or neat to play on a certain side. I would just give him the bass, and he'd take over and play something. We had no animosity at all between each other. And if I felt like I could do something better than him or different than him, I would grab the bass and do it myself; the same kind of thing. But he eventually just eased out of playing bass entirely, and I was just playing bass all the time at American, so that's how that went down."

The name 827 Thomas Street Band came from American's street address. But after the musicians had relocated to Nashville in the 70s, they were eventually rechristened The Memphis Boys. "I'd been in Nashville for years and years and years," says Reggie. "And somebody was talking about us, one of our names would come up, and somebody said, 'Oh yeah, that's one of those Memphis boys.' And this is after I've been here 25 years! So that kind of stuck. And I'm kind of glad it's that instead of saying 'Nashville Boys.' Nothing wrong with Nashville, but I'm still associated with Memphis, the Memphis music that we did. So we just changed it over and called ourselves The Memphis Boys, 'cause that's what they call us over here."

In contrast to Nashville, where an 'A Team' of musicians played sessions at different studios around town, Memphis studios like American and Stax had their own in-house musicians, creating their own distinctive sound, and giving the studios a unique identity. "Nashville was more country," says Bobby Emmons. "And Memphis was blues and rock'n'roll. Just R&B. They just call it R&B, that's what we were. That's what everybody called us, and that's what we called ourselves, so why not?"

The musicians also had a greater autonomy than they might have had elsewhere. "We'd write our own charts and come up with our own arrangements," says Reggie. "We'd worked together long enough to where we sort of all thought alike. That's why we were an in-house group. Somebody might have an idea; 'Well, let's try this.' 'OK.' And there was no time limit; it was really loose. As a band we were like 'player producers.' We offered, I think, a little more than just being individual players. It was a creative band, everybody had great ideas. And we'd toss all that around while we were playing, because there was no time restraint on us. Like Nashville, a session is every three hours. And that's a good thing, too, because every three hours you get paid for another session. Whereas in Memphis it was really loose. We had time to really work out the arrangements."

It was the kind of atmosphere that created a strong sense of camaraderie. "Chips is a great producer, and the band happened to be one of those groups of people that all think from the same piece of their brain," Bobby says. "So we made a team. We didn't have to go in there and compete every day to feel good about it. Everybody had a direction that they went, and the sum of 'em was just a lot better than anybody by themselves. So we made some good records. We had some great songs come in, and we made some good records on 'em."

Recording ended up being less like work than play; "When we would get through with something we'd say, 'Let's call home sick,'" said Chips. "Nobody wanted to leave!" "I think I was in the studio about 28 hours a day back then," adds Bobby. "I don't remember getting to see much of anything else for about three years. I had grown kids by the time I got home to meet 'em!" "If I'm not having fun doing a session, we shouldn't have done the session," Chips observed on another occasion.

With American's track record of hits, and the encouragement of his friends, Elvis soon warmed to the idea of recording there. For his part, Chips had previously expressed an interest in working with Elvis, having said to Marty Lacker and George Klein at one point, "When's Elvis gonna get some good songs, man? When's he gonna quit cuttin' that crap?" On being contacted about the possibility of a session, Chips readily postponed a Neil Diamond session to allow Elvis to get to work right away (in return, Diamond was told they'd try to get Elvis to record one of his songs). Felton Jarvis would also attend the sessions as a secondary producer.

For their part, the musicians working at American shared Chips's views about Elvis's recent work. "I really liked the early Elvis," says Glen Spreen, who played saxophone on the sessions. "Later on I was very disappointed." He'd felt the Comeback Special "was a little more real … but I still didn't hear any songs like I'd heard before, the kind that had really excited me when I was younger."

Neither Mike Leech nor Wayne Jackson (a trumpet player who was part of a group of studio musicians known as The Memphis Horns) felt Elvis had been served well by Nashville. "They Mickey Moused him," says Wayne. "The tracks just sounded real camp and real nice, but certainly not anything creative or innovative at all."

"I didn't like a lot of the songs that came out of Nashville," Mike agrees. "I didn't think they were up to Elvis's standards of records. Even though there were some hits. The stuff with The Jordanaires – all that stuff, I think it took him in a different direction that personally wasn't my cup of tea. I liked his earlier stuff better, and of course I liked the stuff that we did – naturally!"

Though none of them had worked with him, some of the musicians had had encounters with Elvis over the years. Young had played the same shows as Elvis back in the 50s, during his time with Eddie Bond & The Stompers. He also happened to be visiting Memphis radio station WMPS with a friend when Elvis dropped by. "My friend and I and Elvis went down on Main Street and we went in a five-and-ten cent store," he recalls. "And Elvis was flirting with the girl behind the counter. They had some little cheap rings and he bought one, it was probably a quarter or something, and put it on her finger and told her, 'Now we're engaged.' I've often wondered if she ever remembered that! She didn't know who he was then."

Bobby Emmons also remembered Elvis stopping by "our little 1,000-watt radio station in Mississippi" on his early tours. Bobby Wood had met Elvis at Sun in the 50s, and some years later was invited by him to join Elvis and his friends at the Memphis Fairgrounds, the local amusement park Elvis frequently rented out; Chips had also been a part of the gatherings at the Fairgrounds. Wayne Jackson says Elvis would come by Memphis clubs to listen to the Mar-Keys, the house band at Stax, for whom Jackson played: "He would be outside in the parking lot listening to us through the fan – you know the big ol' square hole where the fans was pullin' smoke out of the building? And pullin' our music out too. He would sit out there in his big Cadillac limousine with a couple of his guys, and smoke cigars and listen. And we'd come out on our break; we'd all troop out there to the parking lot and stand around the big ol' Cadillac and talk to Elvis."

But as big a star as Elvis was, the 827 Thomas Street Band had also been working with big name artists themselves for some years. "To be honest, we were kind of 'celebrity tough' then," says Bobby. "We had a lot of big people coming in and out of there, people that you just had heard of all your life. We started calling ourselves the resurrection band there for a while, because we got a hit on people that had been trying, had had big records and then just couldn't get another one off. I knew Elvis was the King of Rock'n'Roll and I agreed with it, but he was cold – he was doing movies and he wasn't really focused on the music end of it. And I missed the '68 comeback [TV show], so I didn't know he was back. So we didn't know enough about it to get nervous."

"Back when he was really hot, it'd be Elvis this and Elvis that," says Reggie. "But then he had that period of nothing but movie tracks and all that stuff, and it didn't ring my bell! If I'm not mistaken, somebody said it had been about eight years since he'd had a hit when he came into American. ['If I Can Dream' didn't peak at Number 12 until early 1969] And we'd been recording, gosh, we had song after song in the chart. I don't know how many songs we had in the Top 40 when he came in. So I don't think any of us was very impressed."

But in a nice touch, Reggie dug out Scotty Moore's Gibson Super 400 CES guitar, which had been used on Elvis's 50s records and was now owned by Chips (Moore having traded it for a classical guitar and a set of vibes Moman owned, along with $80). "I got to thinking, well, Elvis is coming in, I'm going to play that guitar," he says. "We had it worked on so it would be playable really good. So when Elvis came in I played that guitar on most of the stuff we cut with him." (Moman later sold the guitar at a Christie's auction for £58,000.) Perhaps because of Elvis's previous inquiry about using his studio, Scotty hoped he might be contacted for the American sessions, but Chips was only interested in using his own musicians, a decision he later regretted, saying, "If I had it all to do over again, [Scotty] would have been invited to that session."

And so, on the evening of January 13, five days after his 34th birthday, Elvis arrived at American for his first recording session in Memphis in nearly 14 years. Racial tensions in Memphis had increased after Dr Martin Luther King's murder, and guards – both human and canine – made regular patrols around the building (an armed guard was even posted on the roof). The studio was also in a rather run-down condition; rats could be heard scuttling from one dark corner to another.

Reggie Young and Mike Leech were sitting in the studio when Elvis arrived around 7pm (throughout the sessions, Elvis would arrive at the same time, recording until the early hours of the morning). "We were just sitting there talking, shooting the breeze," says Mike. "And the back door of the studio popped open and in comes Elvis with his Memphis Mafia group and everything. And the first words out of Elvis's mouth were 'What a funky, funky studio!' I remember that really well. And then the next thing I knew, it was like a party atmosphere; all the guys in his entourage were cracking jokes and wrestling and playing tricks on each other and stuff like that. It was really not a very serious atmosphere or anything."

The musicians quickly found the attentiveness of Elvis's friends to be somewhat grating. "When Elvis first came in, he had his entourage with him and he was smoking one of those little cigar things, cigarette-type cigars," says Reggie. "And he'd put one in his mouth and there'd be about three or four lighters up there clicking to light his cigarette for him. And they'd go out and get stuff for him and blah blah blah. It was really hard to get to him, 'cause his guys were all around him." Glen Spreen adds, "I wasn't that excited about cutting him, but when those three lighters went up in his face it kind of turned me off. I didn't go into those sessions with a real good attitude."

Nonetheless, they had to admit they also felt a bit of Elvis's star power themselves. "It's funny, because before he came in, I thought, 'Oh well, Elvis is coming in; we're going to do that, then we'll go and do somebody else,'" says Reggie. "But when he walked in, we were all kind of taken aback. I was amazed at my own reaction; I thought 'Man, that's Elvis!' He had that charisma about him, and I think we all kind of backed up a step and went, 'Whoa!' So it took a while to get over that, 'cause he had that star look. You'd know he was in the room when he walked in. He just kind of commanded his space and you definitely knew he was there. We were all kind of taken with him. I was kind of nervous on the first few songs we did, as we all were, I'm sure. I was wanting it to really come off good. So some of those first things we did I'm sure I was a little shaky! Trying too hard maybe."

"When Elvis walked in, he sort of took over," Wayne Jackson agrees. "The building and the lights and the air – everything. It was Elvis! And he looked wonderful. He was at his best in those days, so we were in the room with a sure enough big time star from Memphis who had come home to record and it was a big deal. Big deal for us when we all realized who was standing in the room with us. I hadn't seen him in years. So it was one of those 'uh huh!' moments."

But it quickly became apparent that the musicians weren't going to be, in Reggie's words, "yes men." As everyone listened to the demos that had been submitted, Elvis turned to Reggie at one point and asked, "You like that song?" "No, not really," Reggie replied. "And boy, Felton kind of flinched!" recalls Reggie. "And Elvis asked Bobby Wood, 'Do you like this song at all?' Bobby told him a little stronger than I did ... 'That's a piece of ... that's awful!' And so then me and Bobby got called off to the side by Felton, and he said, 'Oh man, we've got all the songs picked! And they're all out of Hill & Range Publishing. We don't want to make any waves.' I said, 'Well, he just asked a question. I was being honest. I didn't like it.' I still don't! But I think Elvis appreciated us being honest like that." (Chips was equally disdainful of the Hill & Range material, saying, "I don't even want to tell you what I thought of some of those songs!")

Once a song had been selected to work on, Elvis would record a rough vocal with the band, while they worked out an arrangement. "The demos were very basic and we just kind of went our own direction with it," explains Reggie. "That's kind of the way you did it back then. It's more creative that way, instead of having to copy something. And that particular band was a very creative bunch of players. Everybody participated in producing a record, as a player and as a creative person, instead of just being hired as the guitar player, come in and play this and go home. We were involved in it a little more, with everybody that we did at American."

"Sometimes we'd all get a general idea of direction of what we felt the strong points were of the song," says Bobby, "and then we'd all head on out to the control room and just start running it down. Or a lot of times there's more than one idea, so Chips was always our tiebreaker. If there were two things going on, he'd hit the talkback and say, 'Everybody jump on that thing that Reggie's doing' or 'Everybody jump on that thing Bobby's doing.' So he would direct us like that. Or he'd stop us and say, 'Won't you try this or that?' Usually it was just picked from the smorgasbord of what was going on: 'That fill you're doing on drums, do that same thing, but play it on the hi-hat, and play the kick drum part on the snare,' or something like that. Chips was always trying to make a new fresh sound."

"Chips, he's a very musical guy and a really talented producer," says Wayne. "And when he makes comments about the music or the lyric, either one, it's always right. He's just a dead-on musician."

The session began with 'Long Black Limousine,' written by Bobby George and Vern Stoval in 1962, and most recently a country hit for Jody Miller. The stark, funereal tolling of the song's opening piano chords (underscored by the accompanying bell added later) set an ominous tone for this morality tale of big dreams brought to a sudden, tragic end. The song's narrator is a man who has lost his love twice: first when she leaves home for the promise of a glamorous life in the big city, and forever when she dies in a car accident. Her pledge to return to town in a "fancy car" has come true in terribly ironic fashion; it turns out to be the hearse carrying her to her grave.

The song features one of Elvis's most heart-wrenching vocals, heightened by the subtle way it unfolds. Instead of going for an overly dramatic performance – which would have suited the melodrama of the song – 'Limousine' begins with minimal instrumentation and backing vocals for the first minute. A soft drum-roll brings the other instruments in, and from that point on the song slowly but steadily builds in intensity. Halfway through, the horns come in, and by the final verse, with Elvis mourning how his heart and dreams will be forever buried along with his love, the pain of his loss is almost physically tangible.

If Felton hadn't been pleased with the outspokenness of American's musicians, he wasn't any happier with the way Chips worked with Elvis. Early on in the sessions, says Mike Leech, "Chips hit the talkback and said something about Elvis singing a little flat, do it again. And Felton kind of flinched and said not to talk to Elvis like that. And Chips just ignored him. And of course Elvis didn't mind a bit; he said, 'Oh, OK, I'll do it again, no problem.' Of course, I think that scared Felton to death, because he had never talked to Elvis like that."

"That was Felton," says Reggie. "Felton had been Elvis's producer for a long time and kind of catered to him, and his needs, and that was what he wanted to do, I guess. I don't know – I wasn't there whenever he was recording Elvis like that. But I assume that's what went on, because it was like, he seemed to be walking on thin ice, and didn't want to make any waves, like he told us. And Moman wasn't that way at all.

He was just matter of fact, and would tell Elvis if he was singing flat, and 'Let's try this,' or 'Want to try this?' Probably no one had ever talked to him like that. It was a good thing. And I think Elvis really appreciated that, somebody treating him like a human being."

For his part, Chips said he had no problems working with Elvis one-on-one. "[Elvis] obviously hadn't had any direction in a great while," he observed. "If he had, I don't think he would have cut all those junk records he cut ... He took direction great, but I'm sure [he] wouldn't have taken direction over the monitors where 50 people could hear me say he was flat. That would blow things out of proportion. But if you did it quietly, one on one, it was no problem at all." Chips quickly saw that the best way to deal with Elvis was to leave the control room and speak to him directly in the studio.

In any case, it didn't impede the progress of the session. Next came 'This Is The Story,' a downbeat song about a failed relationship that could easily have veered into soppy sentimentality in less skilled hands. But Elvis's delivery gives the song a kind of aching sweetness, while the backing (including the overdubbed strings) is more restrained than it ever would have been in a song used for one of Elvis's films. It was wrapped up quickly in two takes.

A rhythm track was laid down for the mid-tempo 'Come Out, Come Out,' with Elvis intending to record a vocal later, but he never did. The final number worked on that evening, 'Wearin' That Loved On Look' (the first of three songs by Dallas Frazier and Arthur 'Doodle' Owens that Elvis would record at the session), was back in the same soulful groove as 'Long Black Limousine,' with an added element of jauntiness somewhat at odds with the song's theme of suspected infidelity; its opening chord on the organ even leads you to think it might be another of Elvis's well-loved hymns or gospel numbers.

The high notes of the intro gave Elvis some trouble during the early takes, causing him to laugh and curse good-naturedly when his voice cracked. "Somebody asked me one time did I think Elvis had soul," says Mike Leech. "And I said, absolutely. And they said, 'Why do you think that?' And I said, because you get somebody like Pavarotti and throw a high C at him, he'd just hit it without even taking a breath, just go ahead and hit it. But Elvis had to work at hitting those high notes. And sometimes you didn't think he was gonna make it, but he finally would. And that's what in my opinion gave him a lot of soul, because he really worked at trying to hit those notes."

Elvis also had a cold that evening, which gave his voice a touch of hoarseness. This actually works to the song's advantage, adding a welcome element of grittiness. And once the drums kick the song into an up-tempo gear, Elvis's bluesy vocal conjures up a mood of breezy resignation, not outrage, as he lists his partner's many infractions, casually joining in on the "shoop shoops" in the chorus with his backing vocalists.

Elvis soldiered on through 15 takes, and when the session finally ended at 5am his throat was the worse for wear, but he was pleased at how the evening had gone. "Man, that felt really great," he said to his friends while driving in the car back to Graceland. "I can't tell you how good I feel." "It had been a long time since I had seen that look of happiness and satisfaction on his face," Marty Lacker noted.

The musicians all felt the session had gone well, even if they were still a bit surprised by Elvis's personal style. "He had on the slick collars and I don't know, the cape-looking things that he wore," says Mike Leech. "That's the way he would dress in the studio. Most of the other artists, hell, they'd come in in a T-shirt and blue jeans. Elvis was there like he was being filmed, like he was holding up his image. Not on purpose I don't think, that's just the way that he was. He liked to wear that stuff. I thought it looked cool on Elvis, and the other people didn't do that. Like, Neil Diamond was just one of the guys. Elvis was kind of set apart because of his – I don't know – the King of Rock'n'Roll – what can you say? That's the way I looked at him anyway." Indeed, pictures of Elvis at the session show him looking dressier than the other musicians, with a scarf around his neck like he'd worn during the *Elvis* special.

But there was a consensus about the quality of his work. "Oh, I was just blown away by his professionalism and his talent as a vocalist and his feel as a performer," says Bobby Emmons. "Elvis came in there to work. He came in there working harder – he reminded you of a 16-year-old kid that had never had a record, but he wanted one bad. And he just worked like a champion. He was the leader of the band, like he's supposed to be." In Chips's assessment, "He came in there and he was on fire, man. He really was."

Nonetheless, there were a few problems brewing under the surface. Both Chips and the musicians felt Elvis's companions were too much of a distraction. "The entourage when we first started was so big, there just wasn't room for everybody," says Bobby. "But we knew we had to make a record, so we yielded to the sightseers and so forth." "It would be almost like he thought he had to perform for them," Chips observed. "You know, say something cute, do something funny, make 'em laugh."

More problematic was the underlying threat of publishing disputes. When Chips played songs from American's own stable of writers for Elvis, "all the business people started swarmin' in on it," says Bobby, worried about the money they would lose if someone else's song was used. "So they started telling Chips and the writers what they were going to have to give up to get it cut." Adds Reggie, "One of the RCA people cornered Moman, and said that they had all the songs picked – which they did, they brought in all this stuff – and if we cut any outside material they had to have publishing on it."

Chips was not about to put up with such demands. "We had already done some sides, and I said, 'You can take everything we've done so far, be my guest, and just get out of my studio, 'cause there ain't no more sessions!'" he recalled. "I think they were kind of shocked when I stood up to them. They probably had never had anyone ask them to leave the studio before – but I did, and it turned out to be better for Elvis." The issue was resolved when RCA Vice President Harry Jenkins came out in support of Moman, but the bad feelings lingered.

Once the "sightseers" were kept away, the atmosphere improved. "They were asked to leave, after the first day we started," says Reggie. "There were just so many people there. After they left then Elvis would talk to us. And we would sit around, and I remember we reminisced about Memphis, the different clubs and different players and singers and stuff. Anyway, he became one of us, and it kind of took the edge off. And he really got serious about it then."

Elvis, as usual, stayed away from the business disputes, and was back in the studio on the 14th. The first song worked on was 'You'll Think Of Me' by Mort Shuman, who had previously co-written a number of Elvis's better songs of the 60s with Doc Pomus, including 'Viva Las Vegas' (the title song for the film of the same name) and both sides of the single '(Marie's The Name) His Latest Flame'/'Little Sister.' The song had an interesting lyrical approach; despite its title, the narrator sings of the time when his former girlfriend will no longer be thinking of him (Shuman described it as being "influenced by Dylan and the whole San Francisco-type thing").

Elvis's wistful vocal is musically complemented by Reggie Young's sitar line, using the same instrument he'd played on The Box Tops' 'Cry Like A Baby' and B.J. Thomas's 'Hooked On A Feeling.' "I don't know how that came about, but it was there in my arsenal of gimmicks!" he jokes. The mood is bittersweet, Elvis singing that even though he loves his girlfriend he must move on, due to his "heart that's haunted," a feeling echoed both by the mournful backing vocals, and the lyrical suggestion that while the girlfriend is destined to find a new love, the singer apparently isn't.

'A Little Bit Of Green' was next, by the songwriting team of Chris Arnold, Geoff Marrow, and David Martin, who had written 'This Is The Story.' Like that song, it's a rather undistinguished number (unsurprisingly, the 'green' in the title refers to jealousy), though again, Elvis's delivery makes the song seem better than it is. There being little that could be done with the song to make it more interesting, it was completed in three takes (in contrast to 'You'll Think Of Me,' which had run to 23 takes).

After a break for a meal, the mood decidedly picked up when work continued at 2am with 'I'm Movin' On,' a big hit for Hank Snow in

1950 (Snow had been one of Parker's former clients). Elvis turned in a lively version, clearly having fun with the lyrics, tossing in the occasional ad lib ("Move on, baby!"), and sounding almost gleeful at times as he delivers the kiss-off to his one-time sweetheart; the overdubbed horns give the song an additional punch. After a false start, the track was nailed down in one take.

'Gentle On My Mind' was also on the brighter side musically, though a careful listen to the lyrics revealed the song to have an unexpectedly dark streak, fully in keeping with most of the songs recorded at the American sessions. The song had been a minor country hit for its composer, John Hartford (produced by Felton Jarvis), and found greater success with Glen Campbell's version, which won three Grammys. The lyric begins by celebrating the pleasures of having an uncommitted relationship, free of any legally binding ties, but by the final verse an altogether sadder scenario is depicted; the narrator sipping soup in a lonely train yard, imagining that the warm cup he's holding is his lover. That Elvis's vocal is still somewhat hopeful makes the scene even more poignant.

By the end of the session, Elvis's throat was giving him more problems, and it was decided that he should stay home for a few days and let his voice recover. So work continued without him, as the band laid down backing tracks for 'Don't Cry Daddy,' 'Poor Man's Gold,' 'Inherit The Wind,' and 'Mama Liked The Roses' (one of the songs owned by Moman over which there was a publishing dispute) on the 15th, and 'My Little Friend' on the 16th.

When Elvis returned to American on the 20th, he worked on two new songs, one of which would be one of the session's highlights: 'In The Ghetto.' The song was by Mac Davis, and had been submitted on a demo tape of 19 songs for the sessions, also including 'Poor Man's Gold' and 'Don't Cry Daddy' (the latter of which Davis had previously played himself for Elvis at his home in Bel Air).

'In The Ghetto' was a clear 'message song,' a plea for tolerance for those stuck in poverty and unable to find their way out (emphasizing this theme, the song's original title had been 'The Vicious Circle'). The song was inspired by Davis's own experiences, seeing the neighborhoods where African-Americans had lived during his childhood in Lubbock, Texas, and, on watching TV coverage of the civil rights movement, hearing the word 'ghetto' used to refer to primarily black neighborhoods. "I had always thought of ghettos being associated with Europe during World War II," he said. "I had never thought of our slums as being ghettos."

The song hardly espoused radical sentiments, but was still considered possibly too outspoken for a performer who'd never expressed much of a political viewpoint in public before. 'If I Can Dream' had been a step down that path, but ultimately evinced a positive viewpoint, and one could also consider 'Clean Up Your Own Backyard' something of a message song; 'Ghetto' was more critical of a society that left some of its people mired in despair. There was also a question about whether it was even appropriate for Elvis to record the song; "There was some discussion about what people might think about a white guy singing about life in the ghetto," explained Chips. George Klein even initially advised Elvis not to record it. But when Moman said he'd simply give it to another artist, such as former football star Roosevelt Grier, whom he'd just signed to his own American Group Productions record label, everyone reconsidered, and Elvis finally agreed to record the song.

Elvis's concentration is evident from the first take, relating the sad tale with a quiet intensity that's matched by the tasteful restraint of the musicians. Aside from a few mistakes with the lyrics, his delivery never changes; "One is provided with an incontrovertible glimpse of what the process might have been like for Elvis, if only he had been able to approach recording consistently as an art," biographer Peter Guralnick later wrote. His immediate environment undoubtedly provided further inspiration, as Wayne Jackson pointed out: "We were actually in the ghetto, and here was Elvis singing a pertinent song about the South and about the social climate of the day. He's singing, and chills went all over me."

"I can picture myself in the room when it was being cut," says Bobby Emmons, of how the arrangement was worked out. "Reggie was playing that guitar, playing that little pattern that's on it at the start. And I was playing a Hammond M3 organ with a little single-note thing along with it; that was making him a blanket, making him a backdrop for the guitar. And it just built up from the front. It started out with me and Reg and then other people started coming in, I remember that."

"I was nervous on that one," Reggie admits. "'Cause without the overdubs, the first part of that record was just me and Elvis; I played the intro on acoustic guitar. And I remember thinking, 'Gosh, I hope I don't mess up and have to stop and start over.' I was really proud that that turned out so good."

As the song was being worked out over the course of 23 takes (with a change to a higher key after take four), the performances were so compelling that Mike Leech became increasingly anxious to participate. "They were running down 'In The Ghetto' and Tommy [Cogbill] had already taken the bass chair," he explains. "I wanted to play on it, and I couldn't figure out anything to play. Then I noticed the timpani. I rolled it out there, tuned it up, took a microphone and stuck it on it, hooked a cable to it, walked the cable into the control room and plugged it into an input, and showed Chips the slider the timpani was on. I walked back out there and boom-boomed for a couple of seconds, and next thing I heard was 'We're rolling.' And Gene [Chrisman] counted off and I played 'do do la doo' on the timpani. That was a pure accident. If I'd found a spoon or something to make a sound that would be good for that cut, I would have played it. But the timpani seemed like that fitted pretty good."

But it's Elvis's vocal that remains the song's most impressive feature, ranking among his finest vocal performances for its masterful control throughout, as when his voice rises to a slight break on the word "blind" at the end of the first verse, then drops to a near whisper at the end of the next line. "There's not that many artists that can do it the way Elvis could do it," says Bobby. "He could nail a performance on stuff that he hadn't heard that many times either. 'Course I imagine he sang it around the pool, as people used to say. But some of these songs he hadn't heard that much, some of the new songs. Elvis was just phenomenal. He didn't have any tuning machines and we weren't cutting out big chunks of his vocal from another track and making a composite track or any of that stuff. He was just singing it from top to bottom."

There was then a switch to a lighter mood, with Elvis re-cutting his vocal for 'Gentle On My Mind.' The session concluded with the up-tempo 'Rubberneckin',' a sort of pop-soul hybrid. The song was co-written by Dory Jones and Ben Weisman (using his wife's name, Bunny Warren). Weisman had co-written songs for Elvis for years, including such numbers as 'A Dog's Life' (from _Paradise, Hawaiian Style_) and the infamous 'Dominic' (from _Stay Away, Joe_). Weisman himself conceded that these were "weird," though he was quick to add, "I was just doing my job. I wrote those kind of songs because they were needed in the script and I wasn't about to turn down the work." 'Rubberneckin'' was a decided improvement over such material, essentially a song about the pleasures of hanging out, with the overdubbed horns and backing vocals adding a dose of energy.

As if needing a break after the sober emotion of 'Ghetto,' the session on the 21st was more laidback, beginning with a loose version of The Beatles' 'Hey Jude.' With Elvis not knowing all of the words, it was more in the nature of a warm-up song, and remained in the vaults until 1972, when it was used to fill out the album _Elvis Now_. Most of the night was spent on vocal overdubs for songs Elvis had already worked on ('I'm Movin' On,' 'Long Black Limousine,' 'Wearin' That Loved On Look,' 'You'll Think Of Me,' and 'This Is The Story') as well as vocals for songs where the band had already laid down a rhythm track. 'My Little Friend' is a country-pop, discreetly phrased number about losing one's virginity, an occasion that so moves the narrator he vows he'll never love another (a vow that has unsurprisingly been dispensed with by the last verse); Elvis's vocal gives this exercise in nostalgia a melancholy touch. 'Inherit The Wind' was one of two Eddie Rabbit songs Elvis would record at American, with the same I'm-a-restless-spirit theme as 'You'll Think Of Me' and 'I'm Movin' On.'

'Mama Liked The Roses' was written specifically for Elvis by John Christopher, who played bass in a band with Ronnie Milsap, another musician who worked at American. Christopher had given a demo of the song to Chips, and the heart-tugging song about a family remembering their dead mother struck an immediate chord with Elvis, who'd been devoted to his own mother. Elvis took the song home to listen to, and his entourage later informed Christopher, "Man, you got the hit at Elvis's house this week. That's all he's doing, he's playing that song night and day." 'Don't Cry Daddy' was a sort of companion song to 'Roses,' with the narrator's children trying to cheer up their father who is mourning his wife's death. In both cases, the gravitas of Elvis's delivery keeps the songs from becoming too maudlin.

Vernon Presley had come by the session that evening, prompting Elvis to record Ned Miller's 1962 hit 'From A Jack To A King,' one of his father's favorite songs. Elvis's full-bodied version was noticeably tongue-in-cheek, a clear sign he was having a very good time indeed, only needing two complete run-throughs for a final take. (Miller later said Presley's version became his own favorite version of his song.) Elvis also attempted to record a vocal for 'Poor Man's Gold,' but was interrupted by the sound of an ambulance siren outside, and the song was never completed; a 12-second excerpt of the instrumental track was later released on the 1999 set *Suspicious Minds: The Memphis 1969 Anthology*.

Elvis came by American early on the night of the 22nd, having learned that one of his favorite artists, rhythm & blues singer Roy Hamilton, was recording at the studio during the day. George Klein arranged for Elvis to drop by before his own session began. After praising Hamilton's talent, Elvis astonished the musicians by pitching a song he was supposed to record ('Angelica'), like any other songplugger. Hamilton did indeed end up recording the song, which was released as one of his last records; he died a few months later, on July 20, after suffering a stroke. But on this night, Elvis posed for pictures with his idol, smiling broadly in one shot with Roy beside him, as Chips looks on.

When work started on Elvis's own session, the first song recorded was 'Without Love,' first performed in 1957 by Clyde McPhatter, another singer Elvis greatly admired; he once told producer Sam Phillips, "If I could sing like that man I'd never want for another thing." It was the kind of dramatic, show-stopping ballad that Elvis was always partial to, and would become a trademark of his later live shows. It was laid down with dispatch in five takes, then Elvis took over on piano himself on Eddy Arnold's 'I'll Hold You In My Heart,' thoroughly steeping what was originally a country number in the blues. He sings part of the opening line twice before finally completing it, neatly creating a sense of intimacy, as if the band is warming up for its final set of the night, and captured the song in a single take. A passionate yearning comes through in both songs, each of them soulful cries from a lonely heart.

'I'll Be There' (a minor pop hit for its composer, Bobby Darin, in 1960) was far more light-hearted – and disposable – though the strings and horns that were later added gave the song more substance. And then came another song that Chips had been asked to surrender some of his publishing on: 'Suspicious Minds.'

Mark James, a songwriter with Moman's publishing company, Press Music, had released the song himself as a single on Scepter the previous year, and it had not been successful. ("I knew it was Number One in Scranton, Pennsylvania," says Glen Spreen. "I don't know that for sure but Mark told me that!") Asked to come up with material for Elvis's session, he'd suggested it to Chips, who agreed to play it for Elvis, and Elvis immediately recognized the song's potential.

Mark James's version had also been recorded at American with the same musicians that Elvis was using. "'Suspicious Minds' we had a head start on, because we had already cut it with Mark," says Bobby Emmons. "So we just played that arrangement for Elvis; they liked it, and we were all still there to do it. If it had been a hit on Mark, we would have changed [the arrangement]. But that was our best shot then, and since it hadn't ever really got its due we just used it again."

In the early takes, Elvis repeatedly stumbled over a line in the second verse, but by take six he had got it, and take eight became the master. The song concerns a couple being torn apart by distrust, a theme well in keeping with the songs recorded at American, the majority of which were about unhappy relationships. But where the Mark James version featured a more plaintive vocal, Elvis gave the song a driving urgency, especially in the extended fade-out, with Elvis so caught up in his emotional plea he can't let go. Even in its unfinished state, it was clear the track was going to be a winner.

Thus the first round of sessions at American ended on a high note at 7am, with Elvis and Chips immediately doing an interview with the *Commercial Appeal*, which ran later that day. "It all started right here in Memphis for me, man, and it feels so good working in this studio," Elvis enthused to reporter James Kingsley, going on to praise the musicians, who were equally generous toward him. "Elvis hits it hard from the time he comes into the studio until he goes home," Bobby Wood was quoted as saying. "He jokes around to keep everyone relaxed, but he is all business in the session." Chips was just as generous in his praise, telling Kingsley, "He is one of the hardest working artists I have ever been associated with. What energy and enthusiasm he has while working." "We have some hits, don't we Chips?" Elvis concluded. "Maybe some of your biggest," Chips replied.

American's musicians agreed with those sentiments. "Even though we had a good time, we considered ourselves good musicians in the studio," says Mike Leech. "And we were taking great pride in recording these hits that we were doing. We knew when we'd cut a hit. We'd go into the control room and listen to a playback, and Chips would always play it back nice and loud where we could feel it. And he'd be just grinning from ear to ear, and we'd all be just dancing around in the control room, and everybody's mood would be happy and elated, Elvis's included. Big grins and smiles. There was no doubt in our minds, we knew damn well when it was a hit; we'd laugh and give each other high fives and all that stuff, just knowing right then and there that it was a smash. And sure enough it would be."

And despite the occasional tensions over business conflicts, everyone involved recognized that the first sessions at American had produced some extraordinary work. So as Elvis, Priscilla, Lisa Marie, and their friends vacationed in Aspen, Colorado, a second session at the studio was arranged. But there would be no more fights over publishing; no songs were brought to the sessions that hadn't previously been cleared.

With no cold to slow Elvis down, there were no breaks in the sessions; recording began February 17 and ran straight through the 22nd, and, as before, started between 7pm and 9pm and ran till the early morning hours. This round of sessions began with Elvis following a studio tradition, singing a few lines of 'This Time,' a song Chips had written that had been a hit for Troy Shondell in 1961, as the producer arrived in the studio; in his rendition, Elvis found a natural segue into 'It's My Way' and finally 'I Can't Stop Loving You' (the track was later released on *Suspicious Minds: The 1969 Memphis Anthology*).

The session proper began with a decidedly somber love song, 'True Love Travels On A Gravel Road,' another from songwriting team of Dallas Frazier and Arthur 'Doodle' Owens, who had also written 'Wearin' That Loved On Look'; 'Gravel Road' had been a minor hit on the country charts for Duane Dee in 1968. Initially, the song was taken too fast, eventually provoking some chuckles from Elvis. By take six, the tempo was slowed down, enhancing the underlying tenderness, while a subtle instrumental flavor was added when Chips suggested Reggie Young play his guitar through a Leslie speaker, giving it a shimmery quality.

Now thoroughly comfortable with the studio, producer, and musicians, Elvis was noticeably more relaxed, something that also came through on the next number, Percy Mayfield's 'Stranger In My Own Home Town.' Elvis had been listening to the song for a few years, and threw himself into it fully, delighting in the swaggering, bluesy romp to the point that he was freely improvising by the end of the first take, which became the master. The session ended with the gentle pop of Neil Diamond's 'And The Grass Won't Pay No Mind,' fulfilling the promise to Diamond that one of his songs would be recorded during the sessions in exchange for the postponement of his own session at American (Diamond had sent an acetate of the song to George Klein, who played it for Elvis at Graceland). It was one of the few light-hearted songs of the sessions, and put Elvis in a playful mood; at one point, he altered a line about hearing "God calling" to "Chips calling."

The session on the 18th began with the tough braggadocio of 'Power Of My Love.' The song was written by the trio of Bill Giant, Bernie Baum, and Florence Kaye, who had written a number of Elvis's film songs, including such lesser numbers as 'Queenie Wahine's Papaya' (from *Paradise, Hawaiian Style*) and 'Go East, Young Man' (from *Harum Scarum*); their non-soundtrack numbers, like '(You're The) Devil In Disguise' (a chart-topper in the UK) and 'Today, Tomorrow, And Forever,' tended to be much stronger. 'Power Of My Love' freely indulged lyricist Kaye's penchant for double-entendres (accented by the mock groans from the backing singers that emphasize certain lines), and perhaps as a result, some of the between-takes chat got a little fast and loose as well.

'After Loving You' was originally recorded by Eddy Arnold in 1962, though Elvis's version is informed more by Della Reese's 1965 recording. The song was one Elvis had been playing for himself for years, and he had little trouble taking over on piano on the early takes, reveling in the moment. Though ostensibly a song about heartbreak, there's an undeniably ebullient quality to his voice, especially heard on his near scat singing of the line "I'm no good" at the song's end. The last song of the evening was 'Do You Know Who I Am?,' a song about trying to restart a love affair made even more bittersweet when the strings and a gently tapped tambourine were overdubbed on it.

Recording on the 19th began with one of the few songs from the Hill & Range catalogue that Chips admitted he liked; Eddie Rabbitt's

'Kentucky Rain.' Memories differ on Elvis's initial reaction to the song; Lamar Fike (who worked for Hill & Range) recalled him not being particularly "knocked out" with it, while Moman said he "loved" the song and "said yes to it the first time he heard it." Regardless, most of the session was spent on the number, Elvis working hard to find the right emotional tone for this country tale of a man searching for his lost love, to Chips' encouragement; "Elvis, you're singing the hell out of it!" he said after take nine.

The other track recorded that night was the equally emotive 'Only The Strong Survive,' first released the previous November on Jerry Butler's *The Iceman Cometh* album (and co-written by Butler, Kenny Gamble, and Leon Huff); as a single, it reached Number Four in the pop chart and topped the rhythm & blues chart. The touching number was well suited to Elvis, opening with a recitation from a son recounting the advice his mother gave about overcoming a failed love affair. Elvis derided his early efforts, at one point saying during a take: "She said, 'Boy, that's one of the worst jobs of singing I've ever heard you do in your natural life!'" But he pushed on through 29 takes, eventually turning in a deeply affecting performance. Elvis also took the time to sing 'Happy Birthday' to Bobby Emmons, who was celebrating his 26th birthday that night, to Bobby's great delight (Reggie Young remembers him saying excitedly, "Man, I had Elvis sing 'Happy Birthday' to me!").

On the 20th, Elvis began the session with 'It Keeps Right On A-Hurtin',' a song he'd liked since hearing Johnny Tillotson's hit version on the radio back in 1962. The country-flavored song was yet another lament about a failed love affair, but one that Elvis performed with a delicate sensitivity, and wrapped up in three takes. 'Any Day Now' was especially moving, as it has the narrator mourning a love affair that's not quite over but is on the verge of falling apart, a situation heightened by the edge of desperation in Elvis's vocal, especially at the end, as he begs his love to not fly away. The song was originally a hit for Chuck Jackson in 1962; Ronnie Milsap, who played piano and provided back up vocals during the sessions, would go on to have a

Number One country hit with his own version of the song in 1982. But though the song had the right feel from the beginning, there were a few problems in working out the arrangement, causing Chips to exclaim at one point, "We got it, man, we got it! Let's play it like we feel it ... I don't want to lose it, we got it, right now." Take six was ultimately chosen as the master.

Vernon Presley again played a role in the choice of song Elvis recorded next. Elvis had proudly introduced Bobby Wood to Vernon as the man who sang one of his father's favorite songs, 'If I'm A Fool (For Loving You),' a hit for Wood in 1964; then he decided to record the song himself. The song had the hint of a country weeper about it, but Elvis gave it a subdued delivery, gently underscoring the sadness. He'd become far more critical of his performances, however, and dismissed his version of the song as "rotten," perhaps one reason why the track remained in the vault until 1970, when it appeared on the budget album *Let's Be Friends*.

By now, the best material made available for the sessions had all been recorded, and the final two nights yielded few new songs. The only track laid down on the 21st was 'The Fair Is Moving On.' The ballad was by the British songwriting team of Doug Flett and Guy Fletcher, who'd previously written 'Wonderful World,' recorded by Elvis for the film *Live A Little, Love A Little*. Asked to come up with more material, the two revisited the 'fairground' theme they had previously used in 'County Fair,' hoping the new number "might resonate with the Colonel's background," as Fletcher put it. Indeed, one can easily see it being used in one of Elvis's films, perhaps during a romantic moment in *Roustabout*. A funky backing track was also laid down for 'Memory Revival' (another song by the Frazier/Owens team), but Elvis never ended up recording a vocal for it.

On the 22nd, the final night of the sessions, Elvis spent most of his time recording vocal overdubs for 'Any Day Now,' 'True Love Travels On A Gravel Road,' and 'Power Of My Love.' He then recorded one more new song, 'Who Am I?' This was a religious number, originally recorded by The Inspirations in 1964 and later by its composer, Charles 'Rusty' Goodman, with his own group, The Happy Goodmans. (Bobby Wood had also recorded the song.) Though performed with suitable reverence, it was still something of an afterthought, evidenced by the fact that the track remained unreleased for two years, finally turning up on the 1971 budget album *You'll Never Walk Alone*. With that, the American sessions came to an end.

The songs in their 'raw' state – before overdubbing – have since become available on official collections like *Suspicious Minds: The Memphis 1969 Anthology*, among others, as well as on numerous bootlegs; it's here you get a real sense of just how good a singer Presley had become over the years. "A lot of that stuff sounds like a band," says Bobby Emmons. "Before all the strings and horns and background vocals and stuff went on, it was just a little five or six-piece band. A lot of it could have come out and hit just like it was. It would have probably turned music in a different direction. Elvis was plenty strong enough and we were doing plenty good enough to have been a band without all that decoration."

It's an intriguing idea to contemplate, for though the sweetening gave the songs an undeniable commercial sheen, the unadulterated versions are especially powerful. It would also have been a move well in keeping with the trend of artists now eschewing the excesses of the psychedelic movement and trying to get back to their roots. Interestingly, at the same time Elvis was recording at American, in January, The Beatles were trying to get back to basics themselves by attempting to record an album without excessive overdubbing. Elvis's early records had been made in a similar fashion. What would the public response have been to an Elvis Presley album of simple, unadorned songs?

No such plan was considered for Elvis, of course (nor, ultimately, for The Beatles, who later assembled the album *Let It Be* from their January 1969 sessions, layering the music with overdubs). Work on overdubbing Elvis's songs had begun on January 19, and would continue into September, mostly produced by Felton Jarvis. The arrangements were supplied by Mike Leech and Glen Spreen, who each thoroughly enjoyed fleshing out a recording. "We couldn't wait to get a basic track recorded so we could go out there and start putting stuff on it," says Mike, "like overdubbing guitar lines and things like that. To me, the most fun part of recording was the aftermath, that's when the records kind of take form and shape; when you start putting these little extra instruments on there, like putting harmonies on licks you've already played on the basic tracks, stuff like that. That was a total fun time for me."

Glen Spreen approached the arrangements with the intention of broadening a song's musical palette. "I thought that I should always do something different on every song," he says. "The first thing I needed to do was blend with the tracks and yet stand out at the same time. So I did that by every once in a while taking a line that maybe Bobby would play, Bobby Wood or Bobby Emmons, and repeat that with maybe a cello or a horn; I did that maybe once every three or four songs.

"But mainly I wanted to use things that were different. Like Elvis never had strings like cellos and French horns playing together, never had any counter melodies where the track would go one way and the strings would go another way – where the track was going down, the strings are going up. The strings were never syncopated with Elvis, so I wrote a lot of syncopated strings. And I wrote a lot of voicing that was lower, because if Elvis had strings, which he rarely had, they were just real bland, and not very melodic. And I wanted to be a lot more expressive, because of the fact that his strings were never more than just utilitarian kind of instruments. So I wanted to do things a lot different. And I wanted to use cellos, low cellos."

The arrangements worked to add elements of character to the songs. On 'Inherit The Wind,' for example, "Mike came up with an idea for the glissando strings which I liked," says Glen. "Glissando tremolo type strings to sort of mimic the wind." The 'gypsy violin' that plays during the instrumental bridge of 'Any Day Now' "was something that was just thought of in the moment and we asked the guy to improvise," he says; the strings during the rest of the song suggested a feeling of agitation about the failing love affair. The female backing vocals on 'Only The Strong Survive' echo the mother's gentle chiding of her son in the song. And overall, the backing instrumentation gives the songs, even the more upbeat ones, a darker, melancholy feel. "Yeah, that was me at the time," Glen says. "I was just that way. I was very serious and I had a classical background, so that played into it."

Not all of the arrangements worked out to Glen's satisfaction. "If you listen to 'In the Ghetto,' at the end, the strings don't come in on the right beat, and they don't come in together," he says. "The last part, right after Elvis says 'In the ghetto' for the last time and the strings come in; they don't come in quite right and we must have worked on that for 30 minutes.

"And there were a couple songs I refused to write arrangements for," he adds. "Well, not a couple – one: 'Rubberneckin'.' It just reminded me of all those bad movie song that he had cut, and I didn't want to have much to do with it. There were a couple of OK movies he made, like *King Creole*, but most of them were like *Kissin' Cousins*, you know? I watched them, but I came out like, what in the heck does he think he's doing? I was sitting down with Felton, and I said, 'Does Elvis realize how bad those movies are?' And Felton said, 'Yeah, but he gets paid a million dollars a piece for 'em.' And I said, 'Well, this song is just like all those other ones. This is one of the worst songs I've ever heard.' And he said, 'Well, you've got to write some horn parts.' And I said, 'I won't put my name on paper. But what I will do is I'll go out there and hum some parts for the horn players.' So I did and we cut it. It has horns on it, but I refused to put the notes on paper."

The American Sound Studio sessions were the finest of Elvis's career, not so much because of the amount of work they produced (31 sides in 12 days, not counting the rough 'Hey Jude' and the 'This Time'

medley), but rather for the consistent quality of that work. The closest equivalent might be Elvis's first post-army sessions in March and April 1960, when, over the course of two days, Elvis recorded an impressive 18 sides, including such classics as 'Are You Lonesome Tonight?' and 'It's Now Or Never.' Those sessions had helped rekindle Elvis's career, though his absence from the music scene in the previous two years hadn't much affected his popularity; during his years in the service, singles, EPs, and albums continued to hit the Top 20. But before the American sessions, Elvis was in the position to trying to revive a career that had been written off. Making the Comeback Special had helped restore his confidence, by re-establishing the validity of his past work. The American sessions confirmed that he still had validity as a contemporary artist as well.

They were also the last studio sessions to achieve that. Elvis never returned to American, though the sessions at the studio would give him some of the biggest hits he'd had in years. It was obvious he'd enjoyed himself, and he later said he never worked harder in the studio than he had at American.

No one ever pointed to any specific instances of enmity that kept him from returning, beyond a growing distrust between those representing the artistic and business sides of the arrangement. Moman's loyalty was to the music, while Parker's was to the deal, and neither man was prone to backing down when challenged. That Chips had been so obstinate about hanging on to his publishing hadn't endeared him to Presley's manager. Elvis's regular producer, Felton Jarvis, had also worried that he might be losing influence over Elvis. "You know how greedy people and politics and that sort of thing always meander into the artwork," says Bobby Emmons about why Elvis never recorded at American again. "They got stirred up, hard feelings here, and lies told there, and just one thing and another, and it never did happen."

But like the Comeback Special, the American sessions had been a breath of fresh air for Elvis, confirming not just his ability as a singer, but also fulfilling his desire to meet a challenge that was worthy of him. In Mike Leech's assessment, "Everybody just bowed to him like he was a god and everything. And nobody had the nerve to cross him in any way. And we did, and the result was some hits. His biggest hits."

But it would be a few months before any of those hits started materializing. 'Memories,' from the *Elvis* special, had been released in February, but only made it as high as Number 35 (in the UK, the song appeared as the B-side of 'If I Can Dream'). In March came the Easter single 'His Hand In Mine' (recorded in 1960) and *Elvis Sings Flaming Star*, RCA's version of the album Singer had released the previous October, on RCA's budget Camden label. The single didn't chart (it was not released in the UK), and the album just made it into the Top 100, peaking at Number 96, though it did surprisingly sell half a million copies. But neither record was intended to do much more than keep Elvis's name in the public eye.

'Charro!' had appeared as the B-side of 'Memories' to tie in with the release of the film in March (*Variety*: "[Elvis] strolls through a tedious role that would have driven any serious actor up the wall"). The same month also saw work commence on what would be Elvis's last feature film, *Change Of Habit*, as part of the movie and TV special deal Parker had worked out with NBC. Elvis plays a hip doctor working at a free clinic in an urban ghetto, who falls in love with one of the three volunteers who arrive to help him, not knowing they're nuns. The film was a step up from the usual Elvis fare, with plenty of modern touches, though curiously the dilemma faced by Elvis's love interest (Mary Tyler Moore) – will she leave The Lord for Elvis? – is left unresolved. In keeping with Elvis's recent films, there were few songs; just four, including the title number.

The recording sessions were held March 5 and 6 at Decca Universal Studio in Hollywood. On the first night, Elvis recorded 'Let's Be Friends,' an insubstantial romantic number that didn't appear in the movie, and was released in 1970 as the title track of the album of the same name. 'Change Of Habit' had a more contemporary feel (aside from the weak pun of the title, with its reference to a nun's attire), though Elvis's lack of interest in the material is clear. The same could be said of the first song recorded the next night, 'Have A Happy,' though he sounds more engaged on 'Let Us Pray,' perhaps in part because it was the final song of the session. Filming for *Change Of Habit* began on March 12, with one of the highlights for Elvis surely being when he met gospel singer Mahalia Jackson, who came by the set to solicit his help with a fundraiser. Filming was completed by April 29, and with that, Elvis's career as a dramatic film actor came to an end.

The first song from the American sessions was released in mid April, the single 'In The Ghetto.' It quickly showed that the success of the *Elvis* special was no fluke, reaching Number Three in the charts and selling over a million copies, the first single to do so since 1962 (it performed slightly better chartwise in the UK, peaking at Number Two). There was a minor flap over the production credits on its release; *Billboard* listed Felton Jarvis as the song's producer for the first two weeks, then Chips Moman for the next two. Finally Parker stepped in, demanding that no producer be listed, as was the case on Elvis's other records. *Billboard* also gave the record a strong review, simply noting "Elvis at his best."

From Elvis In Memphis was released in June, the cover featuring a shot from the opening sequence of the *Elvis* special, Elvis looking confident, with the trace of a smile on his face, standing in front of the scaffolding with the hundred Elvises caught in their different poses. The final track listing was evenly split between songs recorded at the January and February sessions: 'Wearin' That Loved On Look,' 'Only The Strong Survive,' 'I'll Hold You In My Heart,' 'Long Black Limousine,' 'It Keeps Right On A-Hurtin',' 'I'm Moving On,' 'Power Of My Love,' 'Gentle On My Mind,' 'After Loving You,' 'True Love Travels On A Gravel Road,' 'Any Day Now,' and 'In The Ghetto.' Surprisingly, it didn't fare better in the charts than the *Elvis* soundtrack, peaking at Number 13 (though it topped the charts in Britain) and selling half a million copies. But critically, it was the final proof that, after years of movie soundtracks, Elvis Presley had grown up. The songs on *From Elvis In Memphis* dealt with adult themes; not the fantasy of romantic love common to pop songs, but the kind of perspective that comes with hard experience, the acknowledgment of life's struggles as well as its joys.

"He's never sounded better, and the choice of material is perfect," wrote *Billboard*. Future Presley biographer Peter Guralnick was more expansive in his lead review for *Rolling Stone*: "What is new, and what is obvious from the first notes of the record, is the evident passion which Elvis has invested in this music and at the same time the risk he has taken in doing so ... He needs to have our attention, and it comes as something of a shock to discover that a hero whom we had set up to feel only existential scorn, a hero who was characterized by a frozen sneer and a look of sullen discontent, should need us in the end. It is his involvement after all which comes as the surprise."

Even the sound was better than the often thin production of Elvis's movie soundtracks. When Joan Deary, an RCA executive who'd worked on Elvis's records since he'd signed to the label, first heard songs from the American sessions, she exclaimed to Chet Atkins, "The sound is so superior to what I've been hearing on Elvis I can't believe my ears!" Elvis was pleased by the good reception on all fronts. "Elvis liked the idea of being hot again," says Bobby Emmons. "You can't be as talented as him and work as hard as he did on those sessions and not be pleased that they were received well by an audience that had just been staying away in droves for the last few years."

June also saw the release of 'Clean Up Your Own Backyard,' promoting the upcoming release of *The Trouble With Girls* – though the film itself wasn't due to be released until September. Though better in comparison to a film song like 'Your Time Hasn't Come Yet Baby,' it was decidedly overshadowed by releases like 'In The Ghetto' and *From Elvis In Memphis*, and peaked at Number 35 (released in the UK in September, it reached Number 21). It hardly mattered. By then, Elvis was engaged in his next venture: a full-scale return to live performance.

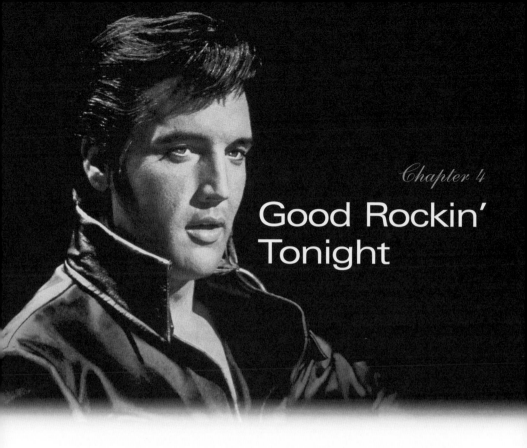

Chapter 4

Good Rockin' Tonight

On February 26 1969 it was announced that Elvis Presley would appear that summer for a month-long engagement at the International Hotel in Las Vegas, which was still under construction. Elvis and his manager came into Vegas that day to sign a contract for the benefit of the cameras; the actual contract wasn't signed until April 15. What Elvis had talked about to reporters so frequently over the last decade was now about to become a reality: he was going to return to the concert stage.

It would not be Elvis's first appearance in the city. He had first played Las Vegas in March 1956, a two-week stint at the New Frontier Hotel's 'Venus Room.' It was an engagement that was something of a disappointment, though not quite the failure it has often been called. The chief problem was that teenagers, Elvis's core audience, were not allowed in the lounge, though a matinee performance was eventually scheduled for them later in the run. Instead, he faced an audience of uninterested adults; on opening night, shortly after Elvis had started his set, one guest had shouted, "Goddamn it, shit! What is all this yelling and screaming?" and promptly stormed out. Parker had been searching for new ways to present his astonishingly successful client, but this was a rare misstep.

But if the Las Vegas response to Elvis had been underwhelming, Elvis himself found much to enjoy about the city. For someone who enjoyed keeping late hours (due in part to the insomnia that plagued him throughout his life), Vegas had a lot to offer, especially in the way of entertainment, and when he wasn't working, he regularly caught other acts in town. The most important part of his trip was undoubtedly when he saw Freddie Bell & The Bellboys at the Sands; it was hearing their cover of Big Mama Thornton's hit 'Hound Dog' that inspired him to record the song at his next session. Over the years, Vegas had become one of his personal playgrounds, and he frequently visited the city between his film commitments. His 1964 film *Viva Las Vegas* had been shot there (primarily on the grounds of the Flamingo and Tropicana hotels, as well as the University of Nevada's gymnasium), and of course he had been married in Vegas in 1967.

But for all Elvis's personal enjoyment of the city, it was still not the most obvious place to launch his comeback as a live performer. Rock was no longer the 'fad' it was presumed to be when Elvis first began touring in the 50s; it was now a well-established big business. Package shows featuring acts playing short 15 to 30-minute sets had been replaced by major rock acts like The Rolling Stones, The Who, The Doors, and Jimi Hendrix playing sets of an hour or more, filling arenas from coast to coast. Though Elvis received many offers of live work after the airing of the Comeback Special, Parker evidently decided it was better to ease his act back into live performance rather than undertake an ambitious, large-scale tour and risk failure. And, with his penchant for securing an impressive deal up front, he couldn't present Elvis's return to performing as simply his next move. It had to be an Event.

Parker had begun negotiating for Elvis's Vegas appearances a week after the Comeback Special aired, and by December 19 had secured the deal with the International Hotel. The International was the latest venture of Kirk Kerkorian, an eighth-grade dropout whose interest in planes and flying had led to his becoming a fighter pilot during World War II and later owner of Trans International Airlines. In 1962 he purchased land in Las Vegas, which he rented to another entrepreneur, who built the massive Caesars Palace casino on the site. He next decided he wanted to enter the casino business himself, buying the Flamingo in 1967 and using it as a training ground for the staff he wished to employ at the new casino he planned to build. The International was at the time the biggest casino in Las Vegas. Its 30 stories (which alone made it the tallest building in Nevada at the time) boasted over 1,500 rooms; its 2,000-seater showroom was just one of three entertainment venues at the hotel; and its casino, with over 1,000 slot machines, was said to be the largest in the world. Even the swimming pool set a record; its 350,000 gallons were said to constitute the second-largest man-made body of water in the state, Lake Mead being the first.

It would not only be an impressive setting in which to unveil the new Elvis, there would also be additional publicity resulting from coverage of the opening of the hotel. But Parker, remaining cautious, elected not to have Elvis open the showroom, not wanting his client to appear in an untested venue; Barbra Streisand would instead have the honour of opening the 'Showroom Internationale.' The final deal called for Elvis to play a four-week engagement of two shows a night, seven days a week, for a fee of $100,000 a week – out of which he would be expected to pay for his own musicians and singers, not to mention Parker.

Elvis put much thought into what kind of show he would like to do; unlike the movies, and even the Comeback Special, the Vegas production would be entirely his own creation. He reached out to nearly every musician he had worked with. "We had a call from Tom

Diskin, Parker's right arm," says Scotty Moore. "All the Nashville musicians – Bob Moore, DJ Fontana and myself, Floyd Cramer I think, and of course The Jordanaires. They wanted us to come and work in Vegas and we'd have to rehearse for a week. And at that time here in Nashville, it was peak recording. The Jordanaires already had sessions all booked. I was working 12 to 14 hours a day engineering, and all the other guys were playing two, three, four sessions a day. And what they were offering, per week – it was just a bottom-line decision we had to make." "We could make more money here in Nashville," agrees Gordon Stoker. "But we hated to quit, because we loved Elvis dearly and we hated to quit him."

Elvis also asked the musicians he'd recently worked with at American if they'd be interested in the gig; they turned him down, because they weren't interested in a joining a band that might end up going out on the road. "Nobody wanted to do that," says Reggie Young. "We all pretty much liked being home at night; we weren't off being a road dog, as they say, traveling up and down the highway. So we all turned it down." "What we aspired to be was session musicians," adds Mike Leech. "And we didn't want to blow that. We had done our share of road work with different groups, and it kind of left a sour taste in our mouth that we were going to be away from home all the time, and the family situation would just be gone, and all that kind of stuff. It wasn't that appealing to us at that time"

Elvis ultimately approached a musician he had never worked with before: James Burton. Burton grew up in Shreveport, Louisiana, and took up the guitar at a young age, joining the *Louisiana Hayride* house band at age 14. (The *Hayride* was a weekly live variety show broadcast over the radio; Elvis had made numerous appearances on the programme in the 50s.) Then he joined swamp rocker Dale Hawkins's band, co-writing Hawkins's classic 'Susie Q' in 1957. Three years later, he was hired to back Ricky Nelson on the popular TV show *The Adventures Of Ozzie And Harriet*, playing with Nelson for two years. He then worked as a studio musician (he'd played on the soundtrack of

Viva Las Vegas), and was in The Shindogs, the house band on TV's rock programme *Shindig!* He had also been approached to play in the band on Elvis's Comeback Special, but had been recording for Frank Sinatra at the time.

Elvis called James at home, and the two ended up talking for several hours, at the end of which James not only agreed to take the gig, but also to put Elvis's band together for him. Elvis explained he wanted versatile musicians, who would also be open to improvisation, while James had his own brief: "I wanted musicians that could play with the same energy, feeling, and soul that Elvis had." He tapped Jerry Scheff, with whom he had played on *Shindig!* and in various sessions, to audition on bass. Scheff had been a session musician in LA since the mid 60s, and had played on the *Double Trouble* soundtrack, though he hadn't met Elvis in person.

"I wasn't going to do it, because I was doing black music, jazz, back then," Jerry says. "I went down there [to audition] just out of curiosity. And here's this guy sitting there, just a really really nice guy, who just welcomed me. He was so gracious. And then he started singing. He was singing all the stuff he thought we would like, blues things and stuff like that. And I was blown away. I thought, you know what? I think I've got something to learn here. And it was like going to school almost." Jerry was so impressed that after he was hired he insisted his wife come to a rehearsal to watch.

John Wilkinson, another studio player, had recently signed a contract with RCA when Burton called and asked if he'd be interested in playing rhythm guitar. Wilkinson was 11 years old when he had first met Elvis. He had found his way backstage when Elvis performed in Springfield, Missouri, on May 17 1956, and brashly informed the singer he could play guitar better than him. He had later moved to LA, where he did session work and appeared as a regular on the TV program *Ninth Street West*, a local teen dance show; Elvis had called to offer him the gig minutes before James Burton phoned him.

Larry Muhoberac was a Louisiana native who'd relocated to

Memphis in 1959 and had worked with Elvis off and on over the years. He served as musical director for Elvis's first post-army live shows, on February 25 1961 in Memphis, and later played piano on a number of Elvis's movie soundtracks.

Larry was also friends with a drummer named Ronnie Tutt, with whom he had worked for the Pepper Tanner Company in Memphis (the commercial jingles company which Marty Lacker ran); Ronnie had since moved back to his native Texas. Larry and Ronnie had both been considering relocating to LA, and when Larry was hired for Elvis's band, he suggested Ronnie come out, as the gig would be a good way to get exposure. "He basically said it'd be a great way to catch the eye of everybody in LA," says Ronnie, "because everybody in the music business and entertainment business would probably be there to see him, since he hadn't been appearing in 10 years. And so he put my name in the hat, and they started auditioning drummers. Then I got a call on a Friday, and he said: 'We've been auditioning everybody in town, and Elvis is not happy with any of the drummers. And I told him about you. Can you get out here tomorrow afternoon?' So I said yeah, I could do that."

By his own admission, Ronnie "wasn't a big fan of Elvis Presley, certainly not his acting career, and not so much even his music either. I was either into R&B or jazz. Having grown up in Texas with the real black R&B stuff, to me he wasn't that much of an authentic situation, in my eyes; I was very naïve about that. And also coming from a jazz symphonic kind of background, I always kind of looked down my nose." He had met Elvis in the summer of 1955, at a show in Fort Worth, Texas, when he was playing in the house band for a radio show called *North Side Jamboree*. He'd been unimpressed with Elvis's attire, but was more perturbed when Elvis broke the strings on his own guitar and then borrowed the instrument of the rhythm guitarist in Ronnie's band. "It was a beautiful old Martin and he just scratched the heck out of it with a pick all the way across the face of it," says Ronnie. "And set it down, and didn't even say 'I'm sorry' or anything. So I didn't have a good impression of him to start out. But I think even more importantly than that was the fact that my girlfriend was with me, and she was gaga over the guy. I mean, she was going nuts."

Now Ronnie hastened to LA for his shot at joining Elvis's band. After setting up his drum set, he was disappointed to find another drummer, Gene Pello, a veteran of numerous Motown sessions, had been scheduled to audition before him. He became even more uneasy when Pello asked to use his drums. "The guys were all nodding in agreement when they heard him play, thinking OK, we've got the guy," says Ronnie. But Larry reminded Elvis that Ronnie had been paid to fly out and audition. "So they said OK, one more song, we got one more guy to listen to."

When he was finally introduced to Elvis, "that's when it all clicked," says Ronnie. "He had such charisma, you could understand truly why everybody was so attracted, so drawn to him. I mean, the guy had it. And just upon meeting him and looking into his eyes, we just clicked. And from that particular moment on, I watched him, and I watched his eyes, I watched his movements, I watched everything he did. And he told me 'What impressed me about you, Ronnie, was the fact that you weren't doing your thing, you were watching me. Everything I did, you got, everything, and accented it.' I've talked with DJ [Fontana] about it, and he mentioned the same thing; we felt like we were working for a stripper. You know, like drummers always accented ladies that did all kinds of movements with their bodies when they danced. So that's what we did with Elvis."

With a band now in place, the rest of the show began to come together. Elvis had a very definite idea of what he wanted to do. "He told me this personally," says Ronnie. "Colonel Parker's original idea was for him to come out with dancing girls, a typical Vegas revue, and he just hated the thought of that. He said that one night he had a dream, and he had seen himself in front of a big orchestra on stage, and behind him would be a hard-driving rhythm section, a black lady soul group, and a white men's gospel group, doing concert stuff. And he said, 'I called the Colonel up, woke him up, and told him that's what I wanted to do. And the Colonel said no, and it's the only time I ever hung up on him. I said, "Colonel, that's the way we're gonna do it, or I'm not gonna do it at all."' So that's a battle he won. And thank God, because when you really look at it, nobody else was doing anything like that. Rockers didn't want to do Vegas because of what they had to do; there was just no real vehicle there of what to do. And so Elvis established this thing, this look, this approach. You'd just watch everything he did, because he wanted us to play to that. He was very, very rhythmical and very expressive in that sense."

But Elvis didn't just stop with hiring a new band. In order to fill out the sound, he also engaged two vocal groups. The Imperials gospel quartet had worked with Elvis on his 1966 sacred album *How Great Thou Art*, though the line-up had changed since then; at the time they were approached for the Vegas engagement, the group consisted of Terry Blackwood (the son of Doyle Blackwood, an original member of The Blackwood Brothers Quartet, one of Elvis's favorite gospel groups), Armond Morales, Joe Moscheo, Jimmie Murray, and Roger Wiles. The group was initially uncertain about how their fans would react to their playing in 'Sin City,' but decided it was an opportunity they couldn't pass up. And though most of them hadn't participated in the *How Great Thou Art* sessions, they knew of Elvis's love of gospel and were fans of his work.

The Sweet Inspirations – The Sweets for short – were an all-black group that had arisen out of the gospel group The Drinkard Singers. By 1967, a core group of Estelle Brown, Cissy Houston (Whitney Houston's mother), Sylvia Shemwell, and Myrna Smith were working as The Sweet Inspirations, providing backup vocals for many artists, including Aretha Franklin. They also released records under their own name, with the single 'Sweet Inspiration' (recorded at American) the most successful, reaching the Top 20 on the pop charts and Top Five on the R&B charts. Elvis was familiar with their work, and the group was signed for the engagement without having to audition. Millie Kirkham, whose graceful soprano had graced many of Elvis's records, was hired as a solo singer. The ever-faithful Charlie Hodge was also made a member of the group, providing rhythm guitar and vocals, as well as seeing to Elvis's needs on stage, making sure he always had water close at hand; he was later responsible for replenishing the supply of scarves that Elvis would pass out to the audience.

Rehearsals with the band (but not the backing vocalists or the International's own in-house orchestra, which was conducted by Bobby Morris) began July 18 at RCA's studios on Sunset Boulevard in LA, just 13 days before the show was set to open in Las Vegas. The band rehearsed well over 100 songs, for Elvis's personal enjoyment as much as seeing which numbers would work best live; among the songs that didn't make the final cut were 'Trying To Get To You,' 'Memphis, Tennessee,' 'Rip It Up,' 'Lawdy Miss Clawdy,' 'Green Green Grass Of Home' (Elvis had been particularly taken with Tom Jones's 1966 version of the song), and 'Release Me,' most recently a hit for Engelbert Humperdinck. "Rehearsals were pretty loose," says Ronnie. "Elvis liked to be just very relaxed ... he liked to just hang out really. It was a chance for him to get out of his world and into the music. That's what he loved most. It was a chance for him to really stretch out musically."

"One of the fun things about playing with him was that as long as it fit you could play pretty much whatever you wanted to play," says Jerry. "He trusted everybody, and I can't remember him really hopping on anybody and saying, 'Don't play that.'" And though the setlist would call for a number of Elvis's 50s hits, he was determined that they sound fresh and contemporary, telling Ronnie, "Don't play like we played those things back then. There weren't even drums on some of that stuff. You play the way you hear it, and if there's something wrong with it, then we'll talk about it. But don't worry about it. You do what you do; that's why you're here." "It was great," says Ronnie. "It really freed me up to try different things."

Rehearsals in Vegas began on July 24, with the band, singers, and orchestra finally rehearsing together on July 29 and 30. Joe Moscheo of The Imperials described Elvis as having "the attitude of a champion racehorse about to go into the gate" and looking exceptionally fit; he had taken to wearing weights around his wrists and ankles while rehearsing. For their part, The Sweets were charmed by their new employer when Elvis began singing their hit single as he walked over to meet them. "We just chimed right in and fell in love with him like that," said Myrna Smith.

As the show came together, Elvis was very specific about what he wanted from the musicians, though never failing to communicate his requests politely. When John Wilkinson had trouble getting a part down, Elvis came over and sang the piece to him; at other times he'd demonstrate what he wanted by playing the piano. "The method was unsophisticated but effective," said Moscheo. "Even though he was largely self-taught as a musician, we were continually impressed by the clarity and single-mindedness with which he pursued the exact sound he had in his mind."

But as opening night drew closer, signs of nervousness appeared. Glen Spreen, who'd written live arrangements for 'In The Ghetto' and 'Suspicious Minds,' noted that during rehearsals a week before opening, the tension had risen. "I do remember every once in a while Elvis would get a little frustrated," he says. "He wouldn't remember the words or something would happen, like the lyrics would drop off the stand and he'd just get angry about that. So he'd get frustrated with himself and the whole thing would stop until he could recompose and get it together." Elvis also talked about his growing unease with his friends, admitting to Sandi Miller, "I went to Vegas and I bombed. What if I bomb again?" "He was scared to death," she says.

Meanwhile, Bill Belew had been working on Elvis's costumes for the show. "I had not realized that the black leather suit [worn during the Comeback Special] was going to have the effect that it did," he says. "I noticed the fans screamed when he came out, but I thought, 'It's Elvis that they're screaming for.' But the second time he came out to perform, I was aware that the wardrobe was a very important part of the persona, because of the reaction of the fans. And I just happened to be close enough to the audience that I heard some of the girls saying 'He's hot!' So when the Colonel called me and said would I do Elvis's Las Vegas show, that was in the back of my mind – he has to be hot!" Belew designed several two-piece suits for Elvis, patterned after a karate 'gi,' the top with a tunic-styled neck that featured herringbone embroidery. In stark contrast to the flamboyant stage wear of later years, the early costumes were unadorned, practically bare; all solid color (white, navy, or black), and simply accessorized with a macramé belt, scarves, and jewelry (Priscilla herself sought out items that she thought would interest Elvis). James Kingsley of the Memphis *Commercial Appeal* referred to the outfit as a "karate tuxedo."

When he wasn't rehearsing, Elvis checked out the other acts in Vegas, and caught the closing night of Barbra Streisand's appearance at the International on the 28th. He observed that the stage was big, but was confident that his own large retinue of band, singers, and orchestra would adequately fill the space. On the back of an RCA press release touting the upcoming shows ("On July 31 1969, a tall, rangy, handsome, and gifted singer-actor-performer will make his first appearance before a live audience in more than a decade when he steps on to the stage of the new International Hotel in Las Vegas"), he made notes of what still needed to be done: "Fix bracelets"; "Record player for dressing room."

There was only one show on opening night; the invitations read "Elvis and the Las Vegas International Hotel take pleasure in inviting you and your lady to our opening show, July 31 1969," further specifying that cocktails would be at 7pm, dinner and the performance at 8pm. For the rest of the engagement, shows would be at 8:15pm (when dinner would be served) and midnight, with a $15 minimum per person. In typical fashion, Parker had drenched Vegas with an array of advertising materials promoting the engagement. One two-page ad featured an illustration of Elvis playing guitar in his Comeback Special leather suit, with copy on the right giving top billing to comedian Sammy Shore (whom Elvis had seen opening for Tom Jones), then The Imperials, The Sweet Inspirations, Bobby Morris, and the members of Elvis's band; a note at the bottom teased "P.S. I'm in the show too! – ELVIS." The marquee outside the International also billed their performer as "ELVIS," with no last name, in letters that were 10 feet tall – larger than those used for the hotel's own name.

Radio and TV ads also continually touted the upcoming shows (some of the radio ads consisted solely of an announcer repeating the name "Elvis!"), with the result that by mid July the engagement was nearly sold out; Parker saw to it that the ads continued to run even after the engagement did sell out. Fans were arriving not just from around the country but from around the world. Kirk Kerkorian flew in a contingent of journalists from New York on his private plane, a DC-9 "remodeled to seat 20 people and make the usual first-class accommodations look chintzy," Ellen Willis wrote in *The New Yorker*. The opening night audience was star-studded, with Pat Boone, Petula Clark, Phil Ochs, Elvis's *Viva Las Vegas* co-star Ann-Margret, Burt Bacharach and his wife Angie Dickinson, Dick Clark, George Hamilton, Cary Grant, and Shirley Bassey among those in attendance; "Paul Anka walked around trying hard to be noticed," the *New York Times* also noted. On each table was a gift box, containing both the *Elvis* soundtrack and the *From Elvis In Memphis* album, a program, and other memorabilia. The waitresses each sported an Elvis button.

The show began with an opening set by The Sweet Inspirations, followed by Sammy Shore. Backstage, Elvis was getting increasingly nervous, still vibrating with energy in spite of the fact that there had already been three dress rehearsals that day. "We went down to his dressing room before the show and hung out with him a little bit," recalls Jerry Scheff. "And he was ready to fly around the room. His leg was going a million miles an hour and his hands drumming on things. He'd get that intense about things. He was nervous about how people were going to receive him after all those years." "He was scared," agrees Ronnie Tutt. "Absolutely scared to death. But that was what the beauty of it was, that he loved that challenge. He loved that adrenaline rush. Because he had no idea what the kind of acceptance was going to be. It was a major deal. And there was a lot of pressure on him." "He was always nervous before every show," said Joe Esposito. "But he was never nervous like that again."

Elvis's set began around 10:30pm, the gold lamé curtains rising, and Elvis, clad in one of his black suits, striding to center stage, grabbing the mic, and tearing into 'Blue Suede Shoes.' The audience was on its feet cheering before he even began to sing, and their enthusiasm didn't let up the entire show. "When we ended that first song, the place went crazy," says Jerry. "And I could see the look change on his face. It's like, 'Oh God, they still love me!' From then on it was too easy for him."

RCA did not begin taping shows for the expected live album until August 21 (nor have any bootlegs of opening night surfaced), and though the setlist varied from night to night, much of it remained the same throughout the run. The first half primarily featured songs from Elvis's past. A brief jazzy orchestra intro segues easily into the opening vamp of 'Blue Suede Shoes,' going on for nearly a minute, and giving the show something of a running start. The song wasn't quite as tough as the Comeback Special's version, lacking the exuberant edge, but it still crackles with its own type of nervous energy, kicking off the show with a bang, as was clearly the intention. A few jokey drawn-out "We-e-e-l-l-ls" finally tumble over into what was invariably the second number, 'I Got A Woman,' the Ray Charles cover that had appeared on Elvis's first album and had been a live favorite on his early tours. Elvis rocks through the song at lightning speed, going so fast he nearly stumbles over the lyrics in the rush to get them out. Nor does the tempo flag on 'All Shook Up,' the first true hit of the set ('Blue Suede Shoes' hadn't charted and 'I Got A Woman' was never released as a single).

It was at this point that Elvis welcomed the audience to the "big ol' freaky International Hotel," always noting the "funky angels" that hung from the lavish showroom's ceiling: "You ain't seen nothing until you've seen a funky angel, boy, I'll tell you for sure." And now he slows down the pace with 'Love Me Tender,' given a light pop arrangement; eventually, this became the number when Elvis took full advantage of bestowing kisses on the women who pushed their way to the stage, sometimes even climbing on other people's tables to get to him.

Then it was back to rock with a medley of 'Jailhouse Rock' and 'Don't Be Cruel,' with Elvis so carried away by the frenetic spirit of the performance that the "knocked out jailbird" of 'Jailhouse Rock' frequently became a "sonofabitch." Elvis's first big national hit, 'Heartbreak Hotel,' was not as chillingly stark as the original single, but was a good deal bluesier, aided by James Burton's guitar solo and the "ooh, baby" accents of The Sweets. As in his 50s live performances, the next song required a special introduction. It was a message song, Elvis patiently explained, going on to detail how he tried to interest a young woman in his "message" one time, his introduction frequently taking longer than the performance of the song itself. Finally, he'd erupt into an explosive 'Hound Dog,' racing through it in a minute and a half, as if trying to set a new record for speed.

After re-establishing Elvis's 50s bona fides, the set moved on to newer material. 'Memories,' first performed during the Comeback Special, was the first song to truly make use of the International's orchestra; in the rock numbers, the orchestra was more evident at a song's conclusion, the brass coming in to sound the final chord. Though insisting "I can't play this more than a little bit," Elvis takes just as much delight in performing 'Baby What You Want Me To Do' as he did during the Comeback Special's sit-down shows, calling out "Play it, James!" before the song's instrumental break. A bright version of Elvis's early Sun hit 'Mystery Train,' often punctuated by his laughter, segues into 'Tiger Man,' also performed for the first time during the Comeback Special's second sit-down show; as Ronnie Tutt pushes the tempo, and James Burton tosses in stinging guitar licks, Elvis's pronouncement that he's king of the jungle doesn't come across as a boast, but a simple statement of fact.

Of the new covers, one of the more unusual choices was Del Shannon's 'Runaway,' a song Elvis imbues with more full-bodied passion than on the original, though it was left for The Sweets to do the falsetto lines Shannon had sung during the chorus. Though he never seriously recorded a Beatles song in the studio (his version of 'Hey Jude' at the American sessions had been an off-the-cuff rendition, and a later recording of 'Lady Madonna' wasn't released during his lifetime) Elvis often included a Beatles song in his shows, beginning in 1969 with 'Yesterday.' The song's sincerity was sometimes undercut by a jokey ad lib (instead of being "half the man," Elvis would sing "half the stud"). It was otherwise a soothingly pleasant cover, though a rather self-consciously 'showbiz' ending was created when the song abruptly segues into the coda at the end of 'Hey Jude' – possibly included because Elvis had just recorded the song, though it wouldn't be released until 1972.

Finally came a reminder that Elvis now had new hits of his own. With the International's orchestra and two backing groups behind him, 'In The Ghetto' understandably didn't have the gravitas of the studio version. But it still offered the audience a compelling illustration of Elvis's musical maturing since the days of his 50s hits. And 'Suspicious Minds' quickly became the show's highlight. The song had not yet been released as a single when the Vegas engagement opened, and Elvis built it into a seven-minute showstopper that virtually guaranteed it would become a hit. The ending has Elvis repeating the song's two opening lines in an extended vamp that rises and decreases in volume, whipping his body propulsively in response, sometimes dropping and rolling on the floor, other times going into a karate routine, but always on his feet, arms held up in triumph, at the song's conclusion. It not only became the show's centerpiece, it also became his signature song of the 70s, one reason why it remained in future setlists longer than 'In The Ghetto.'

Sometimes he kept the energy up by going into another Ray Charles cover, 'What'd I Say,' which featured his most powerful vocal. At other times he went straight into what would become the standard closing number for all subsequent shows, 'Can't Help Falling In Love' from *Blue Hawaii*. It was an effective closer, not only instantly familiar due to the film's success, but also the kind of mid-tempo crowd pleaser that offered a feeling of summation, of the evening arriving at a grand conclusion with a song performed, as Elvis said in his introduction, "Especially for you."

(According to the book *Elvis Vegas '69*, the complete opening night setlist was 'Blue Suede Shoes,' 'I Got A Woman,' 'That's All Right,' 'All Shook Up,' 'Jailhouse Rock'/'Don't Be Cruel,' 'Heartbreak Hotel,' 'Love Me Tender,' 'Hound Dog,' 'Memories,' 'My Babe,' 'I Can't Stop Loving You,' 'In The Ghetto,' 'Suspicious Minds,' 'Yesterday'/'Hey Jude,' 'Johnny B. Goode,' 'Mystery Train'/'Tiger Man,' 'What'd I Say,' 'Can't Help Falling In Love.')

The show was much like the Comeback Special's live shows, with its emphasis on older songs, reintroducing Elvis to an audience that would be most familiar with his biggest hits. But whereas most artists would have been expected to do more songs from their latest release, especially if it was a hit album, Elvis rarely did songs from the American sessions, aside from the singles. Glen Spreen had done live arrangements for 'I'm Movin' On,' 'Any Day Now,' 'Only The Strong Survive' (which were all known to have been rehearsed), as well as 'Gentle On My Mind.' Elvis's own notes indicate he was also considering 'You'll Think Of Me,' 'The Fair Is Moving On,' 'And The Grass Won't Pay No Mind,' and 'Without Love.' A few songs from the American sessions were tried during the engagement: 'Inherit The Wind' at the August 26 dinner show, and 'Rubberneckin'' and 'This Is The Story' at the August 26 midnight show, but they were soon dropped. Perhaps the dark tone of the American material didn't translate well to the glitzy environment of Las Vegas; certainly there was some underlying irony about performing 'In The Ghetto' in a city whose *raison d'être* was the celebration of conspicuous consumption.

Another factor was that the American songs would have been out of place in a show whose star continually emphasized that he didn't take himself too seriously, as in his opening remarks of self-deprecation:

"Before the evening's over I will have made a complete and total fool of myself. And I hope you get a kick out of watching it." There had been a strong element of put-on in Elvis's live performances from the very beginning. Authority figures in the 50s who had been outraged by what they perceived as vulgar movements during Elvis's shows failed to realize the underlying humor; Elvis was trying to provoke a laugh as much as a scream. That he loved toying with an audience's reaction to his trademark mannerisms was clearly evident in the live shows taped for the Comeback Special, and he did the same thing in Las Vegas, as David Dalton noted in something of a back-handed compliment in his review of the show in *Rolling Stone*: "He goes into the classic Elvis warm-up, a deep, guttural, purring, humming of soft internal combustion, revving up as he lurches into epileptic rhythms of 'All Shook Up.' It really blows your mind to see Elvis doing his imitation Elvis. He is very good at it."

Elvis's off-the-wall sense of humor was more fully on display during the lengthy monologue that was a part of each show, in which he gave an overview of his career, from his days as a trainee electrician ("And I got wired the wrong way, is what I did"), to meeting "Colonel Sanders ... Parker!", to the perks of early stardom: "I did *Love Me Tender*, *Loving You*, loving her, loving whoever I could get my hands on at the time." Most of the monologue is laden with similar jokes, though when he discusses how his army service put a momentary end to his career – "Overnight it was all gone, it was like it never happened. It was like a dream" – you get a brief sense of how difficult this period was for him. But then it's right back to a joke: "The guys in the service get awfully lonely, because they call each other mother a lot." Such light-hearted patter continued throughout the performance (Elvis on Gatorade, a sports drink provided for him during the show: "Looks like it's already been used to me, I'll tell you for sure. But if it aids your gator it's all right with me"), with the intention of keeping the atmosphere upbeat.

And the mood was decidedly celebratory when the curtain came down on opening night. Backstage, members of the entourage were taken aback to see Parker with tears in his eyes, as manager and client embraced with a warmth and an openness no one had ever seen before. When Elvis arrived for a post-show press conference at 12:30am, the reporters and photographers gave him a standing ovation as he entered the room, and the look on his face was one of unadulterated delight. He fielded the questions easily, stated that he'd wanted to return to live performance for some time, and admitted he'd been nervous until after getting through 'Love Me Tender': "Then I thought, what the heck, get with it man, or you might be out of a job tomorrow!" He also affirmed he'd like to tour "all over the world," prompting British rocker Screaming Lord Sutch to call out an offer for Elvis to do two shows at London's Wembley Empire for £1 million. "Just put down the deposit," Parker replied, though unfortunately nothing would come of the offer. "This has been one of the most exciting nights in my life," Elvis declared afterwards, draping his arm around Fats Domino, another guest, and graciously proclaiming him the real king of rock'n'roll. The celebrations continued upstairs in Elvis's suite.

The reviews were overwhelmingly positive. "With the opening song on his first night, it was clear that Elvis Presley still knows how to sing rock'n'roll," said the *New York Times*. "He seems, in fact, to have lost nothing in the past decade … He sweated and groaned, and even had the bejewelled thirtyish ladies screaming through their gloved hands." There was further coverage in *Time*, *Newsweek*, *Rolling Stone*, *Billboard*, *Hollywood Reporter*, *Variety*, *The Village Voice*, and *Record World* (UK) among others, including the Memphis dailies. In her piece for *The New Yorker*, Ellen Willis noted that Elvis's humor kept the show from being "burdened by an oppressive reverence for the past. He knew better than to try to be 19 again." Even his performance of 'In The Ghetto,' a song she'd initially dismissed as "weak on beat and strong on slush," won her over: "His emotion was so honest it transformed the song."

Ray Connolly, of London's *Evening Standard*, held nothing back, enthusing, "I've already seen the show three times and I can tell you he is sensational – better than any of us could ever have imagined."

Connolly was also granted a brief interview with Elvis. "He is incredibly handsome, with possibly the best film profile since Rudolph Valentino," Connelly wrote, noting that Elvis was seated on a red couch drinking a soda, with Parker hovering "like a benign mother." Interestingly, while dismissing his past film career, admitting he was "ashamed" of some of his movies, Elvis stated that he expected to continue making films ("But of a more serious nature"), and planned to make another TV special for NBC. He again confirmed he'd been anxious to tour for some time ("It's been building up inside of me since 1965 until the strain became intolerable"), and promised to visit Britain, somewhat mysteriously adding, "But at the moment there are personal reasons why I can't." He also noted his interest in The Beatles, proudly pointing out the good luck telegram the group sent him on opening night, and saying that he'd recorded 'Hey Jude,' though adding he preferred their earlier rockers like 'I Saw Her Standing There.' In the article's most bizarre observation, Connolly wrote, "Marriage hadn't reduced the sexiness of his act. His left knee still trembles when he sings, his guitar still becomes a sort of phallic tommy-gun, while with the microphone he appears to simulate an act of rape" – if rape could be considered "sexy."

The excitement continued throughout the Vegas run, Elvis clearly reveling in his performance. "I thought it was just a one-time occurrence, that opening night," said Myrna Smith. "Because I didn't think anybody could possibly keep packing those people in, two shows a night, for a month. I thought, 'This is phenomenal! But can he do it again tomorrow?' And then the next night came – 'Yeah!'"

"He was almost catlike," recalls Ronnie Tutt. "He was like a black panther out there on stage, his hair was all black, and black clothes, just kind of stalking around. And the showroom was never big enough for what he was doing. He was like a caged animal there in Vegas, just the way he moved around stage and the energy he had was very animalistic. And he had such a tremendous variety of songs that he would just call upon at any moment, in a rehearsal situation or even on the stage. He'd just start singing something, or he'd say 'Give me an E,' and somebody'd hit the chord and off he'd go. He kind of prided himself on the fact that we could all jump in and pretty much make a decent song out of it even though we might not be sure of every little thing."

"That was part of the fun of working with him," says Jerry Scheff. "Because he liked to play 'Stump the band.' And he didn't stump us very often!" Throughout the engagement, the running order of the setlist would change, with new songs being dropped in. Some looked to Elvis's past. 'Johnny B. Goode' was an obvious choice, another breathless rocker, as well as having a storyline that mirrored Elvis's own. His cover of Willie Dixon's 'My Babe' added a welcome dose of grittiness to the show, as did the soulful blues of 'Reconsider Baby,' a wonderful performance of a song that had first appeared on Elvis's other great album of the decade (along with *From Elvis In Memphis*), 1960's *Elvis Is Back!*

Others looked to the future. Both The Bee Gees' 'Words' and Don Gibson's 'I Can't Stop Loving You' (which Ray Charles had also covered) were indicative of the kind of songs he was now interested in, expansive numbers that gave him a chance to stretch out vocally, especially on a song's chorus and the inevitable grand finale. At the other end of the vocally dramatic scale, Willie Nelson's bittersweet 'Funny How Time Slips Away' was another obvious choice for Elvis, his performance creating an intimacy that made you forget you were in a 2,000-seat showroom; he'd record a studio version of the song the following year.

Friends and associates were also on hand throughout the run, at Elvis's invitation. His first producer, Sam Phillips, attended opening night, and, though enjoying the performance, took exception to the inclusion of 'Memories.' "Goddamn, didn't that motherfucker bog down the fucking show?" he told Elvis, only to be met with the disarming response, "Mr. Phillips, I just love that song." His most recent producer, Chips Moman, attended later in the run, as did Glen Spreen, who brought along 'Suspicious Minds' writer Mark James: "We had good seats, the band did well and I liked him, although I thought the karate chops were a little over the top," he says. Gladys Tipler, the co-owner of Crown Electric, where Elvis worked after he graduated from high school, attended the August 22 dinner show and was introduced to the audience. His *Charro!* co-stars James Almanzar and Ina Balin were also invited during the run, seated at a table in front and introduced by Elvis during the show. Jim's wife Lenore was not only impressed by Elvis's performance ("He just sang and sang and didn't stop!"), but also by the "glitter and glitz" of the occasion and the constant parade of women that came to the front to pass Elvis notes and small gifts.

Steve Binder, director of the Comeback Special, also attended, though he was thwarted in his attempts to go backstage and congratulate Elvis, being told by security that they couldn't reach anyone in the dressing room. Chris Bearde had better luck when he attended. "God, I got treated like a king," he says. "And after the show they came and got me and took me backstage. And Elvis was back there and he's got all these people around him, and I come in and he just drops everything. He comes running over and everybody's saying, 'Who the hell is that guy?' And I did a couple of funny things, I did a couple of pratfalls and everything. Elvis loved people like Benny Hill, he just loved pratfalls, he was the pratfall king. And he said, 'Anytime you want to come, you come. And you'll come see me backstage.' I spent two or three hours with him, till about two o'clock in the morning."

As the night went on, the two had a little fun by calling Allan Blye, who had also been invited but was unable to attend. "The phone rings, and I'm in bed with my ex-wife," says Allan. "It's 3:30 in the morning, and I pick up the phone and at the other end of the line I hear, 'Boy, my boy!' And I said, 'Oh my God, what are you doing? It's 3:30 in the morning!' And my wife wakes up and is furious. She said, 'Who's calling at 3:30 in the morning?' I said, 'It's Elvis Presley.' And she said, 'Oh my God, I'm not wearing anything!' And I said, 'Elvis, listen, you've had an effect on my wife that I can't explain.'"

But the longtime fans who'd wondered if they'd ever see Elvis in performance again were undoubtedly the most excited about the show. Darice Murray-McKay, who'd attended the first sit-down performance taped for the Comeback Special, was surprised to find her parents ended up seeing Elvis in a full-length concert before she did. "I never forgave them for this," she jokes. "My parents saw Elvis frequently in Vegas, and never, ever said, 'We're going to Vegas, we've got tickets to Elvis, come on out.' The first time they did it, in 1969, they came back and said, 'Oh, by the way, we were in Vegas.' And I said, 'Oh cool, did you get me my age in silver dollars?' Which is what they would always do, and by now I'm in my twenties so this is a significant amount of money. And they go, 'Yeah, and we went up to see Elvis.' They had the programs and everything. My mother was crazy about Elvis; she was ecstatic because she finally got to see him."

Pamela Des Barres, who'd suffered through Elvis's movie years, was especially thrilled to not only finally see him live, but also to attend the performance in the company of her then-boyfriend, Led Zeppelin guitarist Jimmy Page, along with the rest of the band. "Being there, in between Jimmy and Robert [Plant, Zeppelin's lead singer] in the front row, in those big plush booths just looking at the King strut his shit ... man, it was awesome," she says. "It was beyond a thrill. I mean, let's face it, I was with the modern kings of rock. Seeing the super-duper deluxe king of rock. The eternal king of rock. So I was sitting in between these two gods, watching the greatest god of all. It was quite a combination." Perhaps the band-members themselves were equally overwhelmed by the experience, for when Red West came to their table after the show to invite the group backstage, Page declined. "I have no idea why," says Pamela. "He was the ruler though, and everybody kind of looked at him, and was like, 'Well ... thanks anyway ... ' And I was like 'What?' But they did meet him later, and Robert tells a great story about how, as they were leaving his suite, Robert sang the first line of 'Love Me' in the hallway and Elvis leaned his head out into the hallway and sang the second line. That's one of his great, great stories. And I missed that! I wasn't going out with Jimmy at that point. So I never met the King. It's a big regret."

What was clear to everyone was how good a time Elvis was having on stage, as if he'd been unleashed after years of confinement – which, in a sense, he had been. Photos of the engagement capture him moving athletically; down on one knee, spinning, standing with his legs stretched apart, hunching over his guitar. His monologues and stage patter became increasingly freewheeling, to the point where Parker sent him a memo warning him about using too much "off-color material" during the show, especially the dinner performance, "when there are a great many children." During the August 26 midnight performance of 'Are You Lonesome Tonight?' he became so overcome with laughter he couldn't get through the song's spoken monologue, finally concluding, "That's it man! Fourteen years right down the drain, boy, I'll tell you! Fourteen years, shot, right there man." (This version was released as a single in the UK in 1982 and reached Number 25.) The audience was just as taken with him; from the first performance, women were throwing their clothes at him, begging for kisses, and even trying to climb onto the stage to get to their idol as the curtains fell. Fan Judy Palmer, who attended opening night, recalled a man saying to her, "My cousin says that Elvis is beautiful. I don't know any man who is beautiful." Once the show began, he turned back to Judy and exclaimed, "He *is* beautiful!"

Parker was quick to build on the excitement the engagement was generating. The International immediately wanted to book a second engagement, and Parker roughed out a contract on a tablecloth in the hotel's coffee shop. Elvis's salary was raised to $125,000 a week, and he was booked for two month-long engagements a year through 1974. Capitalizing on the success of the run, the *Elvis* special was re-broadcast on August 17, with 'Blue Christmas' replaced by 'Tiger Man.' On the day the show aired, Parker ran full-page ads gratefully acknowledging all the support, reading simply "Thanks a million, Elvis and the Colonel." Parker also began making plans to take Elvis on the road, booking six dates in Houston the following February, after the next Las Vegas engagement. Elvis had already been discussing the possibility of doing a longer tour. When Pete Bennett, a record promoter who had most recently been working for The Beatles' Apple Records label, saw the show and visited backstage, he told Elvis, "You know, you should tour stadiums, arenas." "You think I'll be as big as The Beatles?" Elvis asked. "Are you kidding?" Pete replied. "You'll sell out bigger." Then, after Pete admired the sparkling rings on Elvis's fingers, Elvis gave him one.

The success of 'Suspicious Minds' was the icing on the cake. There had been a final session of horn overdubs at United Recording in Las Vegas on August 7. "What happened with that is that Mike [Leech] did the original arrangement with the strings and I took that arrangement and tried to copy it," explains Glen Spreen. "I changed just a little bit of it, not much – in fact 90 per cent of it was Mike's. And then Felton called me one day and asked me if I thought anything was missing; he was in Vegas, they were rehearsing. I said, 'Yeah, it's missing power.' So he said, 'What can you do about that?' I said I'd put some horns on it so I wrote the horn part and sent it off to Vegas, and they recorded it there."

The decision was then made to emulate Elvis's presentation of the song in his live show, fading the song out during the extended coda, then fading it back up again (it's been said this may have been inspired by The Beatles' ending for 'Hey Jude'). The musicians at American who'd worked on the record weren't impressed with what they considered to be a gimmick. "We kind of looked at each other in amazement," recalls Glen Spreen. "We went, what in the heck does he think he's doing here? We couldn't believe it. We were also worried about whether it was going to get airplay, because back then you had to have less than four minutes to even have a record played."

"It sounded like a technical mistake, is what it sounded like to me," says Bobby Emmons. "I guess the public liked it. But that was an unusual fade. I mean, most of the time, the older you get, the longer the fades seem. Because when you're young and into it, you can kind of get into listening to the subtle differences in each repeat. It's not like nowadays, where they make a loop and it's actually the same thing over and over. And that'll wear you out, that's like water torture or something. But when there's little nuances of difference in each one of the repeats it really builds a groove; you can stay into the song for a lot longer. And that's the way that song was. And I guess that's the reason they tried to figure out some way to keep it going longer. And it really worked out in Vegas." It worked out beyond Vegas too. 'Suspicious Minds' was released at the end of August and steadily climbed the charts, reaching Number One on November 1, Elvis's first chart topper since 'Good Luck Charm' in 1962; it also sold well over a million copies, and reached Number Two in the UK.

The Las Vegas engagement ended on August 28 on an equally high note; 101,500 people had attended during the run, generating a record $1.5 million. The next evening, Elvis and his entourage attending Nancy Sinatra's opening night show at the International, and at the party hosted by her father, Frank, afterwards, Elvis gave her the engraving plates for the full-page ad he'd arranged to take out in a local newspaper, wishing her luck with the show.

As an additional bonus, the International gave Elvis an all-expenses paid vacation in Hawaii, which he took in October with his family and some of his friends (just prior to the trip, on September 26 at RCA's studios in Nashville, there was a final session of vocal overdubs on songs from the American sessions being prepared for the next release). While in Hawaii, the group decided to extend the trip abroad, and plans were made to fly on to Europe after a stop off in Los Angeles. But Parker insisted such a trip would "offend" Elvis's fans overseas, if he visited their countries as a tourist before playing there. Amazingly, Elvis acquiesced, and (at Parker's suggestion) went off to the Bahamas instead, a trip that ended after a week when a hurricane descended on the islands. His newfound confidence only extended so far.

The Trouble With Girls (And How To Get Into It) was released with little fanfare in September (many cinemas paired it with the grade-B sci-fi flick *The Green Slime*). It was also the last Presley feature film released theatrically in the UK; while *Change Of Habit* was released in the US in November 1969, it wouldn't appear in Britain until August 1971, and then only on television.

Elvis's record releases would find greater success, with his last single and album of the year released in November. 'Don't Cry Daddy,' backed with 'Rubberneckin'' (the latter promoting *Change Of Habit*), was another solid hit, peaking at Number Six (Number Eight UK), and selling over a million copies. Then came the release of an album that in hindsight could be seen as the first misstep in Elvis's comeback, the double-album set *From Memphis To Vegas/From Vegas To Memphis* (which reached Number 12 US, Number Three UK). Instead of simply releasing a live album in the wake of the Vegas engagement, and holding off to release the next studio album until the following year, both were released at once in this set.

Disc one, entitled *Elvis In Person At The International Hotel*, featured 12 songs from the Vegas run, most of them from the August 25 midnight show: 'Blue Suede Shoes,' 'Johnny B. Goode,' 'All Shook Up,' 'Are You Lonesome Tonight?,' 'Hound Dog,' 'I Can't Stop Loving You,' 'My Babe,' 'Mystery Train'/'Tiger Man,' 'Words,' 'In The Ghetto,' 'Suspicious Minds,' and 'Can't Help Falling In Love.' Though short at just under 35 minutes, it effectively captured the excitement of the shows, including some of the less performed numbers ('Johnny B. Goode,' 'My Babe'), the best of the new songs ('I Can't Stop Loving You') and his most recent singles ('In The Ghetto,' 'Suspicious Minds'). Oddly, the cover picture was another shot of Elvis in leather from the Comeback Special, playing Scotty Moore's guitar. First editions of the release also credited 'Suspicious Minds' as being written by "Francis Zambon" – songwriter Mark James's real name.

Disc two, *Back In Memphis* (whose cover shot *did* have a live picture from the Vegas performances) featured more material from the American sessions, two of which had already been released: 'Inherit

The Wind,' 'This Is The Story,' 'Stranger In My Own Home Town,' 'A Little Bit Of Green,' 'And The Grass Won't Pay No Mind,' 'Do You Know Who I Am,' 'From A Jack To A King,' 'The Fair Is Moving On' (previously the B-side of 'Clean Up Your Own Back Yard'), 'You'll Think Of Me' (previously the B-side of 'Suspicious Minds'), and 'Without Love.'

For the most part, the record featured the lesser songs recorded at American; what Moman called "the culls, the throwaways." A better album could have been fashioned by pulling some of the stronger material, like 'Stranger In My Own Home Town' and 'Without Love,' and combining it with good songs from a new session to make an album closer in standard to *From Elvis In Memphis*. But throughout Elvis's career, the policy had always been to eventually make use of every song that was recorded; songs that were not deemed strong enough to release at the time were nevertheless determined to be good enough as filler on an album released years later. Considering the fact that for the previous five years the vast majority of Elvis's albums had been mediocre soundtracks, *Back In Memphis* was a good album indeed. But as Elvis's career now had the chance to move in a new, more adult direction, the old practice of flooding the market with releases should have been reconsidered. At the start of the 60s it was not unusual for major acts to release two or more new albums a year. But as acts – especially those who wrote their own material – began to have more of a say in the process, that standard had changed, with most major acts limiting themselves to one album a year. In contrast, the next year would see a glut of Elvis releases on the market, which would only serve to undercut the artistic gains he'd made in the last two years.

Elvis may not have realized it, but his career was once again at a crossroads.

Chapter 5

Promised Land

In 1970, Elvis furthered the commercial – if not quite the artistic – success he'd achieved the previous year. He also broadened his reach as a live performer, making his first forays out of Las Vegas, and laying the groundwork for the constant touring that would eventually become his primary creative outlet – and ultimately another kind of trap, as making the movies in the 60s had been.

Not that this would have been apparent at the time. Elvis's second Vegas engagement began on January 26, and while some had questioned the wisdom of scheduling another stint so close to his previous season, and during Vegas's off-season as well, it was another sell-out run. There were a few changes in the line-up. Ronnie Tutt, unaware that another Vegas engagement had been scheduled, had taken a job with *The Andy Williams Show* and was unavailable, and Bob Lanning was hired to replace him (Tutt says his absence had nothing to do with insufficient financial compensation, as has been reported elsewhere). Ann Williams replaced Cissy Houston in The Sweet Inspirations, and keyboardist Glen D. Hardin replaced Larry Muhoberac, who had decided to go back to studio work. Glen had been a 'Shindog' along with James Burton and Jerry Scheff, though he had recently been doing more work as an arranger. "I sort of had gotten myself away from playing piano," he says. "I was just arranging music. And I had a terrible feeling I was about to forget how to play the piano, so I decided I'd get back to that." As it turned out, he quickly started arranging for Elvis as well, soon after rehearsals began on January 10.

Rehearsals were held at RCA's studios on Sunset Boulevard, generally running from 7pm to 1am. As usual, the band worked on more songs than were needed. "[Elvis] likes to rehearse anything anybody can name," said Glen, at the time. "If you take off playin' 'Stagger Lee,' he enjoys that and he'll just sing it, man, for about an hour and a half." Sandi Miller, who was among the fans invited to attend Elvis's rehearsals both in LA and Las Vegas, also noticed how practices were sometimes more about just having some fun. "The rehearsals varied from where Elvis just wanted to sit and goof around, and he would accomplish nothing, to where he was really trying to nail a certain song," she says. "So it just kind of depended. If he was in a playful mood, it wasn't even a rehearsal, it was like, let's just go and screw around for two hours. Or there were times when he'd walk into the rehearsal room and he'd go, 'OK, everybody here? Everybody's here ... OK, goodnight.' And there'd be no rehearsal. So you'd just never know. 'But we came here to watch you rehearse!' 'Eh, I don't feel like rehearsing.'"

But when it was time to get serious, she says, "He knew exactly what he wanted. He was in charge. And man, somebody could hit a wrong note behind him, and you wouldn't be able to tell, and he'd hear it. And he'd go 'Whoa! You were low on that' or 'You got ahead of me on that' or 'That was off.' And we're like, what? It sounded fine to me. But he had a very good ear for music and he could pick up on stuff like that that he could have let go; nobody would have known. And there were times when he hit a flat note, and he'd make fun of himself and go, 'OK, that wasn't too pretty.' And a lot of times it was the musicians and the backup singers that were doing more than he was doing; he'd just sit there and listen, and maybe hum along and maybe change things, where he really didn't do an actual lot of singing himself. But he was putting everything in place; he was getting everything ready the way he wanted it. He knew what he was doing."

The setlist was also reworked, cutting back on material from the 50s. Elvis had two new hits of his own to add: 'Don't Cry Daddy' and 'Kentucky Rain,' the latter released to coincide with the Vegas engagement. It reached Number 16 (Number 21 UK) and sold over half a million copies. He also added a number of contemporary hits, such as Neil Diamond's 'Sweet Caroline' and 'Proud Mary' by Creedence Clearwater Revival. 'Proud Mary' (which Elvis performed a year before Ike & Tina Turner would have a hit with the song) and Tony Joe White's 'Polk Salad Annie' added some much-needed funkiness to the set, the latter becoming another set piece that allowed Elvis to go into one of the karate-inspired routines he loved to put into the show. Joe South's 'Walk A Mile In My Shoes' was a rousing slice of country-rock; Elvis frequently recited part of Hank Williams's 'Men With Broken Hearts' before the song, giving it an additional note of poignancy. 'See See Rider' was a blues song first recorded by Ma Rainey in 1924, though it was Chuck Willis's 1957 hit version that inspired Elvis, who rocked up the song to the point where it was almost giddy with excitement. The lushly romantic 'Let It Be Me' (based on the French song 'Je T'appartiens') had first been a hit for The Everly Brothers in 1960, and in Elvis's hands built up to a grand finale.

Elvis swapped around his 50s hits ('Teddy Bear' and 'Love Me' instead of 'Jailhouse Rock' and 'Heartbreak Hotel'), but aside from 'Are You Lonesome Tonight?' and 'Can't Help Falling In Love,' largely overlooked his 60s material. Perhaps songs like 'Good Luck Charm' and 'Return To Sender' were too similar in spirit to 50s songs like 'All Shook

Up,' hits he performed more out of necessity, to please the audience. Elvis preferred to add songs to the setlist by other artists that reflected his new maturity, although he could certainly have found songs in his own extensive catalogue for that purpose, such as 'Guitar Man' or 'If I Can Dream,' both of which would have been familiar from the Comeback Special. And one song that was an obvious contender for the show, one that could have been built up into an energetic showpiece along the lines of 'Polk Salad Annie' or 'Suspicious Minds' was strangely never included: 'Viva Las Vegas.'

Elvis's stage wear also acquired a new look. Instead of two-piece suits, Bill Belew began designing one-piece jumpsuits, which allowed Elvis to move about more freely, and not worry about his shirt coming out of his trousers. Made of a wool/gabardine blend, the fabric was sturdy enough to accommodate Elvis's physical exertions (he'd torn out the seat of his pants at one show during the previous Vegas engagement), but also meant that the outfits were very warm.

The jumpsuits would become Elvis's signature costume, even more so than his 50s drape jackets and blue suede shoes, and the designs were initially simple; one suit had a brocade collar similar to the kind that had been featured on the 1969 suits, while another, seen on the cover of the 1970 *On Stage* album, had no adornment whatsoever; Elvis simply wore an elaborate 'necktie' of thin, macramé-style ropes. The jumpsuits also featured unusually high collars. "The high collar came about because I was a great fan at that period of Napoleon," explained Belew. "And it's what's called the Napoleonic collar. It worked for me, because it framed his face; I was always aware that your eye went to his face, because it was framed with the collar. I started to design his personal wardrobe as well; I had said to him, 'Now Elvis, what we have to do is, the image that we have in the concert, I want to carry that over into your personal wardrobe.'" Hence Elvis frequently appeared as grandiose off stage as he did in performance, with outfits emphasizing his favorite colors. "Mostly, it was off-white, navy blue," says Belew. "He liked blue a lot."

Rehearsals moved to Vegas on January 19, the engagement opening with a single show on January 26, then continuing with two shows a night until February 23. Opening night drew the usual mix of celebrities, including Zsa Zsa Gabor, actor George Chakiris, and Elvis's *G.I. Blues* co-star Juliet Prowse (among the good luck telegrams he received was one from the film's producer, Hal Wallis). Catching sight of Dean Martin in the audience that night, Elvis went into an impromptu rendition of Martin's hit, 'Everybody Loves Somebody.' The reviews were generally positive, and shows from February 15 to 19 were recorded in anticipation of a new live album. But because there weren't quite enough new songs to avoid duplication with the last live album, both 'Release Me,' which had been considered for the previous Vegas engagement, and 'The Wonder Of You,' which Elvis had long been interested in recording, were added to the setlist (unfortunately, official recordings weren't taking place when Elvis performed a rare song from the American sessions, 'True Love Travels On A Gravel Road').

As before, Elvis became more playful as the run continued. During one performance of 'Don't Cry Daddy,' he changed the words and ending up laughing so hard he couldn't get through the number, finally gasping, "Oh man, we gotta end this song!" On the last night, the midnight show ran until 3am, with Elvis in an expansive, relaxed mood, getting behind the piano to accompany himself on 'Lawdy, Miss Clawdy' and 'Blueberry Hill.' During the usual 'kissing' ritual during 'Love Me Tender,' Priscilla got in line to receive a kiss as a joke. "I recognize that girl," Elvis remarked, jokingly adding, "Oh, I forgot to tell you, I got the flu." In keeping with the late night good spirits, at the show's end comedian Sammy Shore came out, fell on his knees in front of Elvis, and began kissing his feet.

Two days later, on February 25, Elvis flew into Houston, Texas, in preparation for his six shows at the Astrodome (the world's first domed stadium) as part of the Houston Livestock Show and Rodeo, holding a short press conference on arrival. The shows would be his first outside of Las Vegas since 1961, and his nervousness wasn't assuaged by the poor quality of the sound system. "The Astrodome was a purty crummy gig," Glen Hardin recalled, describing the venue as "a big ol' giant terrible place to play." Resigned to the situation, Elvis told his musicians, "This is gonna be rather atrocious, so don't fight it, go ahead and play." There had been a further hiccup over the inclusion of The Sweet Inspirations in the show, as the promoters had said they didn't want "those black girls" on the bill. When Elvis insisted they were part of the show and threatened not to perform otherwise, the promoters quickly backed down.

Another press conference was held before the first show on February 27, at which Elvis reconfirmed his interest in making more films, and, asked about the expectation that his shows would set new attendance records, responded, "I hope so. I hope I can give 'em a good show. That's the most important thing." The first show was at 2pm, with Elvis making a grand entrance, driven around the arena waving from the back of a flat-bed truck, showing himself off to the crowd like a conquering hero. Unfortunately, the dome was less than half full (16,708 in an arena that could hold more than 40,000), and, coupled with the poor sound system, left Elvis feeling like a failure. "Well, that's it. I guess I just don't have it anymore," he sadly observed to Gee Gee Gambill (who was married to his cousin, Patsy), after the show. But he was greatly heartened when the crowd more than doubled for the evening show (36,299), and the hoped-for record was set at the February 28 evening show, which drew a crowd of 43,614, a record for the largest indoor rodeo performance. "It was during this weekend that I actually realized that my big brother Elvis Presley was the biggest entertainer in the world," said Elvis's stepbrother David Stanley.

In contrast to the Vegas shows, the Texas shows restored a sizeable number of Elvis's 50s hits to the setlist; no 'Sweet Caroline,' 'Let It Be Me,' or 'Proud Mary.' After the final two shows on March 1, yet another press conference was held. To mark the success of the event, Elvis was given assorted gifts, including a Stetson, a Rolex watch, and a deputy's badge (after noting that he hadn't received any gifts, Parker was given a badge too). He was also presented with a batch of gold records, for the 'In The Ghetto,' 'Suspicious Minds,' and 'Don't Cry Daddy' singles and the *From Elvis In Memphis* and *From Memphis To Vegas/From Vegas To Memphis* albums.

Elvis then had a break of three months, while record releases continued apace, with April seeing the release of the 'The Wonder Of You,' a live recording from the February Vegas engagement. It was the kind of easy listening, middle-of-the-road number that was becoming typical of Elvis's Vegas performances, here benefiting from post-concert vocal overdubs that gave it a vibrant, celestial air. It also proved to be a big hit, reaching Number Nine in the US and selling nearly a million copies, while it topped the charts in the UK. But the first album release of the year was decidedly underwhelming. *Let's Be Friends* was a release on RCA's budget Camden label, a collection of tracks recorded between 1962 and 1969 that hadn't seen official release on a record, primarily movie songs like 'Mama' (from *Girls! Girls! Girls!*) and 'Have A Happy' (from *Change Of Habit*). There was no thought or continuity to the release, which, at a mere nine tracks, was on the skimpy side as well (though it nonetheless sold 400,000 copies).

And just two months later, another album was released, *On Stage*, the live release documenting Elvis's second Vegas season. At only ten tracks, it didn't offer much more music than *Let's Be Friends*, but it was interesting in that none of the songs were numbers Elvis had previously recorded himself; nor would he ever record studio versions of the songs. Despite having added some songs to the setlist, there were still not enough new numbers to make up an entirely different album from the last live release, so two previously unreleased songs from the 1969 Vegas run were included. The album's original running order was: 'See See Rider,' 'Release Me,' 'Sweet Caroline,' 'Runaway' (from the August 25 1969 dinner show), 'The Wonder Of You,' 'Polk Salad Annie,' 'Yesterday' (also from the August 25 1969 dinner show, and minus the 'Hey Jude' coda), 'Proud Mary,' 'Walk A Mile In My Shoes,' and 'Let It Be Me.'

Though a decent representation of the February shows, it was strange to put out a live album just eight months after the release of the previous live record. And especially since by the time *On Stage* was released, a deal had already been made to film the next Vegas engagement for a documentary, which would be accompanied by yet another live album – the third such release in a year. Nonetheless, Elvis's live records remained popular with his fans (the last Number One album of his lifetime would be 1973's live set *Aloha From Hawaii Via Satellite*), and *On Stage* reached Number 13 US (Number Two UK) and sold more than half a million copies. *Billboard* wrote approvingly, "This great package is an illustration of how broad the artist's versatility is."

June also saw Elvis return to the studio for the first time in over a year. There was no thought given to returning to American; Felton Jarvis wanted to be fully back in charge, so the sessions were scheduled at the RCA's studios in Nashville. But Felton did make one important change; instead of the usual crew of musicians who had played on Elvis's Nashville sessions, he engaged some newer, younger musicians from a music scene that was just as legendary as the one in Memphis: Muscle Shoals, Alabama.

Muscle Shoals is actually one of four towns known as 'the Quad Cities' in Northern Alabama, including Florence (where Sam Phillips was born), Sheffield, and Tuscumbia. "It was an out-of-the-way place, but it had loads of talent, loads of it," says drummer Jerry Carrigan. Jerry was born in Florence ("I can stand on my mother's back porch and look at the house where Sam Phillips lived," he says), and had been interested in drums as a child, playing his own makeshift drum set built out of implements he found around the house (an old banjo head served as a snare) until his parents bought him a proper kit. By 1959, Jerry had found his way to Spar Music, a recording studio above Florence's City Drug Store where he met fellow musicians drawn to the only studio in the state at that time. Spar was owned by Tom Stafford, who also owned the town's movie house. "We were just kids who hung out at the theater and the drug store," said keyboardist David Briggs.

"We'd go to the drug store, buy a hot dog, see a pretty girl, get horny, then go upstairs and write a song about it."

"We'd go up there everyday," says Jerry. "When I would get off from school, in the afternoons, I would go straight over to the studio and start playing my drums. We had Arthur Alexander up there doing things, and we were doing demos and all that stuff. I couldn't have a bass drum back then because they didn't know how to mike it. So we had a cymbal and a snare drum, that's all I had. But we made good records with it."

Bass player Norbert Putnam was another young musician who hung around Spar, playing sessions and, with David Briggs and Jerry Carrigan, becoming part of the original 60s Muscle Shoals Rhythm Section. "It was an absolute miracle to get something going in Muscle Shoals," Norbert says. "There is something to be said for a child being brought up in an area with very few options. It allows you to center on something." The three were much in demand, playing sessions and touring the area in The Mark V, later renamed Dan Penn & The Pallbearers. "That was only because we'd found a deal on a Cadillac hearse, and we couldn't find a deal on a van," says Norbert. "We would've been Dan Penn & The Van Menders!" (Penn would later move to Memphis where he worked with Chips Moman, co-writing 'Do Right Woman' with him).

In 1960, Rick Hall, one of Stafford's partners, split with him. Stafford kept the studio, and Hall kept the business name, FAME (for Florence Alabama Music Enterprises). Hall soon set up his own studio in an abandoned warehouse on Wilson Dam Road in Muscle Shoals, and Norbert, David, and Jerry were installed as the house band, getting their first big hit with Arthur Alexander's 'You Better Move On' (the record's B-side, by the studio band's guitarist, Terry Thompson, was the rock'n'roll classic 'A Shot Of Rhythm & Blues'). "We had about three or four mics," Jerry recalls. "I had one mic on my drums and the other guys shared the other mics. And we cut it in that little tobacco barn studio and it was a hit. And Rick borrowed some money and built the studio he has now. The first session done in the new studio was a demo session on a Sunday afternoon; we cut 'Steal Away,' which was a big hit for Jimmy Hughes. The first thing cut in the studio was a hit."

The next few years saw a steady progression of musicians heading to the FAME Studios in the hopes of scoring a hit themselves, including Tommy Roe ('Everybody') and The Tams ('Untie Me'), among others. Felton Jarvis, Roe's producer, suggested to the musicians they'd make out better financially in Nashville. "Felton loved the way we played," Norbert recalls. "We played different from the Nashville guys, probably because of the R&B background. We were not country musicians; we'd never played country music. And at Muscle Shoals, also, we were being paid in a non-union sort of way, so when it was pointed out to us that we could earn four to five times our hourly wage in Nashville we said, 'That's it, we're leaving.' So we went to Nashville and became Nashville's sort of pop-rock rhythm section in the mid 60s."

The musicians were all fans of Elvis while growing up. "If it hadn't been for Elvis, I may never have wanted to play rock'n'roll," says Jerry. Like many others, they'd been dismayed at the material Elvis had recorded during the 60s, but felt the Comeback Special had been a sign his career was getting back on track. "It was great to see him looking good," says Norbert. "I think we were all hopeful." They also enjoyed the work Elvis had done at American, Jerry calling it "The best stuff he's ever done, no doubt."

But though versatile as musicians, the Memphis Boys focused on pop records and rhythm & blues – "They had that in their bones, totally saturated with it," says Jerry – while the Nashville musicians developed a broader musical palette through the numerous sessions they played in Nashville's more rigid studio set up. "I'm working four sessions a day," Jerry says. "I mean, that leaves little time to sleep. Ten to one, two to five, six to ten, and ten to one in the morning. Then you tear down your stuff, you go home, you get about two hours sleep, you get up, and you go do it again. A lot of coffee. A lot of coffee! And man, this went on for years." Felton hoped the new musicians would keep Elvis's sound as fresh as it had been with the Memphis Boys. He was also under some additional pressure himself, having quit RCA in order to work full-time for Elvis, his fee depending on how many tracks were completed.

Some of the musicians engaged for the sessions had previously worked with Elvis. Multi-instrumentalist Charlie McCoy (who would play organ and harmonica on these sessions) played his first Elvis session in 1965; David Briggs and guitarist Chip Young first played with Elvis during the 1966 _How Great Thou Art_ sessions (also the first time Felton had produced Elvis). James Burton, brought in to play lead guitar, was of course in Elvis's live band, but he had never worked in the studio with him. But neither Jerry nor Norbert had even met Elvis before. "I was absolutely terrified," Norbert admits. "There wasn't any doubt that Elvis Presley, in my mind, was the greatest performer of contemporary music in the history of the world. I was wondering if I'd be up to the task. I remember I stood in the bathroom at RCA that night, and just before I went out there I said, 'Dear God, don't allow me to fuck up this session. I'll be back in Muscle Shoals next week!'"

Jerry professed to be more nonchalant. "I was elated, but I thought, 'Ah, won't bother me. I've worked with all of 'em; he's just another star, and I work with stars everyday.'" But it was a different matter when the sessions began, at 6pm on June 4, and he faced the man himself. Felton had wanted the group to be playing when Elvis arrived, so the musicians were jamming on 'Mystery Train' when Elvis and his entourage walked in. "Let me tell you something," says Jerry. "When that door opened and he walked into that room, it was unbelievable. Mouths just dropped open, every one of us. I couldn't believe it. And I quit playing and was shaking. We all quit. You knew a star had walked in the room. You could feel his presence in the room. It was amazing. You could. He was really charismatic."

"Elvis in person was actually more beautiful than he photographed," recalls Norbert. "You notice I used the word 'beautiful.' That's not a word I've ever used to describe another man. If you had designed him, if you'd had Leonardo or someone do the perfect face, it would have been the way Elvis looked when he walked into the room. And the other thing was, he was only six feet tall. He and I were literally the same size. When you put him up against a big man, he looked small. But when he walked in, he looked like he was ten feet tall. There was just all sorts of things going on with Elvis and his aura."

In his usual manner of putting people at ease, Elvis went around introducing himself to each musician, shaking hands, then urged them to continue jamming: "Keep playing! Let's play some more boys, whatcha playing, 'Mystery Train'? Play it!" "We'd start playing and he'd do 'Mystery Train,'" says Jerry. "He stood right in front of me and he'd motion for me to fill, and man, I'd fill too. And he loved it." The jam eventually segued into an equally lively 'Tiger Man' before the session proper began.

The Nashville sessions were done in an entirely different fashion to those at American, where Elvis had sung a rough vocal with the band and laid down a final vocal later; this time, there would be few vocal overdubs. "He liked the live feel, not overdubbing unless absolutely necessary," said James Burton. Nor was there a firm hand like Chips Moman's to guide the proceedings and offer suggestions, which was not Felton's strategy. "Felton had gotten to a point of comfort where he knew Elvis loved him and would listen to him, as much as Elvis listened to anybody," says Norbert. "Felton was careful of Elvis. He didn't really ever criticize him. I don't recall him ever questioning him – a flat or sharp note or anything. He would say, 'King, I think you should do one more,' which meant, 'You probably didn't do it as well as you could.' But then again, Felton Jarvis was not a musician; he was basically a fan of music. He didn't have an ego about him; he would say, 'Hey guys, I think that's the one, come on in and listen and see if you hear any problems.' And he would trust us to point out any irregularities in the rhythm section. He was very good at keeping a positive vibe happening in the room."

Most importantly, the material Elvis was offered was not especially strong, but unlike their Memphis counterparts the Nashville musicians kept their opinions to themselves. "The demos were by a singer who could imitate Elvis's voice," Norbert recalls. "They were usually in Elvis's key, and they were usually the most trite, bullshit songs you've ever heard … I love you, do you love me too, that sort of rhyme scheme." While listening to the demos with the musicians, everyone hearing the songs for the first time, Elvis would begin singing along while looking at the lyric sheet. "He starts singing along with a guy who's imitating Elvis," says Norbert. "It was the most bizarre thing you've ever heard – Elvis imitating a guy imitating Elvis."

Elvis would then look around to gauge the musicians' reactions. "Of course we knew this, so we'd try not to show any emotion, positive or negative," Norbert says. "And it would be a bullshit song, and Elvis would be looking around, and we're not giving him any clue, right? It would get into the last verse and he'd go, 'Lamar, this is a piece of shit!' And he would wad up the lyric sheet and throw it at him. 'Get out of here! Bring me good songs!' And then Elvis would go into this really comedic tirade, pretending he was really upset. And everybody would break up laughing, and then they would bring on another piece of shit, and we'd do the same thing over again, three or four times."

"Elvis would play these things, and man, they were the worst things you've ever heard," agrees Jerry. "He'd take them off, and break them across his knee. He hated 'em, he just hated 'em."

Eventually, Elvis would settle on a song to record. "This guy was a quick study," Norbert observes. "They would play that demo three or four times and Elvis would sing along. Then he would say, 'What key is that in, David?' David would say, 'Well, it's E-flat.' 'Can you move it up slightly? Let's try E natural. OK guys, let's run this now.' And he would take a hand microphone, like you'd have in concert, and he would walk over in front of the rhythm section in the middle of the studio; normally, the singer's behind baffles, you know. And with the lead sheet in one hand, and the mic in the other, the King would start to perform the damn song while we played it out. RCA Studio B was a very small studio, and he's literally ten feet in front of us. And we're not wearing headphones; we can actually hear that vocal, we can hear it loudly. We can hear the timbre of his voice, and we can hear the dynamics come up as he starts to get excited, and we can bring the rhythm section up with it."

Elvis had been able to work quickly from a demo throughout his recording career. He could be painstaking during recording when he wanted to be; in 1956, he had cut 31 takes of 'Hound Dog' before he was satisfied. But if he didn't like a song, instead of demanding better material he would take a more passive-aggressive approach. Rushing through the recording of a song was one ploy. Or, as in these sessions, he'd gamely work his way through the songs served up by his publishers, then veer off in his own direction to play the songs he was really interested in; during these sessions these were older country or traditional numbers that often sprang out of informal jams. It was not too dissimilar to the way he rehearsed for his Vegas shows. "He'd go over and start playing piano and get us started on something," says Jerry. "We just played constantly, from the time he got there until 6:30, 7 o'clock the next morning. We were some tired puppies when we crawled out of there on the 8th [of June, the last day of the sessions]."

The first session began with one of the better newer numbers, 'Twenty Days And Twenty Nights,' a thoughtful, introspective ballad that Elvis performed with great sensitivity. "I remember on the first song, I wanted to play great," says Norbert. "I felt I needed to do something extraordinary and I don't know, I might have added a little 'nother something or other." He was relieved when, during the song's playback, Elvis came over and put his arm around him, saying, "Hey Putt, great part." "That sort of broke the fear I had," says Norbert. "I thought, 'Great, I'm in.'"

Next came 'I've Lost You,' a middle-of-the-road number about a troubled relationship, whose sentiments moved Elvis to tears as he recorded it. Perhaps to lighten the mood, he then broke into something to sing just for fun, the traditional number 'I Was Born About Ten Thousand Years Ago' (which he knew from The Golden Gate Quartet's version) about having been around long enough to have witnessed events in Biblical days, breezing through it in one rollicking take ("That was just kickin' it," says Jerry). The next number, 'The Sound Of Your Cry' was another song about a failed romance, though in a more melodramatic vein than 'I've Lost You' (with the first take falling apart when Elvis couldn't keep from laughing).

After a break, Elvis again went his own way, singing a bit of 'Faded Love,' originally by Western swing outfit Bob Wills & His Texas Playboys. He asked Lamar for the lyrics to record a proper version, but they weren't immediately available, so Elvis suggested they do 'The Fool' instead, a hit for Sanford Clark in 1956. Elvis had made a home recording of the song back in 1959, accompanying himself on piano; now he transformed it into a slice of bluesy funk. On a roll now, he next took up a guitar and launched into Flatt & Scruggs's country romp 'A Hundred Years From Now,' the musicians easily falling in line behind him. "All that and missed the fucking ending!" he exclaimed after stumbling at the end of the first take. "There goes my fucking career, right down the fucking drain!" He worked on the final chords a few times, then the band snapped back to attention, tearing through the song a second time. Not a serious contender for release, it would finally appear on 1995's _Walk A Mile In My Shoes: The Essential 70s Masters_ boxed set.

They stayed in country territory with Bill Monroe's 'Little Cabin On The Hill.' Elvis knew the song well, and had briefly jammed on it back in 1956 during the so-called 'Million Dollar Quartet' session, when he dropped by Sun Studios on December 4 and found Carl Perkins, Jerry Lee Lewis, and Johnny Cash hanging out (he had also cut Monroe's 'Blue Moon Of Kentucky' for his first single on Sun). The final song of the session, which ended around 4:30am, was 'Cindy, Cindy,' brought to the table by his publishers, another traditional number given a rock arrangement that wasn't entirely satisfactory. Both songs were laid down quickly, though still not fast enough for Elvis; at the end of the first take of 'Cindy, Cindy,' Elvis was moved to say, "Fade this motherfucker!"

It had been a good evening's work, with the musicians glad they'd lived up to Elvis's expectations. "That sonofabitch can play, can't he?" he'd remarked to Felton about Jerry's work, which pleased Jerry immensely. "'He's a drumming sonofabitch' is what he called me!" he says proudly. But they were surprised at some of Elvis's personal idiosyncrasies, such as his apparent need to change outfits throughout the sessions. "They would bring his big valet case in with his clothes," says Jerry, "and he would change his clothes three, four times a night, like he was on a show. It was unbelievable."

And they were all a little taken aback by the overly enthusiastic behavior of the entourage. "Even after the first take of a song, the control room would erupt with people leaping into the air and proclaiming Elvis a god, right?" says Norbert. "You can imagine this, they all work for him. He had court jesters that worked for him. It would have been distracting, but we became used to it, you know? And Elvis knew it was kind of bullshit too. But sometimes he would sort of buy into it."

Nonetheless, Elvis wouldn't tolerate the entourage giving his musicians a hard time, as Jerry observed one night when they'd taken a break for a meal. Jerry had innocently reached for a pickle in a cup sitting in the control room when he was stopped by 'Hamburger' James, the member of Elvis's group responsible for providing food at the sessions. "Those are Elvis's pickles," said James, to Jerry's astonishment. "So what man, he doesn't care if I have a pickle!" Jerry replied. "I said, those are Elvis's pickles," James responded, covering them up with a towel. Informed of the matter, Elvis merely shook his head, saying, "Is that right? James, give him that thing of pickles, and go get me some more please. Don't you ever tell one of my boys they can't have a pickle." "He was great," says Jerry. "He was just great."

The June 5 session began with Simon & Garfunkel's 'Bridge Over Trouble Water.' Even from the first take, it was clear that Elvis had studied the song very closely. "Very, very good cut," Jerry says. "It'd be a single today if it were remixed and overdubbed properly. He's into ballads and big long notes. Because he could do it. He could hold 'em and he could hit 'em. He had the feel for that kind of stuff. And he'd draw it out of you too. Because this man commanded your attention so much, when you worked for him, even though you had a chart, you had one eye on the chart and you had one eye on him. You watch him, because if you will, he'll direct you on how he wants it. The best thing to do is play it how the man wants it done." Though it had been a huge hit for Simon & Garfunkel, Elvis easily managed to stamp his own personality on it; as the song's composer, Paul Simon, later observed, "It was a bit dramatic but how the hell am I supposed to compete with that?"

The next song, 'How The Web Was Woven,' was another heart-string pulling ballad, after which Elvis again sought to lighten the mood, bursting into a lively medley of 'Got My Mojo Working'/'Keep Your Hands Off It,' which he stormed through in one take, laughing at his own high spirits at the end. Then it was back to business with 'It's Your Baby, You Rock It,' the first (and best) of the three songs Elvis would record by Shirl Milete at the sessions (he'd previously recorded Milete's 'My Little Friend' at American). The title of the song, sung from the perspective of a man who's tired of offering support to a friend in an unhappy relationship, was inspired by an expression of Elvis's; Lamar Fike had passed it on to Milete, calling him one day to exclaim, "I've got the best title in the world!" Milete duly came up with a song to match.

Then came one of the session's more interesting numbers, 'Stranger In The Crowd,' a breezy number about the joy of love at first sight, enlivened by the brisk Latin rhythms running underneath. 'I'll Never Know' followed, a fairly pedestrian ballad, somewhat redeemed by Elvis's sincere vocal. The session ended with the lushly romantic 'Mary In The Morning.'

It was another productive night, again running until the early morning hours, in part because, although he might arrive at 6pm, Elvis wouldn't get down to work immediately. "We had lots of time telling jokes and cuttin' up time," says Jerry. "Playing football in the parking lot and all that stuff. In June, we had long days, longest of the year; in Nashville, it's light till nearly 9 o'clock in June. He'd get there about 6:30. We'd play ball or tell jokes, stories, and stuff like that, for hours at times. It didn't matter, we were getting paid. That's what Elvis wanted to do. If that's what he wants to do, let's do it. He'd put on karate exhibitions."

"When he would come to the studio, he would walk in and raise his arms up in a 'Come to me, I want to embrace you' way," says Norbert. "He'd say, 'Guys, I've got to tell you what's been going on.' And he would gather us in a corner and start to tell us about all the funny crap that had happened over the last six months; he'd tell stories for two hours, and it was like a reunion of a bunch of high school kids." Eventually, Felton would break up the fun like an indulgent father, reminding Elvis, "You realize it's 10:30 in the evening, and we haven't played a note. We really must do something." "Well guys, I guess we have to record something," Elvis would sigh in response. "What are we doing, Felton?"

It was a sign of an increasingly lax attitude that would in later years take over Elvis's sessions completely – and it was another way for him to indicate his unhappiness at the material he was given to work with. On June 6, Elvis finally took matters into his own hands, kicking off the session by picking up an acoustic guitar and accompanying himself on 'It Ain't No Big Thing (But It's Growing),' a solo record by Charlie Louvin, a member of the Louvin Brothers, an act with whom Elvis had toured in the 50s. While working the song out, a lively jam developed, later entitled 'I Didn't Make It On Playing Guitar,' after a phrase Elvis called out during the number. It later appeared on 1996's *Essential Elvis Volume 4: A Hundred Years From Now*.

This was followed by a song that should have been perfect for him, Dusty Springfield's 'You Don't Have To Say You Love Me.' Instead, his performance was curiously disappointing, the song taken at too fast a tempo, and not building to the kind of dramatic climax that would seem obvious for such a number. 'Just Pretend' was a far more successful depiction of fraught emotion, with Elvis gently restrained during the verses, then fully unleashing his feelings on the choruses (he'd asked Jerry to "Drive me on, it helps me sing better" during the passages with high notes). But the remaining songs had little to recommend them. 'This Is Our Dance' was easy listening schmaltz, with takes breaking down due to Elvis's laughter ("That was our dance?" says Jerry, "I don't think so!"). 'Life' was a story-of-creation number that even Elvis's reverent vocal couldn't keep from dragging. The band struggled through 20 takes, causing Elvis to exclaim at one point "The goddamn thing is as long as life!" in exasperation. 'Heart Of Rome' wasn't much better, a bland tale of separated lovers, dressed up with a touch of Neapolitan flavor to disguise its shortcomings; it was inspired, according to the composers, by the current popularity of *The Godfather*. "It wasn't really a good song, but it was fun to play," Jerry says.

By now, 20 finished tracks had been recorded over three nights – of varying quality, but still an impressive number. One reason for the high turnover was that the songs tended to be laid down very quickly, with all but three completed in no more than nine takes. "In Muscle Shoals, we worked like they did in Memphis," says Norbert. "We literally would do 40, 50 takes, trying to come up with the best arrangement and the best feel. Nashville was a totally different way of producing. We would play a song once, and talk about it for 60 seconds. And it might be, 'Hey David, rather than the keyboard in the intro, what do you think about having James take the intro and you pick it up after the first chorus? You think that's a good idea? Great, let's do it.' So I don't know, it was a different way of working. A lot of the [master] takes were second and third takes. That means we played it once with Elvis as he went through it, then they turned the red light on and started to roll tape. So we maybe played the song two, three, four times. And Elvis would go in and listen, and if it was pretty damn close to being a master, he'd ask Felton to play it again. And we'd go, 'Oh, God.' And he'd ask him to play it again until he sold himself on the fact that the take was good enough and we'd move on to another song." "If it wasn't happening after three or four takes, he'd move on," said James Burton.

While the musicians felt they played well enough, they did find themselves wishing they could spend a bit more time on the songs to make them even better. "There were times I wanted to re-do it, thought it could feel better, thought we could change it," says Jerry. "We all did. But we didn't have the privilege of having our way. They didn't give [engineer] Al Puchucki enough time to work on the drums. I'm used to going in at least an hour early if I can and getting my drums to sound the way they should sound. We couldn't do that on the Elvis stuff. We just put 'em out there and they were miked and we were told to start playing as soon as we got there, and we'd play for hours."

In an attempt to work longer on a song, Norbert and David Briggs soon worked out a little ploy between themselves to get a chance for another take. While listening to a playback, Norbert would nudge Elvis in the ribs and say, "Elvis, look, would you do one more for me? I've got a great idea going into the chorus and I'd really like to be able to do this." Elvis was generally quick to agree, calling out, "Hey guys, could we do one more for Putt?" Then it would be David's turn: "Hey Elvis, would you do one more for me?" "And that way, we could sometimes get two or three extra takes," Norbert explains.

Elvis had already recorded more than enough songs for the one album and two singles that were required by RCA, but it was felt worthwhile to press on and stockpile material for future release. So it was initially discouraging when the June 7 session got off to a less than inspiring start with 'When I'm Over You,' another from Shirl Milete, this time a thoroughly limp pop song. "We didn't like playing them," says Jerry of such material, which reminded the musicians too much of Elvis's movie songs. "They were hard to play. They didn't have any feel, they didn't make sense, they weren't laid out well – nothing was good about the material. You can do just so much. If you don't have a melody or a strong rhythmical feel to go with it, you don't have anything. We wound up with nothing and we'd have to fabricate it all, including Elvis, to even make it what it was."

It wasn't surprising that this became another moment when Elvis wanted to go his own way. "He got tired of it," Jerry explains. "He wanted to cut a bunch of old stuff. That one night he said that's what he wanted to do, and that's what we did. It was fun. We had a lot of fun, lots of fun." The fun began with Elvis suddenly going into Eddy Arnold's 'I Really Don't Want To Know,' giving it the kind of soulful performance that had been noticeably missing from many of the newer songs. Next, he got back to 'Faded Love,' as the lyrics had finally been provided; in contrast to the faster version he'd started recording on June 4, the song was now given a slower rock swing, with Elvis clearly enjoying himself. He was then inspired to turn in a bravura performance of Ernest Tubb's 'Tomorrow Never Comes,' a song that steadily rises in power over four minutes, Elvis sounding oddly triumphant as he hits the final high notes in a song ostensibly about a failed love affair. This wasn't a number that could be knocked off in a few takes; "If I broke there, you can imagine how bad it's going to be later on," Elvis said when one take fell apart during the first verse. He pushed on through 13 takes, later redoing the ending to the final note properly. "Yeah, that was a rockin' beast," says Jerry. "He had those hands out there just goin' at me while we recorded."

There was a step back into a contemporary mode with the mid-tempo 'The Next Step Is Love,' a number with a few lyrical oddities (eg the line about not tasting the icing on the cake "we've been baking with the past"), which sounds flat on record; it was much more successful in live performance. Then it was back to country with 'Make The World Go Away,' a country hit for Ray Price in 1953, and here given a grandiose arrangement that would readily translate to Elvis's live act. In contrast, Willie Nelson's 'Funny How Time Slips Away' was suitably low key, with Elvis's laidback vocal subtly disguising the song's lyrical barbs tossed toward a former lover. 'I Washed My Hands In Muddy Water' was a dizzy pleasure along the lines of 'I Got My Mojo Working,' with Elvis carried away by the propulsive energy. The session ended with an unusual choice, 'Love Letters,' a song Elvis had previously recorded back in 1966 at the same studio. David Briggs, who'd played piano on the original, thought he could improve on this performance and started playing the song, which Elvis readily took up. "Anything you did in front of him, he started singing," says Jerry. "'Love Letters' is fantastic. Good and soulful."

The sessions continued for one more night, beginning with 'There Goes My Everything.' It was the kind of love-gone-wrong song that could easily become overly mawkish, but Elvis turned in a graceful performance that impressed the musicians. "That damn vocal just tells you everything about Elvis Presley," declares Norbert. "He went for it on the first take. He's not being cool, he's not being conservative. It's like he's standing up at the plate and he's already got two strikes, and here comes this fast ball, and he's going for it, and he's going to knock it out of the park. The reason we loved Presley above almost all the others was that he was like a raw nerve. When he got up there, the red light came on, he's going to fucking kill it, he's going to knock it out of the park. He's not holding anything back. And for us, as a rhythm section, it meant we had to be there as well."

But most of the other songs fell short of that standard. 'If I Were You' was thoroughly unremarkable, the vaguely religious 'Only Believe' too lugubrious to be truly inspiring (though Elvis tries to rise to the challenge during the bridge), and despite what Jerry felt was "a pretty melody," 'Sylvia' was simply an undistinguished ballad. But the sessions ended on a high note with 'Patch It Up,' a terrific rocker co-written by Eddie Rabbit (who'd written 'Kentucky Rain' and 'Inherit The Wind,' recorded at American). The song had an urgent drive from the very first take, which made it work well in live performance. "'Patch it Up' is a good tune," says Jerry. "It came out well."

A grand total of 34 songs had been completed, the most productive sessions of Elvis's life. And if there were no break-out singles, there were still a number of creditable performances.

Nonetheless, some of the musicians still had a lingering feeling that they could have sounded better. "I mean, I like all of it because Elvis was such a great guy and I enjoyed playing on it," says Jerry. "But as far as good-sounding records, no, they didn't sound good. They had the equipment to do it with; they just didn't take the time."

On the other hand, for Norbert, the relaxed feel of the songs enhances the performances. "That whole record is loose, you see," he says of *Elvis Country*, the album on which most of the tracks recorded at the June 1970 sessions would appear. "I was amazed at how loose my playing was; I was playing like I had no fear of making a mistake or doing anything wrong. I was sort of going for it all the time, like Elvis was. He really influenced us to be loose – 'Don't worry about it, just go for it!' And for so many of the acts I worked with, I was very meticulous and very precise and thought the part out pretty well. And it really was like a live Elvis concert. We did it so quickly. And you realize the engineer didn't have a chance to work on the songs either. It was like, 'Well, the King's ready to go, I guess turn the red light on and let's hope for the best, you know.' And I think in view of that, those recordings are excellent. In view of the way they were done, and the pressure everyone was under, the fact they could be loose and fluid, it was just a wonderful thing to hear."

Little more than a month later, the first single from the sessions was released: 'I've Lost You.' The chart placing of Number 32 (Number Nine UK) was disappointing, but it still sold over half a million copies. Rehearsals then began for Elvis's next Vegas engagement on July 14. They were initially held at MGM's studios in Culver City, California, so they could be filmed for an upcoming documentary, then with a working title of *Elvis*. The film's director was Denis Sanders, who'd previously won Oscars for the shorts *A Time Out Of War* (1954) and *Czechoslovakia 1968* (1969). "What we're trying to do is capture Elvis the entertainer from the point of view of the fans, the hotel, and the audience," he explained. "Just as Elvis, or any other performer, alternates fast numbers with slower numbers, say, or creates moods, so will I. We'll have a sad scene, a happy scene, another sad scene, and so on."

In the footage of rehearsals, there was the usual playing around that others have described at Elvis's sessions, perhaps enhanced by the presence of the cameras. But one can also see the kind of attention to detail that Sandi Miller had observed, as when Elvis describes to Glen Hardin precisely how he wants the ending of 'Words' to work, and repeatedly goes over a passage in 'Bridge Over Troubled Water' until it matches the arrangement in his head. "It is a surprise to see that he is the guy in charge," a *New York Times* reporter noted, "director, producer, arranger, everything. ... He was a disciplined performer who was having fun in what I've always considered the best possible way to have fun, by working, working very hard with his entire being, belly, blood, and brain to create something." The joy Elvis gets from performing, even in rehearsal, is unmistakable, as he loses himself in a performance of 'That's All Right' that is in some ways more energetic than his rendition in the actual show, or when he throws his body around with such vigor during 'Polk Salad Annie' that he tears out the seat of his pants.

With no scheduling conflicts, Ronnie Tutt was back on drums, and he would remain as drummer for the rest of Elvis's live career. As Elvis had continued to add karate routines to the show, Ronnie ended up studying karate himself. "I found that I had to," he explains. "As he developed more martial arts moves in his songs, and at the end of songs, I found in order for me to quickly follow him and accent and underscore what he was doing, I became very involved in studying it. I'd had some interest in karate, so it just pushed me over the line of wanting to start studying myself. He would even do some katas, as they call them; it's a series of movements like a dance, and he would do some of those onstage from time to time, like a little quick exhibition, just with drums and him."

Rehearsals moved to RCA's studios on Sunset on July 23, and, after a final day of filming back at Culver City on July 29, to Las Vegas on

August 4. Parker had dubbed the event the 'Elvis Summer Festival,' draping the hallways with banners sporting the phrase, along with stuffed hound dogs wearing imitation straw boaters, creating an atmosphere similar to that in Parker's own offices, which were claustrophobically plastered with Elvis memorabilia. Parker even drafted RCA publicist Grelun Landon's teenage son, Chris, to help sell the boaters. "The Colonel grabbed me and thought I looked cute or something," he says. "So we went out front and sold these stupid straw hats with the word 'Elvis' in big bold letters around the top for a dollar to these Japanese tourists as they came off the bus. The Colonel just had to be hustling all the time. And every dollar I got for the hat I had to turn over to Colonel. Here he is with his multi-million-dollar star, but he just couldn't stand not hustling somebody for something. But you had to like him." Even the casino's dealers were used as promotional props, having to wear hats and armbands bearing the word "Elvis." On seeing the dealers so attired while walking through the casino one day, Elvis laughed and said, "Hey guys, it's not my fault!" The hotel's restaurants also offered an "Elvis Special" of "Polk salad" with corn muffins and honey for $1.95.

The cameras were rolling on opening night, August 10, capturing the parade of stars arriving for the single evening show (Sammy Davis, Jr, actor Cary Grant, flamboyant singer/actress Charo), along with Elvis backstage reading telegrams wishing him good luck ("Here's hoping that you have a very successful opening and that you break both legs. Tom Jones"). Bearing in mind the need to avoid repeating songs for the planned live album, the opening shows had very few of Elvis's 50s hits. Opening night itself had just three, including the first song, 'That's All Right.' In place of the urgency of the Comeback Special version, and the manic edge that had infused the renditions of his 50s songs just a year ago, there was now a bold confidence, the sense of a firm hand at the helm, no matter how many goofy adlibs might be dropped in. The 'Mystery Train'/'Tiger Man' medley was just as exciting, with Elvis prone to hanging on to the mic stand and whipping his body back and forth during the instrumental breaks. 'Love Me Tender' continued the ritual of Elvis dispensing kisses to the women in attendance; he was now frequently making forays into the audience himself.

But most of the set on opening night was comprised of new material, with only 'I've Lost You' representing his recent hits. Instead, the show emphasized Elvis's skills as an interpretive artist and live performer. 'Something' had a delicacy missing from his version of 'Yesterday,' enhanced by the angelic solo soprano line sung by Millie Kirkham (who'd provided backing vocals on Elvis's records since 1957, and had been specifically hired for the first week of the engagement). 'I Just Can't Help Believin'' (then a current hit for B.J. Thomas), with its light country flavour, was perfect for Elvis. He threw himself wholeheartedly into 'The Next Step Is Love,' and turned in excellent performances of both 'You've Lost That Lovin' Feelin'' and 'Bridge Over Troubled Water.' It could be said that the show mirrored the rehearsals, in that it was less about showing off his own new work, and more about showcasing songs that Elvis loved, and loved to perform – essentially a celebration of his musical influences. As *Variety* wrote in its review: "Presley is cool and very collected all the way through his full hour, knowing just what to do every minute."

The following day, the engagement went back to the usual schedule of two shows per night, with filming continuing through August 13 (after which Millie Kirkham was replaced by Kathy Westmoreland). 'Polk Salad Annie' had become an audience favorite, with a wonderful spoken word lead-in that explained exactly what the mythical 'polk salad' was ("It looks something like a turnip green"), Elvis punctuating the tale with some body moves: "I said *polk* ... ," when Elvis would pump his fist to the side once, then concluding with "... *salad!*" with Elvis pumping his fist twice, a foretaste of how he would end the song, his hands flying as Ronnie Tutt's drums accented every move, before dropping to one knee on the final chord. It nicely complemented 'Suspicious Minds,' which now regularly preceded the standard closer, 'Can't Help Falling In Love.' Elvis now played around with the coda for several minutes, pumping his fist and body to the side, then, as the song quieted, leaning down to the side on one knee, his other leg straight out, going nearly to the floor, then standing up and leaning down in the other direction (frequently the occasion for him to crack a joke about how tight his suit was), finally leaping back up and spinning around the stage as the song rose to full volume again.

Throughout the run, new songs were dropped in as well; a very bluesy rendition of 'Stranger In My Own Home Town' had been rehearsed but unfortunately didn't make it into the show (it was later released on the *Walk A Mile In My Shoes* boxed set). The recently recorded 'Stranger In The Crowd' made a rare appearance. 'Little Sister' became a regular part of the act, segueing into The Beatles' 'Get Back.' There were also unexpected covers (a medley of Johnny Cash's 'I Walk The Line' and 'Folsom Prison Blues,' a pretty rendition of 'When The Snow Is On The Roses'). And his inclusion of 'Oh Happy Day,' recently popularized by The Edwin Hawkins Singers, was the first step in his bringing more religious-themed songs to his performances.

Still, while acknowledging that "you could tell Elvis loved being out there, the freedom of being able to be on a stage," Ronnie Tutt feels that Elvis was at his best during the midnight show, which was free of the distractions of the dinner show. "Here was probably the most sought after entertainer in all the world at that particular time, right in front of these people's eyes, and they're sitting there having dinner," he says. "There's something real strange about that. You have people ordering, the waiter drops a fork and it makes a loud noise – you can imagine that in a big room full of people. When you think about it, here we are up there singing, playing our hearts out, and these people are sitting there dining? What's that all about? That's why he loved the second show, because it was more like a concert. People were sitting there excited, they were pretty loose by then, there was a great feeling of anticipation, they'd been standing in long lines, the evening was on – it was time to get down."

Jerry Carrigan was invited to Vegas during the run and was highly impressed by Elvis's show. "Oh, Lord have mercy!" he says. "It like was so much energy you thought the building was going to come up off of the ground. It was unreal. That big orchestra. And them all miked well and playing great. Oh man. And they were poppin' 'em, man, just one after the other, just knockin' your head off with it. It was wonderful. And the women, they were rippin' at him, I ain't kiddin.' If they coulda got on that stage, they'd have stripped him naked."

Carrigan was invited up to Elvis's suite after the show, and arrived in a well-lubricated condition. He soon found himself being admonished by Felton Jarvis, also in attendance, who told him "All right, Carrigan. You're drunk. Don't let Elvis see you this way." "And I said, 'Felton, Elvis is a big boy now,'" Jerry recalls. "And then Elvis walked over and said, 'Hey Jerry. Fix yourself a drink.' First thing he said to me! He had this big ol' bar, and I said, 'Thank you Elvis. I think I will.' So I fixed me a big ol' strong drink and he said, 'Come here, I want to talk to you about some overdubbing when you get back to Nashville. You know that song we did? I want you to overdub those triplets again. I loved what you played. Put it on there more for me. Can you do that?' And I said 'Sure, I'll do anything I can for you.' And he said 'I appreciate that Jerry. You have a good time; this is my suite, you can do anything up here you want to.'

"And Felton was standing there like, 'Damn you Elvis, I just told him he couldn't do anything!'" Jerry continues. "He said to me, 'You get your ass over there in the corner and be quiet.' I said, 'Man, how can I do that with all these beautiful girls around here?' I wasn't married at the time. I wasn't working, I was drinking, I had a pocket full of money, out there on Elvis's payroll. I loved it. And there were girls everywhere. I mean, literally, everywhere! Funny how that guy drew 'em!"

Two events marred the engagement. On August 14, a paternity suit was filed against Elvis in LA by Patricia Ann Parker, who claimed she'd become pregnant due to a liaison between her and Elvis during his previous Vegas stint (blood tests later determined Elvis was not the father). More disturbing to him were the physical threats. On August

23, an anonymous caller to the hotel said Elvis would be kidnapped that night, and in the early morning of August 28, Joe Esposito's wife was called at home and told there was a plot to kill Elvis, and for $50,000 the caller would reveal the name of the killer. The FBI was notified, and Elvis was told he could cancel the show. But he chose not to, instead asking members of his entourage who were not in town to fly in and serve as additional bodyguards. He instructed them that if he was killed they should get to the "sonofabitch" before the police did, declaring, "I don't want him sitting around afterwards like Charlie Manson with a grin on his face saying 'I killed Elvis Presley.'" When he took to the stage that night, he had a gun in each boot, and his bodyguards were also armed. During the dinner show, a man in the audience shouted "Elvis!" at one point, and everyone froze. But he only wanted to call out a song request and the show continued without further incident. The would-be kidnapper/killer was never heard from again. But it was a sign for Elvis that stepping outside his cloistered world didn't come without some risk.

Otherwise, it had been another successful, sold-out season for Elvis. Due to demand, an additional 3:30am show was added on the final night, with the band surprising Elvis by sending a basset hound on stage at the beginning of 'Hound Dog.' The International also presented Elvis with a special belt, made of silver and overlaid with gold, sporting a large buckle that read "Worlds Championship Attendance Record" and was studded with sapphires, rubies, and diamonds. The belt had been designed by Nudie Cohn (who had also designed Elvis's famous gold lamé suit in the 50s), and came in an embossed leather case. Elvis wore it proudly, explaining to one reporter, "It's like a trophy but I wear it around. It's just to show off."

There was scarcely any time to rest. On September 8, Elvis attended the opening of Nancy Sinatra's show at the International, then on September 9 he headed out on a six city, eight show tour, that would play Phoenix, Arizona; St Louis, Missouri; Detroit, Michigan; Miami Beach and Tampa, Florida; and Mobile, Alabama. With the exception of The Imperials, who were replaced by The Hugh Jarrett Singers, it was the same line-up of musicians that had accompanied Elvis in Las Vegas. The International's new orchestra leader Joe Guercio was also on hand to direct a pick-up orchestra in each city (along with a single trumpet player from the International's orchestra). The setlist was also largely the same as for the Vegas shows.

Aside from a bomb threat that had been called in for the first Phoenix show (which turned out to be unfounded), the tour went off without a hitch, the venues sold out, the audiences ecstatic. Elvis's new concert promoters, Jerry Weintraub and Tom Hulett, also introduced Elvis to modern day concert sound systems, including onstage monitors so he could hear himself; previously, he'd simply used whatever sound system the venue had.

Everyone enjoyed the chance to escape the rigors of playing Vegas. "Oh, absolutely," says Ronnie Tutt. "We all really felt a release from that. We loved the touring, the going into the cities, and playing in the coliseums – the giant tuna cans, we called them. A promoter's daydream. Yeah, it's much more rewarding to do that."

The tour ended September 14, and another recording session had been scheduled in Nashville for September 21. Though an abundance of material had been recorded in June, there had been enough country songs recorded that it was decided the next studio album would be a country record, and a few more songs were needed to fit in with this theme. Elvis was unhappy about having to go back in the studio, and made his feelings clear by not bothering to show up the first night, and then, when he finally turned up the next day, constantly complaining about how long the session was taking. The same musicians who had worked with him in June were used, aside from James Burton, who was unable to attend; he was replaced by Eddie Hinton.

Elvis quickly laid down four songs in six hours, beginning with 'Snowbird,' a light, upbeat pop song. 'Rags To Riches' and 'Where Did They Go, Lord' (the former, a hit for Tony Bennett in 1953, the latter from the A.L. Owens/Dallas Frazier team that had written 'True Love

Travels On A Gravel Road' and 'Wearin' That Loved On Look') would be paired on a single the following year and each brought out a stirring performance from Elvis. 'Rags To Riches' in particular pushed Elvis to hit some soaring high notes, but he rushed through the song in four takes, reminding everyone he had to leave by 12:30am.

As with much of the livelier material at the June sessions, the cover of 'Whole Lotta Shakin' Goin' On' came about as the result of a jam. "I was over there just foolin' around, playing on the tom toms and the snare and the bass drum," explains Jerry Carrigan. "And he began singing 'Whole Lotta Shakin' Goin On' to that beat, of all things." "Lord, let's cut it that way!" Elvis said, though a first run-through left him with mixed feelings; told it was a good effort, he replied: "OK. That means it's mediocre." His impatience was further evident as he instructed Jerry to come in for the final fade out, "… when I get tired of singing the song. Which is going to be very shortly because I've been singing it too long already." The final version races by so fast it sounds on the verge of going out of control, but Elvis carries on for over four and a half minutes, working himself up to a near frenzy. Like Elvis's cover of Chuck Berry's 'Johnny B. Goode,' it doesn't surpass Jerry Lee Lewis's definitive version ("It's not really good, it's just weird. It's a weird beat," in Jerry Carrigan's view), but it is nonetheless the kind of energetic rocker that would have worked well in his live show.

The final album drawn from the two sessions, *Elvis Country*, released in 1971, would have the following tracks: 'Snowbird,' 'Tomorrow Never Comes,' 'Little Cabin On The Hill,' 'Whole Lotta Shakin' Goin' On,' 'Funny How Times Slips Away,' 'I Really Don't Want To Know,' 'There Goes My Everything,' 'It's Your Baby, You Rock It,' 'The Fool,' 'Faded Love,' 'I Washed My Hands In Muddy Water,' and 'Make The World Go Away,' with 'I Was Born Ten Thousand Years Ago' used as a linking track throughout the album (it was later released in its entirety on 1972's *Elvis Now*). In its way, it was as much a 'roots' album as *From Elvis In Memphis*, spotlighting country instead of soulful rhythm & blues, relaxed and freewheeling where the other album had been carefully crafted.

There continued to be a steady stream of record releases. August saw the release of Elvis's first boxed set, *Worldwide 50 Gold Award Hits Vol. 1*, which reached Number 45 (Number 49 UK), not bad for a four-album set. In October came the release of Elvis's new single, 'You Don't Have To Say You Love Me,' which reached Number 11 (Number Nine UK) and sold 800,000 copies. The release of the *From Memphis To Vegas/From Vegas To Memphis* set as two separate records in November (renamed *Elvis In Person At The International Hotel* and *Back In Memphis*) made sense, as some potential buyers may not have wished to buy the double album. But the October release of the budget collection *Almost In Love*, which contained no previously unreleased material and wasn't a greatest hits collection, only served to flood the market with unnecessary product. Especially as two more album releases followed in November, the budget holiday record *Elvis's Christmas Album*, a repackaging of his Christmas songs, and the album that would accompany the release of the documentary, now entitled *Elvis: That's The Way It Is*.

Though ostensibly a soundtrack, only two songs on the album were actually in the film. And only four songs were live performances; the rest were taken from the June Nashville sessions with applause overdubbed in places. This wasn't without precedent; a number of Elvis's movie soundtracks had featured different versions of the songs from the ones performed in the film, and the version of 'If I Can Dream' heard in the Comeback Special was not the same one that had appeared on the soundtrack album. It's likely most people didn't notice the difference; there were no home videos or DVDs with which to make comparisons.

So, though not presented as such, *That's The Way It Is* could be regarded as more of a studio album than a live release. The running order was 'I Just Can't Help Believin'' (from the August 11 dinner show, and in the film), 'Twenty Days And Twenty Nights,' 'How The Web Was Woven,' 'Patch It Up' (from the August 12 dinner show, and in the film), 'Mary In The Morning,' 'You Don't Have To Say You Love Me,' 'You've Lost That Lovin' Feeling'' (from the August 13 midnight show, and not in the film), 'I've Lost You' (from the August 13 dinner show, and not in the film), 'Just Pretend,' 'Stranger In The Crowd,' 'The Next Step Is Love,' and 'Bridge Over Troubled Water.' The songs showed Elvis's further move away from the brooding material on *From Elvis In Memphis* and *Back In Memphis* (just as the songs on the upcoming *Elvis Country* would). For all the passion of his delivery, the music was closer to pop than anything Elvis had recorded since the movie years (though the songs were decidedly superior). In some ways, the record could be considered a step back, musically – or at least a step to the middle of the road. And though it charted somewhat lower than recent albums at Number 21 (Number 12 UK), it still sold more than half a million copies.

As for the film, Denis Sanders's intention had been to "capture the excitement of Elvis." To that end, he not only filmed rehearsals and performances, he also shot interview footage with fans, personnel at the International Hotel (including vice president Alex Shoofey), and teen magazine *Tiger Beat* editor Ann Moses, among others. Parker objected to the extraneous footage, feeling it took away from his star. But in fact, such scenes give the movie a well-rounded look at the phenomenon that is Elvis, making it more than just a concert film. The fans who say their cat likes Elvis may be comical to some, but their sincerity and low-key manner is surprisingly sweet, and the fact that Elvis can stir such devotion in his fans makes it clear why his popularity has remained undiminished. It is true the film is more observational than insightful, something that could have been different had Elvis, or even the band members, been interviewed, as was noted in some reviews: "What does Presley think and what is he really like?" asked the *New York Times*, adding that the interviews are "simply … random testimonies about how phenomenal is the Wonder Boy still." But given that so few of Elvis's shows were professionally filmed, it's still an invaluable record of Elvis in his prime.

Another short tour was scheduled to coincide with the film's opening on November 11, beginning November 10 in Oakland,

California, and taking in Portland, Oregon; Seattle, Washington; San Francisco, Inglewood (two shows), and San Diego, California; Oklahoma City, Oklahoma; and concluding on November 17 in Denver, Colorado. The Imperials were back, and were excited about being on the road with Elvis's show. "That first tour was exciting," said Joe Mescale. "We felt like history was being made. It was loose, the organization wasn't together yet, but nobody cared, because it was so darned exciting." Parker, concerned that ticket prices be reasonable, had sent the promoters a telegram beforehand, stressing: "We want our fans to be taken care of. When they wait in line for hours and hours they are privileged customers. They come first."

Future music journalist Harvey Kubernik was in the audience at the evening show in Inglewood on November 14. Harvey had grown up in the Los Angeles area, and been interested in Elvis's music since the 50s. "When I heard 'Don't Be Cruel,' it was the thing that made me want to investigate the drums; I was in a surf band briefly called The Riptides in the mid 60s," he says. He regularly saw Elvis's films, impressed that some were filmed at the MGM lot in Culver City, not far from where he lived. "I knew even really young that the plots were sort of silly," he says. "However, if you have the hots for Shelley Fabares or Debra Paget ... I always like looking at hot girls on the screen. And I worshipped *Viva Las Vegas*. Worshipped. Yes, partly for Ann-Margret. But the bottom line is, that movie rocked."

Nonetheless, he admits to being one of the few who found the concert segments of the Comeback Special "corny ... I thought he was dressing like Jim Morrison. And I didn't quite understand all those beehive girls being planted around Elvis, because the chicks I knew were ironing their hair, they were wearing mini-skirts and peasant blouses and stuff. These girls seemed like throwbacks to a sock-hop. But then again, it was just great to see him. And then I just had my mind blown on 'If I Can Dream.' I just thought it was a monumental rock moment in history, that song."

He'd been aware of Elvis's return to live concerts in Vegas, but says,

"The concept of going to Las Vegas for a 17-year-old really wasn't in the cards. I thought it was kind of an adult thing." Indeed, Harvey's parents had already seen Elvis in 1969. "I grilled them about it," he says. "My mom said they were at the blackjack table with him and that he was a 'handsome devil!' And my dad said something like, 'He was good, but I was hoping Julie London was playing.'" But when Harvey bought his ticket for the November 14 show he found that his own friends did not share his enthusiasm. "I remember people saying, 'You're paying $7.50 for that guy?'" he says. "I took a lot of shit for it. I could never get a date to see Elvis. I tried. Girls wanted to see Deep Purple. Or J. Geils or Bad Company. [When Harvey became a rock journalist, he later accompanied Paul Rodgers to Elvis's May 11 1974 show at the Forum in Inglewood; "He had his mind blown ... he kept saying, 'It's Elvis Presley!'"] Elvis was kind of under the radar; he was kind of viewed as yesterday's news by a lot of people. I never could hear him on progressive FM radio or free-form underground radio. But I worshipped 'Suspicious Minds,' and I still think 'Kentucky Rain' is one of my top ten songs of all time. So I went by myself on the bus."

The audience was as ecstatic as others on the tour; "Colonel Parker, I'm sure, liked the 10,000 cameras going off at once," says Harvey. But he was surprised by the short set (which ran under an hour) and the number of medleys in the show. "I didn't anticipate this concept that we now call 'medleys,'" he explains. "I want the full versions. That was throwing me for a loop, because remember I'm seeing John Mayall, Deep Purple, and blues and soul groups, and they would extend their songs when you saw them live. Elvis was doing some bits and pieces, or jamming eight songs all together in one. I got a little too much maudlin and slow songs and not enough rock'n'roll for me. I kinda wanted the raw animal guy that I had seen on the '68 special. And he really wasn't playing guitar; the guitar was a prop, and then there was some shtick, you know, false starts with tunes. Don't get me wrong; I still dug it and he sounded great. I liked hearing his voice in person. I couldn't believe how good 'Can't Help Falling In Love' sounded.

"I also remember something that I thought was distasteful at the time," he adds. "After Sammy Shore did his set, they unrolled this big banner touting the upcoming documentary, *That's The Way It Is*, on the stage. I thought that was a little cheesy. Now we have so much signage on stage it makes sense, but then it was kind of weird."

Unknown to the audience, between the afternoon and evening shows, a process server had served Elvis with papers pertaining to the ongoing paternity suit. Though not explicitly mentioning the incident, during the evening show he protested to the audience, "There have been a lot of things written about me ... and most of it is not true," then went on to cite his record sales and the number of gold record awards he'd received. The shows themselves set yet another record, with ticket sales of over $300,000, easily surpassing the previous record of $238,000 set by The Rolling Stones when they appeared at the venue in 1969. Elvis also wore a unique jumpsuit at the evening show, with fringes on the arms that went nearly to floor (pictured on the cover of the 1973 album *Elvis*); it would actually be the only time he wore the suit on stage, as the fringe kept getting in the way. Fans hanging outside Elvis's home the next day noticed the suit being taken away by a dry cleaner's, and persuaded the driver to stop and take the suit out of his truck so they could take pictures of it.

Though the tour was another sell-out, and the audience reaction was invariably enthusiastic, there were some dissenting voices. Albert Goldman, who would later become infamous for his highly critical biography of Presley, had already cited what he felt was a formulaic quality about Elvis's performances in his review of the February Vegas engagement for *Life* magazine, calling the show a "monodrama," where "Every number ends with a classically struck profile." Other reviewers now echoed this theme. The *St Louis Post Dispatch* described Elvis as "an imitation of swivel-hipped Elvis Presley circa 1956 ... [His] actions and songs were carefully programmed last night to feed the myth." The *St Petersburg Times* stated, "He has frozen rock 'n roll into a kind of parody of what the old, real thing was like, complete with pastel lights, backup singers, a big band, gaudy costumes," while *The Oregonian* (Portland) observed, "Every tune was a lush production that sounded like the previous one." The *Seattle Times* was particularly harsh, calling the concert "disappointing," criticizing the length of time Elvis performed ("perhaps 40 minutes, but it seemed much less"), and concluding with a sense of regret, "The tone of the concert was strange, as Elvis clearly had the talent and ability to have been putting on a top-notch show. But instead of satisfying the audience with his music, he relied on blatant gimmickry to garner applause."

Elvis had of course always had his detractors. And even the negative reviews noted the favorable crowd response and that Elvis was generally in fine voice. But they did suggest that an element of pageantry was becoming as much a part of the show as the music; that, indeed, the crowd's adulation was a distraction from the music, that the show was less a concert and more of a ritual. There were also comments about the carnival-like atmosphere at the shows, especially regarding the perpetual hawking of merchandise. Even in Vegas, not a city to shy away from razzle-dazzle, the amount of Presley memorabilia covering the walls of the International was seen as being tacky, cheapening Elvis's status as a performer who was now being taken seriously once again.

But others expressed different views: "Whatever they say ('they' being the pseudo-sophisticated critics who have forgotten the purpose of music), Elvis sings damned well," Denver's *Rocky Mountain News* assured its readers. "Technically, he has the ability to maneuver through all the songs he chooses with accurate enough intonation and an obviously swinging rhythmic drive." Still, the wild freedom of the '69 shows had now been somewhat toned down.

With nothing to occupy him until his next Las Vegas engagement in January, Elvis was at a loose end. Always in search of a new distraction, he decided to go shopping. Over the first two weeks of December, he bought over $20,000 worth of guns, paid for the weddings of three members of his entourage, bought Joe Esposito a house, paid for renovations on his own home in Beverly Hills, gave Jerry Schilling and one of his girlfriends new Mercedes, and made several jewelry purchases for the upcoming Christmas holidays, many of them featuring his new custom-designed logo, a lightning bolt topped by the letters 'TCB' for 'Taking Care of Business – in a flash' (sources differ on whether the logo was inspired by a similar one used by the West Coast mafia, or the lightning bolt on the costume of comic book hero Captain Marvel). When his father complained about the lavish spending, Elvis tried to mollify him – by buying him a new Mercedes, along with one for Charlie Hodge.

But it was no laughing matter to Vernon and Priscilla, who were now as alarmed as they'd been in 1967 when Elvis had been spending just as extravagantly on his ranch. With Elvis failing to respond to their entreaties, they asked Parker for advice. He suggested they confront Elvis again, which they did on December 19, provoking a fierce argument. Elvis was furious at being told what to do – whose money was it, anyway? Eventually, his anger led him to storm out of the house. Everyone expected him to return in a few hours, but Elvis had decided, in a show of independence, to do something he'd rarely done in adult life: go off on his own.

He caught a plane for Washington, DC, where he checked into the Hotel Washington. But without a ready plan, some of his nerve left him, and he soon checked out of the hotel and flew to Los Angeles. When changing planes in Dallas, he called Jerry Schilling, then living in LA, with the details about his arrival. Jerry duly arranged for a limo to meet Elvis, and the two were taken to Elvis's Beverly Hills home, where Jerry also arranged for a doctor to see him, as Elvis appeared to be suffering an allergic reaction to some medication he was taking.

After the doctor left, Elvis slept, with Jerry becoming increasingly unnerved by the developing drama: "For the first time in 15 years, nobody close to Elvis knew where he was. Except me." When Elvis awoke, he announced he was going back to Washington, and asked

Jerry to go with him. Jerry had no idea what was going on, but felt it incumbent upon him to look after his friend. He did elicit Elvis's permission to call Graceland to let Vernon and Priscilla know he was all right, and Elvis agreed, as long they weren't told where he was; he also asked that Jerry get Sonny West to join them in Washington.

While on the plane, Elvis learned that Senator George Murphy was on board, and went back to speak with him. On returning to his seat, he asked the stewardess for some stationery and began writing a letter. When he handed it to Jerry to read, Jerry was stunned to see that Elvis had been writing a missive to President Richard Nixon. The letter expressed Elvis's wish to be of service to the country and his need for "Federal credentials" to help him in this work. "The drug culture, the hippie elements, the SDS, Black Panthers, etc, do not consider me as their enemy or as they call it The Establishment. I call it America and I love it!" he wrote, underlining the last sentence for emphasis. He also added that he had "done an in-depth study of drug abuse and Communist brainwashing techniques and I am right in the middle of the whole thing where I can and will do the most good."

The desire to serve his country aside, Elvis's real intention was to secure a badge from the Bureau of Narcotics and Dangerous Drugs (BNDD) that would designate him as a Federal Agent. Elvis had first seen this prize the previous month, when John O'Grady, a private eye and former police officer Elvis's lawyer had hired to help out on the paternity suit, had introduced him to Paul Frees. Frees, known for his extensive voice-over work (he provided the voices for "Boris Badinov" in the *Rocky & Bullwinkle* cartoons, John Lennon and George Harrison in *The Beatles* cartoon series, Michael Jackson in *The Jackson 5 Cartoon Show*, and the "Pillsbury Doughboy" in commercials for the food company, to mention a few), was also an undercover narcotics agent, and had such a badge. Elvis, who was building his own impressive collection of badges from police departments around the country, was determined to get such a badge for himself.

On arriving in Washington on the morning of December 21, Elvis dropped his letter off at the White House gates, then returned to the Washington Hotel. He next went to the BNDD offices, where Senator Murphy had promised to arrange a meeting with the Bureau's director, John Ingersoll, as well as FBI director J. Edgar Hoover. Meanwhile, his letter to Nixon was slowly wending its way through the White House bureaucracy. It was first given to staff secretary Dwight Chapin, who quickly brought it to the attention of deputy counsel Egil 'Bud' Krogh. As it happened, Bud had been an Elvis fan since the 50s, first hearing his music while attending prep school in St Louis. "I just loved his music," he says. "I thought wow, this is amazing stuff. I liked his voice. I liked the moves." He also admired the fact that Elvis had served in the army instead of taking an easy way out. "That was a big story for me," he says. "I always respected the entertainers who were able to step out of their careers and contribute their service. I thought he could've got a deferment if he had tried. But he did the job, and I really respected that a lot."

After graduating from the University of Washington School of Law in 1968, Bud went to work for the firm of Hullin, Ehrlichman, Roberts & Hodge, in addition to working alongside John Ehrlichman on Nixon's presidential campaign. When Nixon was elected, he was offered a job in the new administration. "And being given the opportunity to go work on the White House staff five months after you graduate is like a kid being taken to the largest candy store and told 'Have at it!'" he says. His first job was a staff assistant, reading FBI reports; by December 1970, Bud's job was working as a liaison between the Department of Justice, the FBI, and BNDD.

Bud's first response on being told about Elvis's letter was that it was "a joke. Big joke. I should point out, Dwight Chapin, along with about eight of us, belonged to a little group of guys, including Pat Buchanan [later a conservative commentator and presidential candidate, Buchanan was then working for the Nixon administration as a speechwriter and advisor], that played practical jokes on each other. And so when Chapin goes, 'The King is here,' I figure, oh, all right,

Dwight. And he said, 'No, no, really, he's here.' Of course, I'm looking at the President's schedule, and there are no kings on the schedule.

"So the letter is brought over by this messenger with a red tag on it, and I'm going, it looks like it's written by a sixth grader, seventh grader," he continues. "So I figured, OK, this is really good, this is fun, I'll go along with it. But then in the letter, he has the name 'Jon Burrows' [the pseudonym Elvis said he would be using at the hotel], and he's over at the Washington Hotel ... I figure it's pretty elaborate, but I'll go along with it. So I called over there, and Jerry Schilling answers the phone. And I introduce myself, and say I've got this letter and he says, 'Oh yeah, Elvis wrote that letter.' And I'm going 'OK ...' At that point I was sort of thinking this is for real, but also not too sure. And then I said, 'Well, why don't you come over and meet me first. I'm the audition here.'"

Jerry quickly called the BNDD offices, where Elvis was meeting with deputy director John Finlator. He'd been unable to make any headway with Finlator regarding the badge (even offering to make a donation to the Bureau), and had also been informed that Hoover was out of town. So he was thrilled to hear that a meeting with the President was now a possibility. He instructed Jerry to wait in front of the hotel, and he'd pick him up. As Jerry was waiting, Sonny West arrived in a cab, having just flown in from Memphis. Within minutes, Elvis turned up, and the three were soon on their way to the White House.

"I'd set it up so they could come right over," explains Bud. "And then I get a call from a guy at the north entrance, who says, 'We've got somebody here who looks an awful lot like Elvis Presley. And there are two guys with him. What do you want me to do?' And I said well, bring 'em down. So they escorted them down, they walked in, and I knew then that this was not an impersonator. At which point it was like 'Oh boy. OK. He's here.' I mean, my hand is ice cold. It was just like, 'Oh my gosh. It's Elvis Presley!' And of course my secretary, she's just, 'Oh!'

"I thought Elvis was extremely bright and enthusiastic," says Bud of their initial meeting. "But I was really trying to figure out, what is this all about? He obviously wanted something; he had mentioned some kind of credential in the letter. I didn't know that he had been over at the Bureau of Narcotics and Dangerous Drugs earlier and had asked for one and they said no – that came out later." Nonetheless, Bud felt a meeting with the President would be worthwhile. "I figured, Nixon's never met anyone quite like this guy," he explains. "And Elvis never met anyone quite like Nixon, because they are totally unique people. Then it was just trying to figure out, how can I justify this meeting?"

One of the areas Bud worked on was the administration's anti-drug policy. Entertainers, such as *Dragnet* star Jack Webb and radio/television personality Art Linkletter had been tapped to deliver anti-drug statements, and Bud felt if someone with more youth appeal like Elvis could be enlisted it would be a real coup. "It was just part of policy to try to get help from those parts of our society that could be credible," he says. "Because we weren't credible; we were inherently non-credible. You know – 'Don't use drugs!' Give me a break. I felt if Elvis wants to help out, this could be big."

Bud told Elvis he'd try to arrange for a meeting later that day and suggested he wait at his hotel. He then wrote a memo of talking points for the President. "In my letter, I'm waxing on about maybe getting a new theme – 'Get High On Life' rather than 'Get High On Drugs,'" he says. "I mean, I'm trying to come up with something that will get through the system in about an hour." Meanwhile, Chapin wrote a memo to chief of staff Bob Haldeman, recommending Presley as a "perfect" example of the kind of bright young person the President might wish to meet; Haldeman wrote "You must be kidding," on the memo, but agreed to the meeting. It was ultimately arranged for Elvis to come in during the President's 'Open Hour,' a time period set aside for brief, informal meetings. Elvis was contacted and told to arrive at the White House at 11:45am.

And so, 48 hours after leaving his home in Memphis in a fit of pique, Elvis Presley was about to meet the leader of the free world, an event Bud Krogh agrees was "Totally unique. It was a confluence of a lot of different forces going on. If I had not been an Elvis fan, this would never have happened. It would have just been 'Fine, we'll take the message in.' Or as Chapin said, 'We could pass him off to the Vice President. 'Cause he's already met the Vice President. [Elvis had met Vice President Spiro Agnew the previous month in Palm Springs] Why does he need to come and see the President?' But I was just enthralled with the idea of these two guys meeting each other."

Though dressed in sober dark colors, Elvis's outfit still stood out in stark contrast to the conservative, buttoned-down atmosphere of the Nixon White House. Elvis wore one of the two piece karate-style suits he'd worn during his 1969 Vegas appearances, along with the championship belt he'd recently received; draped over his shoulders was the velvet jacket he'd worn during the 'Guitar Man' production number of the _Elvis_ special (some accounts have mistakenly called this a cape). "He sure wasn't wearing the standard attire for male guests to the Nixon White House," Bud would later note. Of more immediate concern was the fact that Elvis had brought a commemorative Colt .45 to give to the President as a gift. Bud informed him he could not bring a gun into the Oval Office, but it would be held on the President's behalf and given to him later (it's since gone on display at the Nixon Presidential Library).

When it was 12:30pm, Jerry and Sonny waited in the Roosevelt Room while Elvis was escorted across the hall to the Oval Office, with Bud on hand to oversee the meeting. "It's a high-wire act when you have somebody go in and talk to the President," Bud explains. "One thing people don't realize is that when you are the sponsor for a meeting, you're basically validating that this person's OK. That he's not going to do anything weird." Elvis and The President were introduced and shook hands, Elvis then making small talk, showing Nixon the photos he'd brought of his wife and child as a gift, along with his collection of police badges, while Ollie Atkins, the White House photographer, took pictures.

Nixon thanked Elvis for his offer to help with the administration's anti-drug program. "I think you can reach young people in a way no one in the government can," he told him. "I do my thing just by singing, Mr. President," Elvis replied. "I don't make any speeches on stage. I just try to reach them in my own way." He then unexpectedly attacked The Beatles for being "kind of anti-American," making good money in the US, then criticizing the country from the safety of their homes in England.

Elvis's remarks left both the President and Bud perplexed. "I don't want to say Nixon didn't know about The Beatles," says Bud, "but when Elvis started talking about them, he goes 'Beatles?' And I go, 'They're a singing group, popular.' Nixon liked Rachmaninoff, he liked classical music. I mean, I don't know quite how much he knows at this point. And when Elvis said they were saying things that were sort of un-American, Nixon goes 'What?' Elvis didn't mention that [in his letter]. And then he mentioned brainwashing, which I was trying to figure out: why is he telling the President about how he's done a study of brainwashing? And I could see the President, he looks at me like, you know, 'What am I doing here now?'"

Then Elvis got to the heart of the matter, saying, "Mr President, can you get me a badge from the Narcotics Bureau? I've been trying to get a badge from them for my collection." "I was frankly taken aback when Elvis asked him directly," says Bud. "And the President doesn't say yes immediately. He turns to me and says 'Bud, can we get him a badge?'" Bud opted to respond by leaving the matter open for the President to decide: "Well sir, if you want to give him a badge, I think we can get him one." "I'd like to do that. See that he gets one," Nixon affirmed.

"And once that was said, as is clearly the case with the President, a card laid is a card played," says Bud. "In other words, we're going to get him a badge now. And of course Elvis was just, 'mission accomplished.' And he hugged him! He hugged him. I'm just going Oh, gee, no, nobody hugs the President! That was a real surprise to both Nixon and me. Because president hugging wasn't the norm at that time. Ever. You just didn't get that close to the body. Unless you're Secret Service."

Elvis then asked if Nixon had time to meet his bodyguards, and Jerry and Sonny were escorted in. "To them, it was like Elvis can do anything," says Bud. "'He got us in to see the President!'" After introductions were made, Nixon went to his desk to get souvenirs for everyone, from a special gift drawer that was arranged sequentially, with less expensive items, like golf balls and small cuff links with the presidential seal on them in the front, and items of greater value, like 16-caret gold cuff links, at the back. "Those are for heavy hitters," Bud explains. "And Elvis just marched behind the desk with the President, and he's reaching in and the President is reaching in. Then he said, 'Remember, Mr. President, they've got wives.' And so back into the drawer. He's hitting up the President for more swag! And it occurred to me, he didn't get to be the king of rock by not knowing where the gold is! And I'm just watching and the President looks up at me, and the message was, 'He's cleaning me out!' It was four days before Christmas and they scored."

Bud then escorted Elvis, Jerry, and Sonny to the White House mess for lunch, pointing out the Situation Room on the way, causing Elvis to joke "No fighting in the War Room!" a reference to one of his favorite films, _Dr. Strangelove_. "You can't believe how exciting it is for me to take these guys to lunch in the White House mess," says Bud. "People are jaded around there, because you go to a lunch there or even breakfast, and you're going to see the Speaker of the House, Movie Star A, Movie Star B, all famous celebrities. To get invited to the White House mess is a big deal, because now you're having lunch in the inner sanctum of political power. And so I came in with three of them, and plopped ourselves down at a table right in the middle. And there's a round table where all of the staff are eating, and they were staring. A woman came up afterwards and asked for an autograph."

After lunch, everyone returned to Bud's office, Elvis causing a little more excitement, saying hello to people and giving a secretary a hug. At 2pm, John Finlator arrived with Elvis's badge, designating him as a Special Assistant for the BNDD. After thank yous were exchanged,

Jerry was dropped off at the airport to return to LA. Elvis returned to Memphis with Sonny the next day.

"It was an amazing day," says Bud – all the more amazing because it wouldn't be until January 1972 that the public found out about the meeting, in Jack Anderson's 'Washington Merry-Go-Round' column in the *Washington Post*. Both the President and Elvis had indicated they wanted the meeting to be confidential. "So I'm thinking, how does he become a spokesperson for a meeting that never happened?" says Bud. "I was disappointed, because I had hoped that there was going to be some follow up and then I'd be able to talk to Elvis and work with him. And once I heard that they wanted this to be secret, I felt, OK, that means he's not going to be our spokesperson. And then Elvis said, 'I can do the best I can just by singing.' And I realized OK, he doesn't want to step outside his comfort zone. So I wrote the notes up and I put them away."

But of course, Elvis's real reason for meeting with Nixon had been to get a badge. "To Elvis, that's the real deal," says Bud. "And that's the important thing. And I know when I give something the President has authorized, it's going to mean something to that person. However we might see it, it's how he intends to use it or carry it. That's the thing. Still, overall, I loved the meeting."

Though no one at the White House would have been aware of it, the unorthodox meeting also provided something of a rebuke to Vernon and Priscilla's complaints about Elvis's spending; his response to being told what to do was to show how he could meet with the President of the United States on what was little more than a whim. And as a final statement, on returning to Memphis Elvis went right back to doing the very thing that had prompted the argument in the first place – he bought four more Mercedes and another batch of guns. Nixon later wrote Elvis a letter, dated December 31 1970, thanking him for the gifts of the gun and family photos, noting, "I am delighted to have them for my collection of special mementos."

Elvis returned to DC on December 30, still hoping to meet with

Hoover, and was offered a tour of FBI headquarters the next day to compensate for the fact that Hoover was still out of town (though an FBI memo dated December 30 made the Bureau's feelings on the subject clear: "Presley's sincerity and good intentions notwithstanding he is certainly not the type of individual the Director would wish to meet. It is noted at the present time he is wearing his hair down to his shoulders and indulges in wearing all sorts of exotic dress"). The memo by the agent who gave Elvis the tour noted that he again criticized The Beatles for having "laid the groundwork for many of the problems we are having with young people by their filthy unkempt appearances and suggestive music," and offered to report to the FBI if he was approached by entertainers "whose motives and goals he is convinced are not in the best interests of this country." By that evening, he was back at home, hosting a New Year's Eve party at Memphis club TJ's. Hoover later acknowledged the visit in a letter dated January 4 1971, writing: "Your generous comments concerning this Bureau and me are appreciated, and you may be sure we will keep in mind your offer to be of assistance."

In meeting the President and getting his BNDD badge, the year had ended for Elvis on an unexpectedly high note. His final single of the year, 'I Really Don't Want To Know' from the upcoming *Elvis Country*, only reached Number 21, but still enjoyed sales of nearly 700,000 (the single's B-side, 'There Goes My Everything,' was released as the A-side in the UK, and reached Number Six). On December 28, at Sonny West's wedding reception at Graceland, Elvis had a picture taken of himself surrounded by his entourage, all displaying their police badges, with Elvis seated proudly in the middle, exuding an understated satisfaction that shows he is clearly master of his domain.

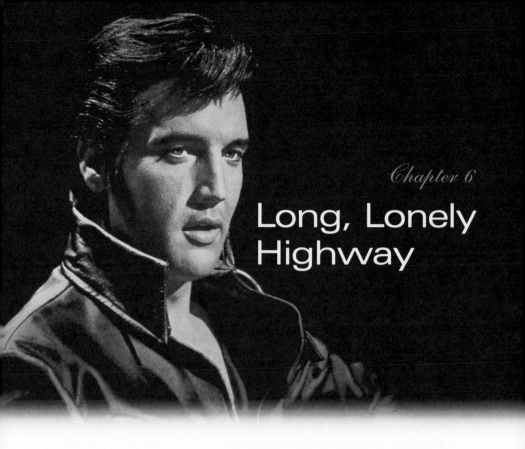

Chapter 6

Long, Lonely Highway

The last six years of Elvis Presley's life were a slow fade; a gradual slide into what some would see as ignominious caricature. But Elvis's physical appearance during his later years – the frequent target of much derision – was only a sign of a greater, deeper, malaise. By the end of his life, it seemed as if Elvis had lost the most precious thing that a performer has: faith in his talent and in himself.

Ironically, the seeds for Elvis's decline were sewn by the very thing that had initially rejuvenated him and his career – his return to live performance. His 1969 Vegas engagement had offered him a worthy challenge, but the thrill was gone all too soon. "People like Lamar Fike talked about how quickly Elvis got burned out on Vegas," said Peter Guralnick, reflecting on the interviews he'd done for *Careless Love*, the second volume of his Elvis biography. "And I'd thought they meant over a period of five years. But I think by the time he came back to

Vegas for the second time, he was no longer as interested. He had
proved that he could do it; he had conquered Las Vegas, he had been
restored on the pop charts. And it wasn't that he ever lost his love for
performing, because I think the connection with the audience was one
of the most important things in his life. But as far as engaging on the
level that he had at the first Las Vegas shows, I don't think it ever
happened again."

Vegas had quickly become a routine – what Ronnie Tutt later
described as "the ultimate gilded cage." And the performing schedule
remained heavy; from 1971 to 1973 Elvis played Vegas twice a year, in
seasons running close to 60 shows each. "It's a peculiar situation when
you're that hot," says Wayne Jackson, the Memphis Horns player who
worked with Elvis at American. "You don't want to stop, 'cause it's good
to you too. But that's what two shows a day will get ya. I mean, come
on, you tune it up and push it as hard as you can, and you have an hour
and a half or two hours, and all that goes out of you and it's a physical
outpouring of energy. Then you stop for an hour, and you go back
and do a second one. Where did that come from? It takes so much out
of you."

Eventually the strain began to show. In 1974, each run was scaled
back to fewer than 30 shows. In 1975, his summer engagement was cut
short after five shows due to illness, and in 1976 he only managed one
engagement of 15 shows. "The paradox is that Las Vegas was a place
that gave Elvis new life, even as his success in Vegas would ultimately
endanger his life by putting him on a treadmill he couldn't get off,"
observed Priscilla.

Subsequent US tours were more extensive than they'd been in
1970, and for a while they still offered new opportunities for Elvis to
rise to the occasion. In 1972, he sold out four shows at Madison Square
Garden, and his January 14 1973 appearance in Honolulu, broadcast
live via satellite to the Far East, and later seen in Europe and the US,
generated great excitement around the world. Both shows also
produced top-selling live albums (*Elvis As Recorded At Madison Square*

Garden reaching Number 11 US, Number Three UK, *Aloha From Hawaii* reaching Number One US, Number 11 UK).

An obvious move would have been to let Elvis tour abroad, but his manager always demurred, despite being offered fabulous sums of money. After Elvis's death, it was revealed that Parker was in fact an illegal immigrant, born Andreas Cornelis van Kuijk in Breda, the Netherlands, in 1909. It has been suggested that, because he did not have a valid passport, Parker couldn't leave the country and didn't want Elvis to tour without being able to be by his side. But one would think a man with Parker's influence (and money) could have easily surmounted this obstacle, especially considering the fees he was being offered for a tour. Perhaps, having so long concealed his real identity, Parker didn't want to risk bringing any undue attention to himself.

As he had done throughout his career, Elvis expressed an interest in touring overseas to those around him. In December 1973, during a session at Stax Studios in Memphis, Norbert Putnam recalls Elvis saying to him, "Putt, we've had offers to come and play Wembley in London. I've never been there. I'd love to go to London, and they want to me to come. But the Colonel says no. The Colonel says the only reason I'm so huge in Europe is because of a lack of exposure. If they see me live, I could lose that. Putt, what do you think?" "And I'm sitting there, you know, eating my meal, trying to figure out, 'Do I want to get in the middle of this?'" says Norbert. "But I knew he was questioning Colonel Tom's reasoning. There was a huge offer to play Australia, and to play Japan, and Colonel Tom was saying no." The matter was left unresolved, Elvis ending the discussion by saying, "OK, I guess it's time to go back to being Elvis Presley."

The vast number of Elvis's live shows that have been released, officially and otherwise, clearly reveal how his performance style changed from the nearly manic shows of 1969 to the more subdued pace of the mid 70s, aside from his big rock'n'roll hits, which were usually presented in a medley that was always taken at a brisk clip.

"Personally, I think what was too much for him was the fact that he didn't want to be a rock'n'roll singer anymore," says Jerry Scheff. "He would reduce all his rock'n'roll songs to a medley in the show and that was it. He couldn't get through them fast enough! Some of them, like 'Hound Dog,' are so fast, actually they're ridiculously fast. He wanted to be respected for his voice, and rock'n'roll didn't do that for him. He wanted to do stuff like 'Impossible Dream,' which he loved, and all those songs where he could really get emotional in them and also show off his range. He wanted to be respected as a vocalist, and I'm sure that he thought he was too old to do the rock'n'roll thing anymore. That's my opinion."

Jerry had noticed a shift in the energy level of the live performances, citing the _Aloha From Hawaii_ show as a turning point. "We were like a punk lounge band," he says. "We had played just screaming so many times, just rocking it as hard as we could. And it was really refreshing to go to Hawaii … [but] everybody got a little more conservative. Not so much in what they played, but in the tempos, the feel of the thing. It was like we'd been driving a car along in second gear and the engine's just roaring for a couple of years, and then all of a sudden we push it into drive."

Jerry left Presley's band in 1973, and when he returned two years later, he saw the pace of the show had changed even more. "When we started [the show], I was used to doing it in second gear and I started hopping on it," he says. "And Elvis turned around and he took his hand, and went 'Whoa whoa whoa!' 'Cause they had dropped into drive permanently. We'd get crazy once in a while after that, but for the most part, things had dropped back just a notch, tempo wise. Which I thought was really good. Well, I was older too!"

The shows also became locked into something of a routine, in terms of the songs being performed. "There was one time I remember where we had a whole slew of material that was fairly new," says Ronnie Tutt, recalling the opening night performance of the 'Elvis Summer Festival' in Vegas on August 19 1974, which included songs like 'Down In The Alley,' 'Good Time Charlie's Got The Blues,' and 'My Baby Left

Me.' "We rehearsed all this new material and tried to sequence it all, get it all together. He did it the opening show, but people kind of sat on their hands, and so that was it. For the next show we got the call, 'Hey, last night's setlist, we're not going to do that same one. Elvis doesn't want to do that again.' He was insecure enough that he just didn't trust sometimes more than just the reaction of the day, of the moment. Which is a shame. Because there was a lot of great material that could have been worked up and performed."

Instead, the spectacle of the event was emphasized. In 1971, Richard Strauss's 'Also Sprach Zarathustra,' better known to modern audiences for its use in Stanley Kubrick's film *2001: A Space Odyssey*, was introduced as Elvis's own 'theme music,' booming out as he took the stage with regal authority, and generally segueing into 'See See Rider.' His jumpsuits also became increasingly extravagant. "In Vegas, I think he got just wrapped up into that competitive thing of trying to outdo Sinatra, trying to outdo Tom Jones, the most shows sold out in a row," says Ronnie Tutt. "And he got more into doing the big orchestral show tunes. If you even look at his wardrobe, which is I think a good indicator, he did have the one piece suit, then later on it got that there was just no turning back, it got to be more and more. Pretty soon he was a walking jewel with a cape up there, just every color of the rainbow, and he started having one after the other made in different colors. I mean it was amazing work, Bill Belew did some phenomenal wardrobe stuff, but it just shows you how the perspective changed from the first year all the way to the end." Having set the bar high with jewel-encrusted suits, Belew was next planning to design a suit that would shoot out laser beams, operated by a remote control. As Priscilla observed, "It was as if [Elvis] were determined to upstage himself instead of relying on his raw talent."

Things had changed in the recording studio as well. In 1971, there had been another 'Nashville marathon,' with Elvis recording 32 tracks in a week, though even then the musicians had sensed a lack of interest on Elvis's part. "I felt Elvis was kind of bored coming to the studio," says

Norbert. "And he sort of had to get himself charged up for it. So we'd sit there for two hours. Eight o'clock, the King comes in and he wants to tell stories, tell jokes, do a little karate, clown around until ten. And I think that was as much for him as anything else; he got loosened up, there was the camaraderie with the band, and then suddenly, 'Ah, I guess we have to make a record. Show me the songs, and let's do it.'"

But in subsequent years, Elvis spent less and less time in the studio, and his lack of interest in the proceedings became increasingly apparent. The creative drive seen in 1968, when he asked the studio lights to be dimmed so he could pour his heart into 'If I Can Dream' while writhing on the floor, or 1969, when he pushed himself through 23 takes of 'In The Ghetto,' was gone. There was a single, three-day studio session in 1972 that resulted in a mere seven songs. And at his 1973 sessions at Stax Studios in July and December, the musicians encountered a very different Elvis than the one they'd worked with previously.

"It wasn't anything even close to American," says Reggie Young of the July sessions. "We were set up, we'd been there all night long waiting for him to show up. And when he came in, he had his entourage with him, and The Stamps Quartet [the gospel group who had replaced The Imperials for Elvis's tours and recordings] was there, and everybody was just kind of hanging out with him. And I don't think we even talked. It wasn't anything like American. American was so personal and one-on-one kind of thing. This was just a roomful of people. It wasn't that 'Let's sit around and work up some songs' or sit around and just talk about stuff."

Reggie was more taken aback at being told how he was supposed to behave while waiting for Elvis to arrive. As the hours ticked by and everyone grew tired, Reggie made the mistake of yawning, only to find himself being scolded by Felton Jarvis, who sternly told him, "Reg, no yawning on the sessions." Thinking it was a joke, Reggie burst out laughing, saying, "You've gotta be kiddin'!" "No," Felton replied soberly. "It wouldn't look good if the King walks in and you're yawning." "And I thought, 'He's really serious!'" says Reggie. "Anyway, I laughed and said, 'Well, I'll try not to yawn.' And then he went around and told everybody else the same thing. That became kind of a joke because it got back to my buddies in the studio world, and they'd say to me, 'Hey Reg, no yawning on the session!'"

And when Elvis did arrive, his lack of commitment was evident to all. "He didn't know the songs," remembers Jerry Carrigan, who also played during the July sessions. "They were weird old songs and just weren't good; I mean, they were really bad. And he just didn't care about it. And all those people around ... it was very unpleasant. And very distracting, 'cause we didn't know who these people were. We'd never seen 'em before. And Stax, at that time, had a chain link fence around it and guards with guns everywhere. And that was very distracting. You were afraid to walk out in the lobby, afraid you'd get shot, you know? These guys, boy, they would put that gun across the door and 'Wait a minute man, I'm on the session.' 'Oh, OK.' I mean, it was gettin' weird, gettin' too weird. Those were some weird sessions in a lot of ways."

"It wasn't as friendly. It was too businesslike," says Reggie. "OK, we'll cut this song, and then go on to the next song. Like at American we'd pick it apart and talk about stuff, and maybe change the key, and maybe stop, take a break and talk. There wasn't any of that at Stax."

"That's the way it was for me too," agrees Bobby Emmons, who played organ on the sessions. "You can't just take a good song and throw it at the tape machine and expect it to stick. It's not like pasta on the refrigerator; you have to mess with 'em a bit. You can't just punch a clock, play a little while and sign out."

"It just got to be no fun," says Jerry. "No fun at all. We were getting nothing. The tracks weren't good; a few of 'em we could use, a few of 'em we couldn't. Just was too weird. And I hated to see Elvis look the way he looked. He looked like he was miserable, both in health and in life."

There were no studio recording sessions at all in 1974, the first year that had happened since 1959, when Elvis was in the army. His final session in a proper studio was at RCA's Hollywood facility in March 1975, after which he seemed disinclined to record again. In desperation, RCA set up recording equipment in the den at Graceland, today known as the 'Jungle Room' because of its Tiki-style furnishings. Two 'Jungle Room' sessions were held in February and October 1976, though there was still the problem of getting Elvis motivated enough even to put in an appearance. "We'd have to wait for him to come down," says Norbert, who played the February session. "And of course we were told to be there at eight in the evening or something. And sometimes he'd come down at midnight, and sometimes Felton would come out at midnight and say, 'Well, he's not coming down.' And so we'd all go back to our hotel. It was not the best of times. And I remember when he did come down, he was really out of shape. He was wearing a big jogging outfit, and he was bloated. And he was talking to me a lot about numerology, and all the stuff he was into; he certainly didn't seem to be thinking that much about the music." Even so, there were moments when Elvis recaptured his old fire, as in his towering rendition of Roy Hamilton's 'Hurt.'

The October sessions were also plagued by distractions. One night the musicians, including bassist Jerry Scheff, were waiting downstairs as usual for Elvis to show up, when Charlie Hodge approached Jerry and told him "Elvis wants to see you up in his bedroom." Jerry duly went upstairs and knocked on the door, and Elvis invited him in. "He took me into his closet, which was the size of my living room," he says. "And he started going through these clothes in his closet. There were these five suits, and they were just the loudest, weirdest looking suits you ever saw in your life; they had fur cuffs, and they had felt hats to go with them with rhinestone belt buckles." Elvis pulled a suit off the rack for Jerry to inspect. "Where in the hell did you get that?" asked Jerry. "Oh, we'd be walking down the street, and I'd look in a store and say, 'Hey! look at those suits!'" Elvis told him. "And then Red West would go back and say, 'Give me five of those in Elvis's size.' I never wear 'em. Here, try this on.'"

"So I went into the bathroom and put it on, and I just swam in it," says Jerry. "It was way too big for me. So he found a velvet jacket that fit me, and a scarf and some other stuff, and he dressed me up, and sent me downstairs. And Charlie went and got Ronnie Tutt, and the others, and he dressed everybody in a costume out of his wardrobe. And when he got to J.D. Sumner and The Stamps, those suits, they looked like _Superfly_ suits. And they fit The Stamps perfectly. We started to record, everybody all dressed up, and we couldn't record. Every time we'd start to record a song, if one of us looked over at Elvis or if he looked over at us, we'd start laughing."

Jerry had hoped Elvis would record a song he had written, a mid-tempo rocker called 'Fire Down Below.' But though the rhythm track was laid down, a vocal was never completed. "We worked on it for an hour or two," Jerry says. "And then Elvis said, 'I don't feel good, I'm going to have to go upstairs for a few minutes.' I went in and shot some pool in the pool room with somebody for maybe an hour, and then Charlie came and got me and said, 'Elvis wants to see you in his bedroom.' And I went up to his bedroom, and he said, 'Jerry, I just don't feel good, I can't do it anymore. You guys cut a track and have Sherrill [Sherrill Nielsen, one of the backing vocalists and formerly a member of Voice, one of the vocal groups that toured with Elvis] put a scratch vocal on it and I promise I'll cut it.' And of course he never did. Felton went around for a couple of months with the master tape for that trying to get Elvis to put his vocal on it. 'Cause a lot of people believed that that would've been a hit for him. It was sad. I knew he was bored to death during the Stax sessions and later on at the mansion he was just tired. Sick and tired." It was Elvis's last recording session.

Undoubtedly some of Elvis's reluctance to record was due to his inability to get songs he was excited about. "I think he had musically gotten into a rut because he was finding himself doing the same thing over and again," says Ronnie. "He was throwing his old rock stuff away, doing a little bit of the newer rock stuff, but it was more orchestrated and it didn't quite have the heart of some of the newer stuff that we were trying to get him to do. A song like 'Burning Love' came along and we wanted him to do more things like that [released in 1972, the single was a Top Ten hit in both the US and UK]. Jerry had written a song for him to do, called 'Fire Down Below,' and that was the kind of thing that we were trying to get him more into doing. It was kind of tragic in a way, because Felton Jarvis his producer, he told me one time, 'Ronnie, I'm just there to make him happy.' And that's true, we all were there to support him, but sometimes you have to tell people the truth and say, 'This is not as good as this,' or 'Let's do this,' or whatever. It was kind of a shame to see him surrounded by people who were trying to feed him songs that were songs that they had connections with, that they owned, they were getting monies from or were pushing to get paid, that kind of thing."

Elvis had also become increasingly unhappy about the sound of his recordings. At one of the Jungle Room sessions, he called Ronnie upstairs to his bedroom and told him "I want you to listen to this," first playing Ronnie one of his own records, then a few recent recordings by other artists. "I can't remember who they were, but they were current pop-rock hit artists," says Ronnie. "It might've been Three Dog Night or Led Zeppelin. And the sound difference was amazing. It filled the room; it was big, it was gigantic, it was the way things are supposed to be mixed. And he says, 'Why don't my records sound like that?' He didn't know enough musically to be able to ask more pointedly as far as production is concerned as to why, but he knew his records just didn't have that impact and that drive and that kick.

"And there again the Colonel had the say-so on how his records sounded," Ronnie continues. "He'd go to RCA himself and have them mix them with his, quote, 'boy' louder than everything else, because he wanted to hear his boy. ... You know, you can hear every little fault, every little mistake in his voice, every little shake. It begins to sound very unnatural. ... And of course Elvis wanted the records to sound good, he wanted them to flatter him, not make him sound worse than he actually was. So anyway, I think that was the frustration of actually recording. And that's why when we recorded he really hated to do even vocal overdubs. He just wanted to get it on the first take and let them capture what it was. It was a spontaneous experience to him."

Elvis, of course, wasn't powerless to effect change in his life. But he was easily intimidated. At the end of his 1973 summer Las Vegas engagement, an argument had broken out between Elvis and his manager, not, ironically, due to any career dissatisfaction on Elvis's part, but because one of his favorite employees at the Hilton (formerly the International) had been fired. The argument ended with Elvis firing his manager, Parker storming off to his suite, calculating what he felt Elvis still owed him, and presenting him with a substantial bill. Elvis was dismayed by the large amount, but didn't verify that Parker's accounting was accurate. Nor apparently did he search for another manager to possibly buy out the contract, though Jerry Schilling has contended, "Nobody would touch him, because they were afraid of the Colonel."

Perhaps, though it would seem that Elvis was more afraid of his manager than anybody else. The success of the Comeback Special had spurred Elvis to exert more control over his career, first by choosing to record at American, then in putting together his live show for Las Vegas to his own specifications. But the confidence he regained during this period was short-lived. And Parker was not interested in having a client who thought too much for himself. "I'll tell you my opinion," says Chris Bearde. "And I don't know how to put it any other way. I believe that the Colonel saw he was losing influence over Elvis tremendously during our [Comeback] Special. And Elvis was like a schoolboy toward the Colonel; I mean the Colonel owned him lock, stock, and barrel – and brain. And I think the '68 Presley special was a big shock to the Colonel that Elvis had the gumption to move a little bit from him. Not just the music or the movies and everything, but away from the Colonel. And the Colonel was a guy who wanted to stay in control."

Such control led to Elvis missing out on what might have proved a career-changing opportunity. On March 28 1975, Barbra Streisand and her then-boyfriend Jon Peters had attended Elvis's midnight show in

Vegas. On meeting with him afterwards, they asked if he'd consider co-starring with Streisand in a remake of *A Star Is Born*. Elvis was immediately interested, but Parker just as immediately began planting seeds of doubt, pointing out Peters's lack of experience as a filmmaker (he was to be the producer), speculating that the film might favor Streisand over Elvis, and raising other objections. Negotiations rapidly fell apart. (Kris Kristofferson was eventually cast in the role offered to Elvis, and the film was released in 1976.) "I knew it wasn't going to happen, because it didn't come through the machinery," Jerry Schilling said. "By the time Elvis got smart, business-wise, the machinery was built. And they only wanted him to work the machinery, they didn't want him to change it."

And as Schilling has also pointed out, "It's a combination of business and creativity if you want to have a career." By focusing on the former at the expense of the latter, Parker did a great disservice to his sole client. "I feel a lot of Elvis's problems came from the frustration of not being able to do the things that he should have been allowed to do," says Ronnie. "The Colonel, in my opinion, didn't know how to deal with the artistic nature of Elvis. He knew how to promote in a marvelous way, to bring somebody from where Elvis was at up to the level that he brought him to. It was phenomenal what he did. But on the other hand, he had no clue how to keep him sane and healthy as an artist." "We lost Elvis because of creative disappointments," Schilling observed.

In any case, the two soon made up and Parker was reinstated as manager. No sooner had the managerial crisis been averted than Elvis faced another difficult situation; the formal dissolution of his marriage. Priscilla had left Elvis at the end of 1971. It had never been an easy relationship. Prior to their marriage, Elvis was away much of the time making films; now he was increasingly away on tour. And where wives and girlfriends had once been welcome during the Vegas engagements, they were now limited to attending only opening and closing night. "It was the day Elvis suggested I come to Vegas less often that I became really upset and suspicious," Priscilla said. Elvis had never been entirely faithful to her before or after the marriage; now that they were growing apart, she too began to lead her own life. At the time she and Elvis separated, she was involved with karate instructor Mike Stone; ironically, she had become interested in the sport in the hope that it would bring her closer to Elvis. The couple finally divorced on October 9 1973.

Six days later, Elvis was admitted to Baptist Memorial Hospital in Memphis, suffering a severe reaction to the drugs he'd been taking. As during the movie years, the frustrations in his life and career led to an increase in Elvis's drug use; the vicious cycle of taking stimulants to pump himself up before a performance and depressants to calm down afterwards had returned with a vengeance. Though often seen as the cause of Elvis's problems, the drugs were really just a symptom of them, though drug addiction of course eventually becomes its own problem. "Whenever Elvis caught a clear glimpse of himself and realized what he was doing, he became so depressed he had to take more pills to feel better," said Joe Esposito. Elvis's sizeable weight gain was also a sign he was becoming increasingly ill. Some weight gain was due to drug use, but it was also due to Elvis's diet, which was largely made up of fatty foods. As a young man, Elvis had been able to keep his weight down through rigorous performance; the metabolism of a 40-year-old man worked less efficiently in this regard. Nor did he partake of much regular exercise. His health problems, including hypertension and intestinal difficulties, were also exacerbated by his drug use.

As Elvis's ill health began affecting his performances, his appearance was commented on in reviews, as were his frequently rambling monologues and his tendency to pass out jewelry to the audience to provoke a reaction. In a 1975 story for the *Los Angeles Times*, Robert Hilburn called Elvis's shows "sloppy" and suggested he consider retiring. Harvey Kubernik regularly saw Elvis's shows in the LA area, and had been a witness to the excitement Elvis continued to incite in audiences. At one show he attended with DJ Rodney Bingenheimer, the two men were startled to see their female companions burst into tears when Elvis took the stage. "I said, 'Why are you crying, did we do something wrong?'" says Harvey. "They said 'No – it's Elvis!' And I realized he had this primordial connection to girls still. Mostly he reminded them of the 50s, when they were happier people ... I mean, people liked him because they could go back to a simpler time."

But an April 25 1976 show in Long Beach that he reviewed for *Melody Maker* left him saddened. "The screaming never stopped," he wrote. "He still gets 'em hot. But his movements are now so restricted that at times the concert is sluggish and pathetic." "It was a bad show, and he looked bad," he says. "My parents had just seen him in Vegas and they said 'Elvis Presley's got some medical problems.' He had canceled some shows in Vegas for the first time, which was unheard of. And in my mind I was going, what's going on here? 'Cause I'd never seen performers drop the mic, or forget the words to a song. Something was wrong."

Bill Burk, a *Memphis Press-Scimitar* reporter who had known Elvis since the 50s, wrote that Elvis looked "terribly tired" during the December 1976 Vegas shows he saw: "Even his famed swiveling hips, which don't swivel all that much anymore, seem programmed." Elsewhere he observed: "One walks away wondering how much longer it can be before the end comes, perhaps suddenly, and why the King of Rock'n'Roll would subject himself to possible ridicule by going on stage so ill-prepared." Burk later wrote that when Elvis read the review he brought some fans in from outside Graceland and asked them if they agreed with it. The fans said no, and were rewarded with a new car. Burk also heard through an associate that Elvis was going to contact him, an interaction Burk welcomed; but the call never came.

Those around Elvis were concerned, but no one knew how to deal with the problem. His primary physician, Dr George Nichopoulos, tried regulating Elvis's drug use by administering placebos, a gesture that was as ineffective as it was well-intentioned; Elvis simply patronized other doctors, who were often unaware of the various medications he'd already been prescribed, resulting in a potentially dangerous mix of drugs. Nearly everyone close to Elvis has gone on record as saying they tried to confront him about his drug use, only to be told it either wasn't a problem or was none of their business. "Why he did the drugs?" said Sonny West. "I guess because he was bored."

Others who were thought to have a good influence on Elvis were also asked to help. Chris Bearde, who kept in touch with Elvis by seeing him in Vegas, says Charlie Hodge often approached him. "Charlie kept confiding in me," he says. "He'd say, 'Chris, you've got to do something. Elvis is this, Elvis is that.' And I said, 'Well, I can't do anything, I'm just this writer.' He said, 'No, no, no, he really likes you, he'd listen to you. He's putting on weight and he's doing this and blah blah blah.' I tried to get to him after that, but I couldn't. He was totally surrounded by people. But I did try to get close to him. 'Cause I know if I had, I probably would've been able to speak to him a little bit. Whether it would've changed anything, who knows?"

But there was little that could be done. Those close to Elvis became resigned to his self-destructive habits. "He was going to go ahead and slowly kill himself, no matter what I did," said Linda Thompson, Elvis's primary girlfriend after his divorce. "I couldn't make him happy, and I knew he wasn't going to change. So I left." "I felt sorry for Elvis, and at the same time, I hated him for being drugged and out of control and wasting his wonderful gifts," said Joe Esposito. "I prayed the real Elvis would return. Talking to him did no good, and it was frustrating because I didn't know what else to do about it."

A firm managerial hand might have refused to send Elvis back on the road until he was healthy, thus cutting off his chief source of income and providing the incentive to make some changes. But no one had the nerve to make such a move. Norbert Putnam's last Elvis-related session was on June 9 1977, when he overdubbed a bass part on a live recording of 'Unchained Melody.' During the session, at which Elvis was not present, Norbert asked Felton Jarvis how Elvis was doing. "Oh Putt, you know how Elvis is, you can't tell him nothing," said Felton. "Yesterday for breakfast he had a dozen biscuits, a pound of bacon, an eight-egg omelet, and the day before he had 16 banana splits. He goes on these binges." "My God!" said Norbert. "Can't anyone do something about this?" "No," Felton replied. "You can't tell him anything. He'll fire you!" "That was a bad situation," says Norbert. "Because everyone around him worked for him. Felton was afraid to say anything. Elvis's own father was afraid to say anything. They were all afraid, and it was a sad situation."

It left Elvis with a terrible sense of isolation he didn't know how to address. Ronnie recalls how Elvis reached out to him one evening in LA, using the pretext of the drummer having problems with his shoulder. "It was 12 at night," he says. "My wife and I were just getting ready to go to bed, and I get a call – 'Ronnie you want to come over? I've got an acupuncturist coming ... ' Well, what it was, he wanted to talk. He took me upstairs, went into the bedroom and he sat down on the bed and he said it was basically just driving him crazy, and he didn't have people to talk to. He couldn't talk like you and I are talking, or we'd talk with friends. He surrounded himself with a bunch of 'yes guys,' so he never could bounce things off of them. He said, 'I know you've been through this,' because I had gone through a divorce. And he said, 'I just can't believe that I am who I am, and I can't believe that Priscilla wants a divorce.' I mean, on an emotional basis it's like, 'Wait a minute. Who am I? I'm the dream of all these millions of women around the world and yet ...' I only say that to give a better picture of the frustration that was going on in his life. It happened to him on so many different levels. I guess that's my point."

Elvis might have been surprised to learn who exactly was interested in helping him break out of his sheltered environment. In the mid 70s, Norbert was in England, producing Splinter for George Harrison's label, Dark Horse, and spending a lot of time with Harrison at his home at Henley-on-Thames. One night Norbert had asked so many questions about The Beatles, George finally told him, "Well, I'll make you a deal. You answer all of my questions about Elvis, and I'll answer all of your questions about The Beatles." Norbert readily agreed, listening with fascination as George told him, "Norbert, I have been in Elvis's presence a few times. When [The Beatles] went out to California and we went up to his house [on August 27 1965], we were so paranoid that we got stoned in the car. And then when we came into his house, we couldn't talk in any sort of lucid manner … he thought we were a bunch of idiots. A few years later, I went to see him play a concert and I went backstage and I'm waiting in line and Elvis comes up and I couldn't talk! He thinks I'm an idiot!" "Did all of you feel that way about Elvis?" asked Norbert. "Oh yeah," George assured him. "Lennon, Paul … Elvis was it. Everyone else was secondary."

Norbert was also interested to see how George could go around his neighborhood on his own without being hassled, unlike Elvis, who felt he couldn't go anywhere without his entourage. Norbert had accompanied George to the local pub and seen for himself the nonchalant reaction of the patrons. "We'd walk in and I would watch everyone in the bar turn and see George, and then immediately move their vision back to the person they were talking to," he says. "They would never approach George. He and I would sit there and talk, as though no one had noticed a Beatle walked in the room, you know?" On one occasion, an elderly gentleman followed the two back to their car and politely requested an autograph "for my nephew." George complied and the man went on his way. Watching him go, George turned and said, "Norbert, tell Elvis to come stay with me in Henley. We can walk the streets of Henley. You've seen this, Norbert, and no one will bother us!" "I remember standing there, trying to imagine George Harrison and Elvis Presley walking up and down the streets of Henley, looking in windows and no one bothering him," says Norbert. "I said, 'I'll mention it to Elvis, George.' But not for one moment did I ever think that would be possible."

But Elvis was still Memphis's favorite son; in 1972, the stretch of US Highway 51 South that passed in front of Graceland was renamed Elvis Presley Boulevard. He still had a loyal fan-base that could be counted on to attend his live shows. And for every off night, there were still performances when his voice could thrill the crowd. "If you listen to some of the shows, even right before he died, there'd be some of 'em that he wouldn't sing very well, but then there'd be other ones that were the best renditions of those songs that he'd ever done," says Jerry Scheff. Pamela Des Barres and her then husband saw such a show during Elvis's last Vegas engagement, in December 1976, and she was as impressed as she'd been on first seeing him in concert in 1969. "We got put right in the very very back of the showroom," she recalls. "We were so green about how you tip people and move up. So we tipped this guy 20 dollars and he moved us about halfway down, and we realized oh, we should've given him 50, and we could've gotten closer. Oh God, he was great though. Spellbinding. Mesmerizing. Ecstatic. Every moment. And his voice was never better. He was a big heavy guy then, but his voice just continued to get better. I don't know how that happened. It was the one thing the good Lord let him keep."

"I think he got stronger and stronger over the years, as far as being able to really have strength and power in his voice," says Ronnie. "I don't think he ever lost that. In fact, I saw it increase, up till maybe the very last. He was one of the most resilient men I've ever seen. He could really look out of condition, then all of a sudden he was like Clark Kent jumping into a convenient phone booth. He'd pop into this phone booth, and out would come the guy with the big freshly dyed black hair and eyebrows and eyelashes, and the suit with the cape. And there he was – Elvis Presley!"

Two of Elvis's concerts on his last tour, June 19 in Omaha, Nebraska, and June 21 in Rapid City, South Dakota, were filmed for use in an upcoming TV special. In the concert footage, Elvis looks ill and out of shape, his face swollen and beaded with sweat, his speech slow and quiet, like a man who can't shake off his drowsiness. His lack of engagement is most obviously seen in his performance of 'Are You Lonesome Tonight?' during the June 21 show, when he stumbles over his words during the spoken monologue and begins speaking gibberish and cracking jokes, finally laughing the moment off by saying, "Aw, the heck with it" and going back into the song. (This performance was originally included in the theatrical version of the 1981 documentary

This Is Elvis, but was cut from the home video release.) It's this moment that Albert Goldman, of all people, cites as an example of Elvis "fighting to the last, with crack-brained audacity, to break free of his imprisoning image."

But the sentimentality that Elvis sends up in 'Lonesome' is addressed with complete sincerity in his performance of 'My Way' from the same show; aside from the poignancy of hearing Elvis sing about the end being near, it's a song he delivers with gentle, heartfelt authority, a number that clearly resonates deeply with him. He also turns in a powerful performance of Roy Hamilton's 'Unchained Melody' (included on *Elvis: The Great Performances, Vol. 1*), accompanying himself on piano as Charlie Hodge holds up a microphone, as lost in the moment as if he's playing in his own living room instead of before a crowd of several thousand, giving a growl of pleasure at the song's conclusion, then grinning at the audience for approval.

Elvis spent much of 1977 on tour. "Yeah, I used to call it the 'tour of the month band,'" says Ronnie. "We were gone a few weeks out of every month." The February tour began in Florida and took in Alabama, Georgia, the Carolinas, and Tennessee. The March tour began in the Southwest with Arizona, then moved on to Texas, Oklahoma, and Louisiana. In April and May he played North Carolina, Michigan, Ohio, Wisconsin, and Illinois. After a two-week break he went back on the road, hitting Kentucky, Maryland, Rhode Island, Maine, New York, Pennsylvania, Louisiana, Georgia, and Alabama, a tour which continued into June. After another two weeks off, he was on tour for the rest of June, playing Missouri, Nebraska, South Dakota, Iowa, Wisconsin, Ohio, and finally the Market Square Arena, in Indianapolis, Indiana, on Sunday, June 26. "I think that that was the only time that he really felt at home, so to speak," says Jerry Scheff. "I don't think it was so much the music as the contact with the people, and the reassurance that the people gave him. The people still loved him." All in all, he performed 56 shows in the first six months of the year.

In July, the album *Moody Blue* was released, a mix of songs from the Jungle Room sessions and Elvis's recent live shows. Elvis's last few albums hadn't even cracked the Top 40, but his big concern that summer was not the fate of his new album but the upcoming release of a tell-all biography. The previous July, Red and Sonny West had been fired, along with Dave Hebler, a newer member of the entourage. Vernon Presley had always thought Elvis spent far too much on his 'Mafia,' and the official reason given for the men's dismissal was the need to "cut back on expenses" (unofficially, it was felt that the bodyguards' roughness with the public had resulted in too many lawsuits). It wasn't surprising that Elvis would leave it to Vernon fire his friends, but, adding insult to injury, they were only given a week's severance pay. Nor would Elvis take their calls when they later attempted to get a hold of him.

Soon after the firings, the three had a book contract, working on a memoir with Steve Dunleavy of the tabloid *The Star*. Elvis's lawyer contacted the men and offered them money not to go ahead with the book, but they would not be dissuaded, contending that they hoped the book would serve as a wake-up call for Elvis. As Red put it, "If we can scare him enough, maybe he'll clean up." The book, entitled *Elvis: What Happened?*, was serialized overseas, beginning in June 1977, and published on August 1. Today, stories of drug use and bad behavior by celebrities are commonplace enough to be a cliché, just one stage along the well-worn trajectory of rise-fall-redemption in the lives of the rich and famous. Back then, people were shocked to read about what the book's breathless style painted as the rampant drug use, disturbing violence, and constant womanizing of Elvis and his friends; all of these were quite at odds with Elvis's image as an all-American, clean-living, God-fearing country boy.

Longtime fans denounced the book. But Wayne Jackson feels the book's intentions were made clear by its title. "I like that book because it was written by his good friend," he says, referring to Red West. "Someone who really knew him, and knew how to get to him, and knew how to say what it was he wanted to say – hey, what happened man? That's what he wanted to say and that's what he did say. And that was the only thing that was important. The rest of it's all a bunch of garbage. Looking at the world scope of what Elvis did is huge, but really it can all be folded back down into – what happened? What happened, man? How'd you let that shit get away from you like that? The book Red wrote was a real missive from his heart to Elvis."

Nonetheless, Elvis was still hurt by what he saw as a gross invasion of his privacy and a betrayal by his closest friends (especially in the case of the Wests, whom he had known since the 50s). He was especially worried as the date for his upcoming tour approached; it would begin on August 17 with a performance in Portland, Maine, and would be his first public appearance since the book's publication. "He just anguished over this something awful," said Billy Smith, Elvis's cousin. He eventually had an impromptu speech planned, if he was heckled, in which he'd admit he wasn't perfect, and planned to take time off "to get myself straightened out."

It was something he'd spoken of regularly in his final months. At one point he'd told Larry Geller, the hairdresser who was now back in the fold, "I want to quit touring for at least a year. I'm going to go to Hawaii, I'm going to rent a house, I want to run on the beach, and exercise, and come back and make a movie as an actor." "This was his vision of the future," Geller said. "And if he would've right then and there took the bull by the horns and made those dramatic changes, perhaps he'd be alive. But he waited. And I know he had contracts, he had to fulfill his obligations. But he didn't do it. He didn't do it."

Sandi Miller also recalls Elvis telling her during his last visit to Palm Springs in January 1977 that he was going to take six months off and "make some changes." "He was very non-specific," she says. "And then there was going to be a surprise; he was going to do something that was going to be different and that would be a surprise. And for whatever reason, I never asked any questions. I'm mad at myself for not asking questions, but I figured, oh well, he'll tell us next time." Mentioning the conversation when having dinner with J.D. Sumner and The Stamps a decade later, she was surprised when Sumner said, "Yeah, you know what it was? He was going to go on a gospel tour with us."

Elvis may only have been expressing his desire to change, rather than referring to any plans that were actually in the works. In Lamar Fike's account, he was the one to suggest Elvis needed time off right before the August tour, only to be told, "I need the money. I've got to keep everything going ... Lamar, I'd love to do it, but I've got this obligation."

"There is a big question mark about who would Elvis have been had he just one day said, 'Well folks, that's it for Elvis,'" says Wayne Jackson. "'I'm calling it off. I'm going back to Memphis, and I'm just going to live my life.' What would he have been? Well, I don't know if you can not be Elvis, if you've been Elvis all your life. He was never anything but Elvis."

But before Elvis was able to go ahead with any changes he might have been thinking about, his time ran out. He woke up around 4pm on August 15. He visited his dentist at 10:30pm that evening, then returned to Graceland, playing racquetball at the indoor court in the grounds with his girlfriend, Ginger Alden, and his cousin Billy and his wife, Jo. After serenading his friends at the piano, the last song of which was Willie Nelson's 'Blue Eyes Crying In The Rain,' he and Ginger retired to his bedroom to get some sleep before leaving for Portland the next day. Unable to sleep, he took three packets of his prescribed sleeping medication, and told Ginger he was going to read in the bathroom.

Ginger awoke around 1:30pm on August 16, and soon after found Elvis face-down on the bathroom floor. He was rushed to Baptist Memorial Hospital, where efforts were made to revive him, but he was finally declared dead at 3:30pm. The news was flashed around the world, and fans and media descended on Memphis in the thousands, eventually estimated to number as many as 80,000 people. But in spite of the accumulating crowds and the ensuing tumult, the banner headlines and the media frenzy, and the sudden flurry of activity as Elvis's slumping record sales began to climb, the headline of the *Memphis Press-Scimitar* on August 17 was sadly appropriate: "A Lonely Life Ends On Elvis Presley Boulevard."

Chapter 7

Today, Tomorrow, And Forever

Ironically, the state of Elvis's career when he died in August 1977 was not too dissimilar to what it had been in 1967. His last Top Ten single had been 'Burning Love' in 1972, which not only reached Number Two, it also sold more than a million copies, the last single to do so in his lifetime. The 1973 album *Aloha From Hawaii* topped the charts and sold more than half a million copies. From that point on, his sales fell, and Elvis became increasingly less of a presence on Top 40 radio. (His chart placings were often better in the UK, and toward the end of his life his records also began doing better on the US country charts; the 1976 album *From Elvis Presley Boulevard, Memphis, Tennessee* only reached Number 41 on the pop charts, but topped the country charts.) Ten years after the renaissance that had tentatively begun when he recorded 'Guitar Man' in September 1967, it was as if few gains had been made at all over the last decade.

Nor was Elvis's legacy then regarded as something that would have much longevity. The first few years after his death were consumed with tabloidesque scandal. The pronouncement that the cause of Elvis's death was a heart attack was met with skepticism, in part because the statement was made while the autopsy was still going on. When it was later learned that Elvis had 14 different drugs in his system when he died (mostly depressants like Placidyl, Codeine, Quaaludes, and Valium), it was assumed his death was due to a drug overdose, or was at the very least drug-related, a speculation seemingly confirmed by the revelations in the book _Elvis: What Happened?_ about his drug use. And when _Elvis In Concert_ was broadcast on October 3 on CBS, the fact that something was not right with Elvis during the final months of his life was made explicitly and painfully clear (the accompanying soundtrack reached Number Five US, Number 13 UK).

In an era before celebrities freely discussed their substance abuse problems in interviews and memoirs, the notion that Elvis Presley could have been a drug abuser was controversial. Drug addiction was perceived by many to be a moral failing, rather than a health disorder. And a 'drug addict' was seen as someone who abused illegal drugs, not medication that had been prescribed by a doctor. Thus, to some, to call Elvis a drug addict was to impugn his memory. In an effort to quell the debate, in 1994 the state of Tennessee enlisted Dr Joseph Davis, a former medical examiner from Florida, to review the autopsy materials. Davis declared Elvis's death was indeed due to a heart attack, though without elaborating about what brought it on. But as Priscilla put it, "The last year of his life was rough … I knew he was having all sorts of heartache. He wasn't happy. As a result, he abused his body. It was that abuse that killed him."

A steady stream of gossipy books followed in the wake of _Elvis: What Happened?_, written by family members, former employees, and other presumed 'insiders.' Companies eager to capitalize on the demand for Elvis memorabilia issued a wide range of items, going well beyond the standard t-shirts and posters to include such items of dubious value as an Elvis Presley flyswatter, not to mention that ultimate artifact of kitsch, the Velvet Elvis – a portrait of Elvis painted on velvet. Such items, many of them unlicensed, were sold in the gift shops that sprang up across the street from Graceland. Along the fringes of fandom, rumors began circulating that Elvis was still alive, resulting in such front page headlines as "I'VE SEEN ELVIS IN THE FLESH" in the tabloid *Weekly World News*, alleging that Elvis had been spotted in a Burger King in Kalamazoo, Michigan. (Perhaps not coincidentally, another headline on the page read "EXPERT'S ADVICE: It's okay to be fat so eat junk food to your hearts content.") There was the possibility that the continual association of Elvis with the sensational and the tacky would sideline serious consideration of his accomplishments.

A key moment in the turnaround of the handling of Elvis's legacy came in 1980. Elvis's will had named his father, Vernon, as executor of his estate, and his daughter, Lisa Marie, as the primary beneficiary. When Vernon died, on June 26 1979, the new executors, accountant Joe Hanks, the National Bank of Commerce in Memphis, and Priscilla Presley, were prepared to let Elvis's manager continue to handle Elvis's business affairs, as he had done for Vernon, and petitioned the court to that end. Instead, probate court Judge Joseph Evans, concerned over the high percentage of the estate's income Parker received for his services (50 percent), appointed Memphis attorney Blanchard Tual as a guardian *ad litem* (guardian for a minor) for Lisa Marie, and ordered him to conduct an investigation into Parker's business dealings with Elvis.

Tual's subsequent reports (filed in 1980 and 1981) lambasted Parker for the size of his commission (calling it "excessive, imprudent, unfair to the estate, and beyond all reasonable bounds of industry standards"), criticized the deals he negotiated for his client (calling a 1973 deal by which RCA purchased Elvis's royalty rights on all recordings prior to March 1 1973 for $5.4 million "unethical, fraudulently obtained and against all industry standards"), and cited numerous conflicts of interest, charging both Parker and RCA with "collusion, conspiracy, fraud, misrepresentation, bad faith, and over-reaching." In the light of Tual's findings, on August 14 1981, just shy of the fourth anniversary of Elvis's death, Judge Evans ordered that the estate sue Parker. In response, Parker countersued. The legal battles continued until 1983, when the estate settled with Parker for $2 million, Parker giving up all claims to the estate's future earnings. "Had I realized that the Colonel would live as long as he did, I would never have settled," Tual said. "If Elvis had lived and we tried a case against the Colonel, Elvis would have won." In 1990, the estate paid another $2 million to purchase Parker's extensive archives. Parker died on January 21 1997 in Las Vegas of a stroke.

In the meantime, the estate had been experiencing its own financial difficulties. At the time of Elvis's death, his estate was valued at $7 million, and though additional monies had come in due to sales of records and other merchandise, there were rising expenses; it took half a million a year to maintain Graceland, and there were substantial inheritance taxes. Vernon had already sold off Elvis's two planes, a Convair 880 named *Lisa Marie* and the Lockheed JetStar *Hound Dog II*, to help pay the bills, but the estate was in danger of facing bankruptcy; by the time Lisa Marie came into her full inheritance at age 25, there might be nothing left.

Priscilla was advised to sell Graceland. But she had no wish to sell off her daughter's first home. Instead, she hired former investment manager Jack Soden (now the CEO of EPE – Elvis Presley Enterprises) to help her plan the opening of Graceland to the public. Tours of the grounds began on June 7 1982, and in the first year drew over half a million visitors. Graceland was on its way to becoming a major tourist attraction, and is now the second most-visited house in the country (the first being the White House). The businesses across the street were eventually purchased by EPE and remodeled to accommodate its own array of shops and museums (showcasing Elvis's many cars and motorcycles, and his two planes, which EPE repurchased in 1984). Fans flock to Memphis on the anniversaries of Elvis's birthday, January 8, and especially during the week he died, in what's now called 'Elvis Week,' which culminates in the 'Candlelight Vigil' on August 15, where fans walk past the graves of Elvis and his parents in Graceland's Meditation Garden.

Elvis's status as a cultural icon was thus assured. Now his musical career was due for a reassessment. Some posthumous releases had given a measure of thought to placing Elvis's work in an historical context, such as the *Elvis Aron Presley* and *A Golden Celebration* boxed sets and the *Essential Elvis* album series, but these were the exceptions rather than the rule. An attempt to 'modernize' Elvis came with the 1981 *Guitar Man* album, with producer Felton Jarvis pairing Elvis's original vocal tracks with newly recorded backings. Along with the title track, the album included 'After Loving You,' 'Too Much Monkey Business,' 'Just Call Me Lonesome,' 'Lovin' Arms,' 'You Asked Me To,' 'Clean Up Your Own Backyard,' 'She Thinks I Still Care,' 'Faded Love,' and 'I'm Movin' On.' Despite the fact that some of the musicians were those who'd actually played with Elvis (including Chip Young, David Briggs, Mike Leech, and Jerry Carrigan), the overall sound was generic, as if Elvis was singing along to a karaoke track. Still, a single of 'Guitar Man' reached Number 28, a higher position than the original recording had reached, as well as topping the Country charts (and reaching Number 43 UK), while the album reached Number 49 (Number 33 UK); a second single, 'Lovin' Arms,' reached Number Eight in the Country charts. Jarvis died on January 3 1981, the same month the album was released, perhaps the reason there was no follow up. In 2000, an expanded collection, *Too Much Monkey Business*, was released, featuring the songs that might have been issued at the time had Jarvis been around to oversee their release: 'Burning Love,' 'I'll Be There,' 'I'll Hold You In My Heart,' 'In The Ghetto,' 'Long Black Limousine,' 'Only The Strong Survive,' 'Hey Jude,' 'Kentucky Rain,' 'If You Talk In Your Sleep,' and 'Blue Suede Shoes.'

The 1992 boxed set *The King Of Rock'n'Roll: The Complete 50s*

Masters was a major leap forward in quality; a five-CD set of every master recording Elvis had released during the 50s, including a disc of rarities, and a booklet with a detailed sessionography, discography, and an essay by Peter Guralnick. The set was a commercial success, quickly selling over half a million copies – an impressive number for a boxed set. It also provided a welcome reminder of why Elvis had become a phenomenon in the first place: "Presley the singer emerges as a workhorse, a student – finally, unarguably, an artist," said *Rolling Stone*. "If anything in pop history deserves this kind of completist treatment, this is it."

The boxed set was co-produced by Ernst Jorgensen and Roger Semon, who have since overseen dozens of thoughtfully compiled releases. The boxed sets *From Nashville To Memphis: The Essential 60s Masters I* and *Walk A Mile In My Shoes: The Essential 70s Masters* followed in 1993 and 1995, respectively. New album reissues usually featured bonus tracks; the *Elvis* Comeback Special soundtrack was reissued as *Memories: The '68 Comeback Special* (1998) and the *From Elvis In Memphis* and *Back In Memphis* albums were reissued as *Suspicious Minds: The Memphis 1969 Anthology* (1999), each set featuring the original album and a disc of rarities. A set like *Tomorrow Is A Long Time* (1999), which compiled Elvis's non-soundtrack material recorded from 1966 to 1968, shows that the period was not as much of a musical wasteland as had previously been thought. Even the movie soundtracks were decently packaged, in the *Elvis Double Features* series, which compiled songs from two or more Elvis films on each release. In 1999, a collector's label, Follow That Dream (named after the 1962 Elvis film), was established, a mail-order-only venture that sells CDs of live shows and studio outtakes to hardcore fans.

For most of the general public, there are two Elvises – the slim Hillbilly Cat of the 50s and the paunchier jumpsuit-clad superhero of the 70s; even Elvis impersonators ('Elvis Tribute Artists,' or ETAs, in today's parlance) have largely tended to emulate one of these two characterizations. In 1992, the American public was able to vote for which Elvis they wanted to grace a US postage stamp, the young 1956 era Elvis, or the 1973 *Aloha From Hawaii* Elvis; young Elvis won handily, receiving 851,200 votes to the older Elvis's 277,723. But until recently, not as much consideration has been given to the 'middle period' Elvis, the link between the two polarities; and the main Elvis narratives have either concerned his historic rise or his tragic fall.

The ten-year anniversaries for the Comeback Special, the American studio sessions, and Vegas debut passed with little notice. The Comeback Special was first unearthed and rebroadcast as part of a *Memories Of Elvis* package on November 20 1977, hosted by Ann-Margret, combined with footage from the 1973 Hawaii concert. It was the first time the show had aired on television since August 17 1969, and, Steve Binder notes, included the 'bordello' sequence once deemed too risqué; now it aired without comment.

On January 5 1985, just shy of what would have been Elvis's 50th birthday, fans got a special treat when HBO aired *One Night With You*, the complete 6pm sit-down show taped on June 27 1968. Joe Rascoff, then EPE's business manager, had been talking to Steve about ideas for upcoming projects, and was surprised when Steve told him about the Comeback Special's 'out-takes' – the two full sit-down shows. "You have to realize this is years later, after it's all history," Steve says. "And so Rascoff said, 'Well, I'm on the East Coast, would you mind going to Bekins' vault in Hollywood and pulling out what you're talking about and send it to me?' So I said, 'Fine,' and I trudged by myself over to Bekins, went into the vault, and there's all these Elvis tapes there from all his shows. And they gave me a read out, and I pulled the two out-take reels. So I sent 'em to Rascoff in New York. He calls me up and he said, 'Listen, we just looked at one with RCA executives and everybody's questioning, is it worth anything?' And I said, 'Joe, I can't believe you're asking me that question. Show it to anybody in the Elvis Presley world and you'll be amazed.' So the next phone call I got from Joe was, 'Well, you'll never believe this, but we just sold it to HBO for a million dollars. Would you mind going in and fixing it with titles and so forth?' Thank you!"

The show was subsequently released on video and DVD, as was the Comeback Special. But not all editions were complete; for example, 'Are You Lonesome Tonight?' was left off some versions because of licensing issues. And when the Comeback Special was shown on television, it was often edited, something Steve admits is a "sore spot" for him. "There have been so many 'edited' versions of the original, it's hard to even keep track of how many," he says.

In 2004, the *Elvis: '68 Comeback Special Deluxe Edition* DVD set was released, including seemingly all the footage shot for the show that is available. The three discs contain the special itself (though despite what the booklet's credits state, the 'Guitar Man' production number is missing 'It Hurts Me,' with a karate style dance segment in its place), both sit-down and stand-up shows, and out-takes for all the production numbers. This was followed in 2006 by a single disc 'special edition,' featuring yet another edit of the special, with the original show expanded to 94 minutes by including more performances from the sit-down/stand-up shows (and this time the 'Guitar Man' production number does have 'It Hurts Me'). "I actually would have loved to do a re-edit from the original material myself," says Steve. "I certainly saw some changes I would like to have made, since when I shot the special there were only two extra tape machines to record, and I actually cut each sequence live on tape in the control room at the actual time we were shooting. I specifically would have loved to fix the lip-sync portion of the gospel segment that Elvis refused to sing live-to-track on." Ironically, none of the officially released versions of the special have featured the original edit of the show that aired on December 3 1968 – the actual program that initially generated all the acclaim.

In 2008, the four-CD boxed set *The Complete '68 Comeback Special* provided an audio counterpart to the DVD set, featuring the original soundtrack album, both sit-down/stand-up shows, and two rehearsals. The set's liner notes were written by Harvey Kubernik. "When I saw Elvis Presley perform, I never had an idea I would be writing about him in the liner note or multi-CD boxed set arena," he says. "In some ways, writing the liner notes for the '68 Special boxed set did bring things full circle. The liner note gig was a reward, like a fiscal dividend, for all the investment I gave to Elvis over the years."

The box also contained the version of 'A Little Less Conversation' that had been recorded for, but ultimately cut from, the special. In 2002, a remixed version of the song became an unexpected international hit. Dutch DJ Tom Holkenberg had been asked by an advertising agency to work on a Nike commercial to be used in their advertising during that year's World Cup soccer tournament. Holkenberg felt an Elvis song would be a good choice for a commercial, given his broad cultural appeal, and felt the lyrics of 'A Little Less Conversation' in particular were "really spot-on for football."

Work on the dance-rock-styled track was nearly finished before the song was officially licensed by EPE. Holkenberg, who worked under the name Junkie XL, also agreed to change his name credit on the single to "JXL." "When I ask people here in Holland how they remember Elvis, they always say that they remember him being too fat and doing drugs and all this," he told *Rolling Stone*. "But that was just the last few years of his life, when he had this horrible contract to perform two or three times a day in Vegas. And that's too bad, because musically he did amazing stuff, and his performances were amazing. So changing my name for this single was about respecting Elvis and his fans."

Released in June 2002, the remix gave Elvis his 18th Number One in the UK, and it topped the charts in over 20 other countries; while it reached Number 50 in *Billboard*'s main Pop Singles chart, it did top the magazine's Singles Sales chart. A year later, a single of 'Rubberneckin',' remixed by UK producer/DJ Paul Oakenfold, reached Number 94 in the US, Number Five in the UK. The first dance remix of an Elvis track was actually producer/DJ Kenny Jaymes's take on 'Suspicious Minds,' released in May 2001 to DJs only, which appeared on the compilation *Mastermix Issue 178* (by Music Factory of Rotherham, UK). Another song from the special, 'If I Can Dream,' was given new life in 2007, when Celine Dion was shown in a video duet with Elvis that aired on *American*

Idol; the clip quickly became the most downloaded video on iTunes at the time.

American Sound Studios closed in 1972, and most of the 827 Thomas Street Band, aka The Memphis Boys, moved to Nashville, continuing to play sessions, and, in 1990, releasing their own album, _The Memphis Boys_. In the new century, Elvis fan clubs in Europe asked the musicians if they'd be interested in playing shows together overseas. "The Elvis fans wanted to meet the musicians that had played on these records," Reggie Young explains. "And well, yeah, we'll do that. And so we got our group together and went over there and hired singers from whatever country we were playing in; not Elvis clones, just really good singers. And it was amazing. We did most of those songs that we recorded with him, the exact way that we recorded them, same licks, same fills and everything. And after the first show they said, 'We want to do an autograph session.' We're going to sign autographs? Yeah. Gosh, it lasted for about three hours. I mean, they wore us out. They had us set up at tables and we had photos and we signed albums and all kinds of stuff. And I thought, 'All because of Elvis.'

"Someone said that because he never went over there, this is probably as close as they're ever going to get to him, through the people that worked with him," he continues. "But what was really amazing was that it was like seven, eight year old kids to eighty, ninety year old people. Boy, he had a fan base that was something else. Still does, you know."

"We got reviews, and then we got phone calls saying, 'Can you come back? We'll do ten concerts instead of two,'" says Bobby Emmons. "And then the next one was can you do 15 shows, and we wound up working a good gig over there. And it wasn't by the Grateful Dead standards a big concert tour, but it was little fan club things and we felt really good about being there. Because we'd play a little 90-minute concert and people would hang out for two hours getting us to sign pictures and autograph albums that they'd bought for the last 30 years, and they'd line up around the building with us sitting at a table to come up and say hello and shake hands and have us sign something. That's bound to make you feel good, and it did every time. I mean we were side men – no one ever gave us the time of day."

In 2009, Chips Moman finally received official recognition for his accomplishments when he was awarded a brass note on the Beale Street Walk Of Fame, once the legendary 'Main Street of Negro America' in Memphis, and today the heart of the city's entertainment district. At a presentation during Elvis Week 2009, Moman and the Memphis Boys were inducted into the Grammy Hall Of Fame for their work on 'Suspicious Minds.' And the Memphis Boys continue to plays shows at home and abroad.

"I'm surprised we're all still alive," says Mike Leech. "There's a joke going round – if I'd known I was going to live this long, I'd have taken better care of myself. It's great to be around my pals. You couldn't be any more of a family than we are. We're the best of friends and have been for years, and whenever we get to play together and do something together, it seems like that magic is still there. Something just comes out. And we're still quite capable of recording a hit record on just about anybody that might jump in there, you know?"

The 1970 documentary *Elvis: That's The Way It Is* also came in for a makeover, reissued in a new 'special edition' edit in 2001. It was not a director's cut; director Denis Sanders had died in 1987. Instead, Sanders's work was reshaped so that the movie became less a documentary about Elvis and more a straight concert film; most of the interview footage (especially interviews with fans) was cut, though rehearsal footage was retained. It was certainly welcome to get new performance footage, and the film was also beautifully restored. But the original film was a snapshot of its era as much as it was a look at Elvis; its integrity could have been maintained by simply fashioning another film from the unused footage instead of rejigging an existing work to fit new specifications (as was done with the documentary *Gimme Some Truth*, drawn from unused footage from the film *Imagine: John Lennon*). For some years, the 2001 cut was the only version of the film available on DVD. But in 2007, the original version was also released on DVD, in a two-disc set that also included the 2001 special edition version.

In the strangest development, Elvis finally got to give the world tour he was never able to while he was alive, via the production *Elvis In Concert*. The concept was the idea of Todd Morgan, a marketing major at the University of Mississippi who started out at Graceland as a tour guide and worked his way up to be EPE's Director of Media and Creative Development. Morgan wanted to stage a reunion event for the 20th anniversary Elvis Week celebrations, and decided to make it a concert. Footage of Elvis performing (primarily taken from *That's The Way It Is*, the 1972 documentary *Elvis On Tour*, and the 1973 Hawaii concert) was projected on a large screen, with his vocal track isolated. Live music was then provided by the original musicians and singers who had played with Elvis in the 70s.

The musicians all agreed to participate, but were uncertain as to how it would come off. "We pretty much were not very enthused about it and could not imagine how it would be anything other than something that was pretty hokey," says Ronnie Tutt. But everyone felt better when they began to work with the show's producer, Stig Edgren, who'd produced numerous large-scale events as well as an innovative video for 'Unforgettable,' in which Nat 'King' Cole appeared to duet with his daughter, Natalie. "Once he came aboard and started talking to me, I started getting the idea that, hey, this might be possible," says Ronnie. "We even talked over the idea of holograms."

"I thought, there's no way that this is ever going to work," says Jerry Scheff. "And then Stig talked to us all, and told us, 'Yeah, it's going to work, it's going to work.' I still had my doubts, but when I went down there to start the rehearsals I started seeing the virtues of it."

"It was very difficult to do at first," says Glen Hardin. "Ronnie took the tapes to a studio and put some count offs and some clicks and some other things to guide us through it. You had to pay attention to the count offs, make sure to play the intro, because obviously this tape is going to play with or without you. But once we got the hang of it, it became very easy to do." There were also TV monitors placed on the stage so the performers could watch the video footage of Elvis as it played. "I just hear the count offs, and then we watch Elvis," explains Jerry. "And let's face it, that's what we did in the old days; all we did was watch him, follow him. It's like being in the slipstream; you just put yourself right in Elvis's slipstream and off you go. And that's the way we did it."

It also proved to be a more emotional experience for the performers than they'd expected. Joe Guercio, the show's musical director and conductor (the same position he'd held at the International/Hilton during the 70s), recalled that while rehearsing 'Bridge Over Troubled Water,' The Sweet Inspirations had been overcome. "The Sweets could not get through it," he said. "It's an emotional song and there he is on a screen, and here are all the original guys, so they just lost it. We took a break, we came back, and we've been laughing ever since." During the show's first performance, August 16 1997 at the Mid-South Coliseum in Memphis, the emotional quotient was heightened due to the surprise screening of a video Edgren produced of Elvis and Lisa Marie duetting on 'Don't Cry Daddy.'

Since then, the show has played across the US, and around the world, in Britain, Europe, Australia, New Zealand, Japan, Singapore, and Thailand. In 1998, the show received a designation from Guinness World Records as "The first live tour headlined by a performer who is no longer living." One difficulty, especially in the US, has been explaining to people exactly what kind of show it is. "A good buddy of mine and his family were coming to see the show when we decided to take it to the Hilton," says Ronnie. "He was staying at the hotel, and he walked up to the box office, and he was next in line behind somebody, and this guy was saying, 'What's this Elvis thing all about? Who's the imitator?' And the lady that was selling tickets could not explain what it was, so my friend finally said, 'Well, it's the original cast, and Elvis is on film and on this big screen,' and had to give the rundown himself. And the guy said, 'Oh, that sounds great,

I'll take four tickets.' Even the people that were involved with it didn't really understand how to promote it, and how to explain it. I think the curse of that show is that there's been so many imitators. I know they had that problem in Japan. I talked to the promoter over there, a really nice lady, and she found it very difficult to try to explain to people what it's all about."

"It was incredible overseas," says Glen. "In the USA, people didn't understand what it was about. There's just so many misconceptions about it. People think there's an impersonator involved, or they think it's a video of the last concert he ever did. Just all kinds of strange things that people think. It's hard to snap 'em out of that, and hard to explain what this thing is about."

Even though Elvis is only an image on a screen, the show is just as engaging as any other concert. It's also surprisingly moving, undoubtedly due to the participation of the original performers, who imbue the show with a sincerity and a deep affection born from the hundreds of hours they spent on stage with Elvis from July 31 1969 to June 26 1977; the excitement is such that you forget that you are, essentially, watching a movie with live accompaniment.

"It's just amazing how audiences respond," says Ronnie. "I mean, you would think he was there, the way they're waiting for us back at the stage door for autographs; there'll be hundreds of people. It's crazy. And overall the effect of the show is pretty amazing. I don't understand it myself, because I'm driving the bus up there, if you will, and I can't see it. I'm underneath the screen, so I'm back behind everything, and I don't have any idea. All I can judge by is by people whose opinions I respect; they've seen it, and they say, 'Man, this is the most amazing thing I've ever seen. You just become totally wrapped up in it.' And so hearing all of that, I feel good. So many people will say, 'Man, one of my greatest regrets is that I never got to see a live show, never saw him in concert.' And I say, 'Well, this is as close as you'll ever be able to get.' If somebody ten years ago told me I'd still be doing some touring with Elvis ... yeah, right!"

During the later years of his life, Elvis was said to have wondered if his work would even be remembered. It's a kind of insecurity common to most artists. But perhaps in Elvis's case it also reflected his feelings that his later work had not often lived up to his own high expectations, his knowledge that he was capable of achieving so much more. That Elvis had fought his way out of total obscurity to dazzling fame in the 50s was extraordinary enough. Performers who are able to coast on their fame after their hit-making years, touring and releasing records that are no longer huge but still sell in respectable amounts, consider themselves to be quite lucky.

But Elvis's undeniable talents would not have him taking that path. What the entire Comeback period of 1968 to 1970 showed was that Elvis's skills as an entertainer had never left him; they just hadn't been given a suitable vehicle for expression. That he ultimately failed to live up to the promise the Comeback period rekindled was not due to any diminution of talent on his part, as the studio recording of 'Hurt,' from the Jungle Room sessions, or his 1977 live performances of 'How Great Thou Art' and 'Unchained Melody' confirm. Rather, it was the simple fact – often forgotten about those who have achieved such monumental fame – that he was no more or less human than the rest of us, and just as prone to making brilliant decisions or fateful errors.

What remain are sounds that still captivate, images that are still potent. The vibrant performer in his physical prime, whipping his body back and forth with such force during the coda of 'Suspicious Minds' it's as if he never wants the moment to end. The singer who conjures up an almost unbearable sadness during 'In The Ghetto,' his quiet dignity underscoring the pain of being trapped in circumstances beyond one's control. The earnest young man, in a pristine white suit, unleashing all the passion in his soul as he sings of that better land we can find if we never forget the power of our dreams, holding his arms aloft until the final notes of the song fade away, then addressing his audience in a voice that reveals both the strain of his exertions and a pride in his accomplishment: "Thank you. Good night."

End Notes

PROLOGUE FOLLOW THAT DREAM
18 "Do you believe in the afterlife?" Author interview, 2009
19 "When he came out of the army" All quotes from Gordon Stoker, author interview, 2009
20 "He was good in the beginning" All quotes from Julie Parrish, author interview, 2002
21 "He was obviously uncomfortable" Guralnick, *Careless Love*
22 "He wanted to see the world" Unless noted, all quotes from Scotty Moore, author interview, 2002
22 "One of the first things I want to do" Gilbert King, 'Presley: The Living Legend,' *Melody Maker*, September 12 1959
24 "I saw him protest the scripts" Gillian G. Gaar, 'Cross Paths: When Elvis Met The Beatles,' *Goldmine*, August 14, 2009
24 "He was absolutely perfect" Author interview, 2009
25 "I had never known him to do that before" Guralnick, *Careless Love*
25 "We lived on amphetamines" Esposito, *Good Rockin' Tonight*
25 "Eventually Elvis' consumption of pills" Presley, *Elvis And Me*
25 "Larry, I've finally found someone" Geller, *If I Can Dream*
26 "I'm gonna meet him one day" Author interview, 2009
29 "Elvis had to sing a song" Clayton, *Elvis Up Close*
30 "Elvis at the top of his form" Guernsey's *Elvis: The Official Auction Catalogue*

CHAPTER 1 WILD IN THE COUNTRY
31 "As with anything he enjoyed" Presley, *Elvis And Me*
31 "It was impossible for him to say" Schilling, *Me And A Guy Named Elvis*
31 "What Elvis did to the horse market" Clayton, *Elvis Up Close*
32 "He bought 22 trucks in one day" Nash, *Elvis And The Memphis Mafia*
33 "He was tanned" Clayton, *Elvis Up Close*
33 "I'm having fun, Daddy" Presley, *Elvis And Me*
34 "Of the early songs in the movies" Author interview, 2008
34 "That night he seemed kind of depressed" Guralnick, *Careless Love*

35 "Suddenly it was open season" Geller, *If I Can Dream*
35 "I think he'd reached a point" Klein, *Elvis: My Best Man*
36 "A Tired Little Color Clinker" Howard Thompson, *The New York Times*, June 15 1967
36 "Strong rhythm entry" *Billboard*, May 6 1967
36 "[He] gives a pretty fair account" *Variety*, April 5 1967
37 "I'll have you in and out of here" Clayton, *Elvis Up Close*
37 "I wish I'd had the strength"/"It seemed that as soon" Presley, *Elvis And Me*
38 "Good, strong, rugged stories" Guralnick, *Careless Love*
40 "It's a make-believe story" Sharp, *Writing For The King*
40 "Sing the living stuff out of it, El!" Jorgensen, *Elvis Presley: A Life In Music*
40 "I'll put it to you this way" Guralnick, *Careless Love*
42 "Elvis' latest movie track" *Billboard*, November 25 1967
42 "Elvis' songs are as forgettable" *The Los Angeles Times*, November 1 1967
42 "Part Hud, part Alfie" *Los Angeles Herald Examiner*, April 3 1968
42 "It wasn't so much being on the set" All quotes from Sandi Miller, author interview, 2009
44 "Things got jokingly rough" Guralnick, *Careless Love*
44 "It was sad to watch Elvis" Schilling, *Me And A Guy Named Elvis*
44 "Doesn't anyone have some goddamn material" Schilling, *Me And A Guy Named Elvis*
45 "It's not you" Presley, *Elvis And Me*
45 "She's a little miracle" Guralnick, *Careless Love*
46 "To get enough 'gold'" *Billboard*, February 17 1968
46 "Caters to out-dated prejudice" *Variety*, March 8 1968
47 "I can picture him in my mind" Author interview, 2009
48 "In all honesty 'A Little Less Conversation'" Sharp, *Writing For The King*
48 "He put his hand on my head" Guralnick, *Careless Love*
48 "Just Another Presley Movie" Renata Adler, *The New York Times*, June 14 1968

CHAPTER 2 LET YOURSELF GO

51 "The story of Presley as the initiator" Guralnick, *Careless Love*

51 "He wants everyone to know" Guralnick, *Careless Love*

52 "I heard that if you get a job" Author interview, 2003

52 "If you've seen any of the *Hullabaloo*s today" Author interview, 2008

53 "I was kind of unhappy" Author interview, 2008

53 "And it was like a light went on" All quotes from Bones Howe, author interview, 2009

54 "I think Finkel wisely" Author interview, 2003

54 "I don't relate to Elvis" Related by Steve Binder, author interview, 2008

54 "My initial instinct" Author interview, 2003

55 "The Colonel dominated" Author interview, 2008

55 "Here. I want you to have this" Related by Steve Binder, author interview, 2008

55 "I had absolutely no intentions" Author interview, 2003

56 "What career?" Author interview, 2003

56 "If you do this special" Author interview, 2008

56 "I think that very first meeting" Author interview, 2003

57 "And the reason I asked him" Author interview, 2003

57 "My turf is in a recording studio" Related by Steve Binder, author interview, 2008

57 "I've never believed" Author interview, 2008

58 "It was quite an amazing thing" All quotes from Chris Bearde, author interview, 2009

59 "Well, I'll tell you one thing" Related by Chris Bearde, author interview, 2009

61 "I didn't know Jerry Reed" All quotes from Allan Blye, author interview, 2009

61 "Wouldn't it be great" Related by Steve Binder, author interview, 2008

61 "I took it to Bob Finkel" Author interview, 2008

62 "I was one of the few people" All quotes from Bill Belew, author interview, 2003

63 "The gospel segment was twofold" Author interview, 2008

63 "I'd just come from this amazing controversy" Author interview, 2008

65 "I used to joke with him" Author interview, 2003

65 "Billy, I have to be honest with you" Related by Bill Belew, author interview, 2003

65 "Looked more carnival than cool" Mundy, *Elvis Fashion From Memphis To Vegas*

66 "What does so-and-so do?" The conversations in this and the subsequent paragraph related by Allan Blye, author interview, 2009

67 "I was doing the best job" Author interview, 2003

67 "The Colonel didn't want to acknowledge" Author interview, 2008

68 "Thrilling … he was on such a high" Guralnick, *Careless Love*

70 "I really felt, here's this guy" Author interview, 2008

70 "The Colonel kept insisting" Author interview, 2003

70 "You've been around Elvis" Author interview, 2003

71 "They played it three or four times" Author interview, 2003

72 "I talked to Earl about his writing" Author interview, 2008

72 "Anyone who hears 'If I Can Dream'" Love, *My Name Is Love*

72 "Elvis sings this song like a gospel singer" Moscheo, *The Gospel Side Of Elvis*

73 "It was this huge studio" Author interview, 2003

73 "As soon as we finished" Author interview, 2008

74 "I didn't want to recreate it" Author interview, 2008

74 "The whole special was to let Elvis" Author interview, 2003

75 "He just out of the blue called" Author interview, 2001

75 "I'm usually the 'goody goody'" Steve Binder, *If I Can Dream*, unpublished manuscript

75 "The director told us" Author interview, 2001

75 "Steve, the only thing" Author interview, 2003

76 "He implied that he was going to fly a 747" Author interview, 2008

77 "All you had to do was write to NBC studios" All quotes from Sandi Miller, author interview, 2009

77 "He said 'Oh, go ahead'" All quotes from Darice Murray-MacKay, author interview 2008

79 "Do you think they'll like us?"/"Elvis, all you've gotta do" Gillian Gaar, 'Guitar Man,' *Goldmine*, January 9, 2004

79 "Steve, I can't do it"/"What do you mean" Related by Steve Binder, author interview, 2008

84 "Tuned into the darkness" Guralnick, *Careless Love*

85 "You're never going to believe this!"/"That was true" Related by Steve Binder, author interview, 2008

88 "When I looked up at Elvis" All quotes from Chris Landon, author interview, 2008

92 "How was I?"/"I'm happy with it" Related by Sandi Miller, author interview, 2009

95 "Originally, I edited the show" Author interview, 2008

95 "And after they reexamined the production number" Author interview, 2003

96 "What I was trying to say" Author interview, 2003

96 "I got a call" Author interview, 2008

96 "We have a problem, Steve" Related by Steve Binder, author interview, 2008

96 "They were scared to death" Author interview, 2003

97 "We saw it with everybody" Author interview, 2008

98 "Steve, I'll never sing a song again" Related by Steve Binder, author interview, 2003

98 "I'd seen so many instances" Author interview, 2008

98 "No, I could never do that" Related by Steve Binder, author interview, 2008

98 "It was unbelievable" Author interview, 2008

99 "Elvis was completely shut off" Author interview, 2003

99 "We just didn't have the wherewithal" Author interview, 2008

100 "Potent and timely lyric message" *Billboard*, November 23 1968

101 "I felt sorry for him" Author interview, 2008

102 "I was so naïve in those days" Author interview, 2008

102 "I want the wardrobe thrown out"/"You have no idea" Related by Bill Belew, author interview, 2003

103 "The films and ballads" Robert Shelton, *The New York Times*, December 4 1968

CHAPTER 3 A LITTLE LESS CONVERSATION

104 "They had a contest" All quotes from Sandi Miller, author interview, 2009

105 "They ultimately decided" All quotes from Lenore Bond, author interview, 2009

105 "[Presley] seems determined" Roger Greenspun, *The New York Times*, September 4 1969

105 "A lovely, warm, bright, nice person" Robert Blair Kaiser, 'The Rediscovery of Elvis,' *The New York Times*, October 11 1970

105 "Residents are enjoying Presley" *The Superior Sun*, August 1 1968

106 "Audiences may grow a little weary" *Motion Picture Herald*, October 2 1968

106 "I'd like to make one good film" Simpson, *The Rough Guide To Elvis*

107 "He said 'Would you guys like'" Author interview, 2001

108 "Magazines like *Billboard*" All quotes from Bobby Emmons, author interview, 2008

108 "That was what I was into" Guralnick, *Sweet Soul Music*

109 "It sounds more important" All quotes from Reggie Young, author interview, 2008

111 "Tommy kind of ascended" All quotes from Mike Leech, author interview, 2008

112 "When we would get through with something" 'LaGrange Native Chips Moman Talks About His Life In Music,' georgiarhythm.com, November 16, 2008

112 "If I'm not having fun" Guralnick, *Sweet Soul Music*

112 "When's Elvis gonna get some good songs, man?" Clayton, *Elvis Up Close*

113 "I really liked the early Elvis" All quotes from Glen Spreen, author interview, 2009

113 "They Mickey Moused him" Unless noted, all quotes from Wayne Jackson, author interview, 2009

115 "If I had it all to do over again" Dickerson, *Mojo Triangle*

116 "'You like that song?'" Related by Reggie Young, author interview, 2008

117 "I don't even want to tell you" Clayton, *Elvis Up Close*

119 "[Elvis] obviously hadn't had any direction" Dickerson, *Mojo Triangle*

120 "Man, that felt really great"/"It had been a long time" Nash, *Elvis And The Memphis Mafia*

121 "It would be almost like he thought" Clayton, *Elvis Up Close*

121 "We had already done some sides" Clayton, *Elvis Up Close*

122 "Influenced by Dylan and the whole San Francisco type thing" Sharp, *Writing For The King*

124 "I had always thought of ghettos" Collins, *Untold Gold*

124 "There was some discussion" Clayton, *Elvis Up Close*

124 "One is provided" Guralnick, *Careless Love*

124 "We were actually in the ghetto" Clayton, *Elvis Up Close*

126 "I was just doing my job" Sharp, *Writing For The King*

127 "Man, you got the hit" Sharp, *Writing For The King*

128 "If I could sing like that man" Simpson, *The Rough Guide To Elvis*

129 "It all started right here" All quotes in this paragraph from James Kingsley, 'Relaxed Elvis Disks 16 Songs in Hometown Stint,' *Memphis Commercial Appeal*, January 23 1969

132 "Knocked out" Nash, *Elvis And The Memphis Mafia*
132 "Said yes to it the first time" Clayton, *Elvis Up Close*
133 "Might resonate with the Colonel's background" Sharp, *Writing For The King*
138 "[Elvis] strolls through a tedious role" *Variety*, March 12 1969
139 "Elvis at his best" *Billboard*, April 26 1969
140 "He's never sounded better" Peter Guralnick, *Rolling Stone*, August 23 1969
140 "The sound is so superior" Clayton, *Elvis Up Close*

CHAPTER 4 GOOD ROCKIN' TONIGHT
142 "Goddamn it, shit!" Guralnick, *Last Train To Memphis*
143 "We had a call from Tom Diskin" Author interview, 2001
144 "We could make more money" Author interview, 2009
144 "Nobody wanted to do that" Author interview, 2008
144 "What we aspired to be" Author interview, 2008
145 "I wanted musicians that could play" Sharp, *Elvis: Vegas '69*
145 "I wasn't going to do it" Unless noted, all quotes from Jerry Scheff, author interview, 2001
146 "He basically said it'd be a great way" Author interview, 2002
146 "Wasn't a big fan of Elvis Presley" Unless noted, all quotes from Ronnie Tutt, author interview, 2009
150 "The attitude of a champion racehorse" Moscheo *The Gospel Side Of Elvis*
150 "We just chimed right in" Guralnick, *Careless Love*
150 "I do remember" Author interview, 2009
150 "I went to Vegas" Related by Sandi Miller, author interview, 2009
150 "He was so afraid" All quotes from Sandi Miller, author interview, 2009
150 "I had not realized" All quotes from Bill Belew, author interview, 2003
151 "Karate tuxedo" Guernsey's *Elvis: The Official Auction Catalogue*
151 "On July 31 1969" Press release included in Robert Gordon's *The Elvis Treasures*
152 "Remodeled to seat 20 people" Ellen Willis *Beginning To See The Light*
152 "Paul Anka walked around" Mike Jahn, 'Elvis Presley's Comeback Gets Off To Exciting Start,' *The New York Times*, August 18 1969
153 "He was always nervous" Guralnick, *Careless Love*
153 "Big ol' freaky International Hotel" All stage patter taken from Osborne, *Elvis: Word For Word*
157 "He goes into the classic Elvis warm-up" David Dalton, 'Elvis Presley: Wagging His Tail In Las Vegas,' *Rolling Stone*, February 21 1970
158 "Then I thought, what the heck" All press conference quotes from elvis.com.au
158 "With the opening song" Mike Jahn, 'Elvis Presley's Comeback Gets Off To Exciting Start,' *The New York Times*, August 18 1969
158 "Burdened by an oppressive" Willis, *Beginning To See The Light*
158 "I've already seen the show" Ray Connolly, *Evening Standard*, August 2 1969
159 "He is incredibly handsome" Ray Connolly, *Evening Standard*, August 2 1969
159 "I thought it was just a one-time occurrence" Clayton, *Elvis Up Close*
159 "He was almost catlike" Author interview, 2002
160 "Goddamn, didn't that motherfucker"/"Mr. Phillips, I just love that song" Guralnick, *Careless Love*
161 "He just sang and sang" Author interview, 2009
161 "God, I got treated like a king" Author interview, 2009
161 "The phone rings" Author interview, 2009
162 "I never forgave them for this" Author interview, 2008
162 "Being there, in between Jimmy" Author interview, 2008
163 "Off-color material" Guralnick, *Careless Love*
163 "My cousin says that Elvis" Bendewald, *My Treasured Memories Of Elvis*
164 "You know, you should tour stadiums"/"You think I'll be as big" Related by Pete Bennett, author interview, 2008
164 "It sounded like a technical mistake" Author interview, 2008
167 "The culls, the throwaways" Bob Mehr, 'Chips Moman Gives a Little More Conversation on Elvis' 1969 Creative Rebirth,' *The Commercial Appeal*, August 14 2009

CHAPTER 5 PROMISED LAND
169 "I sort of had gotten myself" Author interview, 2002
169 "[Elvis] likes to rehearse anything" Hopkins, *Elvis: The Biography*
169 "The rehearsals varied from" All quotes from Sandi Miller, author interview, 2009
171 "The high collar came about" All quotes from Sandi Miller, author interview 2003

172 "Oh man, we gotta end this song" Bendewald, *My Treasured Memories Of Elvis*

172 "Oh, I forgot to tell you" Osborne, *Elvis: Word For Word*

173 "The Astrodome was a purty crummy gig" Hopkins, *Elvis: The Biography*

173 "This is gonna be rather atrocious" Hopkins, *Elvis: The Biography*

173 "I hope so" Jerry Osborne, *Elvis: Word For Word*

173 "Well, that's it" Guralnick, *Careless Love*

173 "It was during this weekend" Stanley, *The Elvis Encyclopedia*

175 "This great package" *Billboard*, June 13 1970

175 "It was an out-of-the-way place" All quotes from Jerry Carrigan, author interview, 2009

175 "We were just kids" Guralnick, *Sweet Soul Music*

176 "It was an absolute miracle" All quotes from Norbert Putnam, author interview, 2008

179 "Keep playing!" Related by Jerry Carrigan, author interview, 2009

183 "That sonofabitch can play" Related by Jerry Carrigan, author interview, 2009

183 "Those are Elvis's pickles" Related by Jerry Carrigan, author interview, 2009

184 "It was a bit dramatic" Simpson *The Rough Guide To Elvis*

184 "I've got the best title in the world!" Sharp, *Writing For The King*

185 "You realize it's 10:30"/"Well guys, I guess" Related by Norbert Putnam, author interview, 2008

186 "The goddamn thing" Jorgensen, *Elvis Presley: A Life In Music*

190 "What we're trying to do is capture" Hopkins, *Elvis: The Biography*

191 "It is a surprise to see" Robert Blair Kaiser, 'The Rediscovery of Elvis,' *The New York Times*, October 11 1970

191 "I found that I had to" Author interview, 2002

192 "The Colonel grabbed me" Author interview, Landon

192 "Hey guys, it's not my fault!" Sharp, *Elvis: Vegas '69*

193 "Presley is cool and very collected" *Variety*, August 19 1970

194 "You could tell Elvis loved" Author interview, 2002

194 "Here was probably the most" Author interview, 2002

196 "I don't want him sitting around" Clayton, *Elvis Up Close*

196 "It's like a trophy" Mundy, *Elvis Fashion*

197 "We all really felt a release" Author interview, 2009

200 "Capture the excitement of Elvis" Robert Blair Kaiser, 'The Rediscovery of Elvis,' *The New York Times*, October 11 1970

200 "What does Presley think" Howard Thompson, 'What's Opened At The Movies,' *The New York Times*, December 27 1970

201 "That first tour was exciting" Hopkins, *Elvis: The Biography*

201 "We want our fans" Guernsey's *Elvis: The Official Auction Catalogue*

201 "When I heard 'Don't Be Cruel'" All quotes from Harvey Kubernik, author interview, 2008

203 "There have been a lot of things" Glass *Elvis Presley Paternity Suit Uncovered!*

203 "Every number ends with a classically struck profile" Albert Goldman, 'A Gross Top-Grosser: Elvis Presley at Las Vegas,' *Life*, March 20 1970

203 "An imitation of swivel-hipped" Thomas B. Newsom, 'Imitation of 1956 Elvis Brings Squeals at Keil,' *St Louis Post Dispatch*, September 11 1970

203 "He has frozen rock 'n roll" Jack McClintock, 'Elvis: Audience Shares His Past,' *St Petersburg Times*, September 14 1970

204 "Every tune was a lush production" John Wenderborn, 'Old Elvis Comes Through To Delight of Devotees,' *The Oregonian*, November 12 1970

204 "The tone of the concert" Janine Gressel, 'Presley's Show No Blockbuster,' *The Seattle Times*, November 13 1970

204 "Whatever they say" Thomas MacCluskey, 'Elvis Fans Turn Out – 11,500 Strong,' *Rocky Mountain News*, November 18 1970

205 "For the first time in 15 years" Schilling, *Me And A Guy Named Elvis*

206 "The drug culture" Krogh, *The Day Elvis Met Nixon*

207 "I just loved his music," Unless noted, all quotes from Bud Krogh, author interview, 2009

210 "He sure wasn't wearing" Krogh, *The Day Elvis Met Nixon*

211 "I think you can reach"/"I do my thing just by singing" Krogh, *The Day Elvis Met Nixon*

212 "No fighting in the War Room!" Schilling, *Me And A Guy Named Elvis*

213 "I am delighted to have them" Flippo, *Graceland: The Living Legacy Of Elvis Presley*

214 "Presley's sincerity and good intentions"/"Laid the groundwork" Federal Bureau Of Investigation *Elvis Presley: The FBI Files*

214 "Your generous comments" Flippo, *Graceland: The Living Legacy Of Elvis Presley*

CHAPTER 6 LONG LONELY HIGHWAY

215 "People like Lamar Fike" Gillian G. Gaar, 'Elvis, What Happened?,' *Goldmine*, January 15 1999

216 "The ultimate gilded cage." Stuart Bailie, 'King Of The Road,' *Uncut Legends: Elvis*, 2005

216 "It's a peculiar situation" All quotes from Wayne Jackson, author interview, 2009

216 "The paradox is that Las Vegas" Ritz, *Elvis By The Presleys*

217 "Putt, we've had offers" Related by Norbert Putnam, author interview, 2008

217 "And I'm sitting there" All quotes from Norbert Putnam, author interview, 2008

217 "Personally, I think what was too much" Unless noted, all quotes from Jerry Scheff, author interview, 2001

218 "There was one time I remember" Author interview, 2009

219 "In Vegas, I think he got just wrapped up" Author interview, 2002

219 "It was as if [Elvis]" Presley, *Elvis And Me*

220 "It wasn't anything even close" All quotes from Reggie Young, author interview, 2008

220 "Reg, no yawning" Related by Reggie Young, author interview, 2008

221 "He didn't know the songs" All quotes from Jerry Carrigan, author interview, 2009

221 "That's the way it was" All quotes from Bobby Emmons, author interview, 2008

222 "Elvis wants to see you" Related by Jerry Scheff, author interview, 2001

223 "I think he had musically" Author interview, 2002

224 "I want you to listen to this" Related by Ronnie Tutt, author interview, 2002

224 "I can't remember who" Author interview, 2002

224 "And there again the Colonel" Author interview, 2009

225 "Nobody would touch him" Gillian G. Gaar, 'All Things Elvis,' *Goldmine*, August 4 2006

225 "I'll tell you my opinion" All quotes from Chris Bearde, author interview, 2009

226 "I knew it wasn't going to happen" Gillian G. Gaar, 'All Things Elvis,' *Goldmine*, August 4 2006

226 "It's a combination of business" Gillian G. Gaar, 'Crossing Paths: When Elvis Met The Beatles,' *Goldmine*, August 14 2009

226 "I feel a lot of Elvis's problems" Author interview, 2009

226 "We lost Elvis" Gillian G. Gaar, 'All Things Elvis,' *Goldmine*, August 4, 2006

226 "It was the day Elvis suggested" Presley, *Elvis And Me*

227 "Whenever Elvis caught a clear glimpse" Esposito, *Good Rockin' Tonight*

227 "Sloppy" Hopkins, *Elvis: The Biography*

227 "I said, 'Why are you crying" All quotes from Harvey Kubernik, author interview, 2008

228 "The screaming never stopped" Harvey Kubernik, *Melody Maker*, May 8 1976

228 "Terribly tired" Burk, *Dot … Dot … Dot …*

229 "Why he did the drugs?" Ben Fong-Torres, 'Broken Heart For Sale,' *Rolling Stone*, September 22 1977

229 "He was going to go ahead" Guralnick, *Careless Love*

229 "I felt sorry for Elvis" Esposito, *Good Rockin' Tonight*

229 "Oh Putt, you know how Elvis is" Related by Norbert Putnam, author interview, 2008

230 "It was 12 at night" Author interview, 2009

230 "Well, I'll make you a deal" Related by Norbert Putnam, author interview, 2008

232 "We got put right in" Author interview, 2008

232 "I think he got stronger" Author interview, 2002

233 "Fighting to the last" Goldman, *Elvis*

233 "Yeah, I used to call it" Author interview, 2002

233 "I think that that was the only time" Author interview, 2002

234 "If we can scare him enough" West, *Elvis: Still Taking Care Of Business*

235 "He just anguished over this" Nash, *Elvis And The Memphis Mafia*

235 "I want to quit touring"/"This was his vision of the future" Gillian G. Gaar, 'Elvis' Spiritual Search,' *Goldmine*, January 11 2002

235 "Make some changes"/"He was very non-specific" Author interview, 2009

236 "I need the money" Nash, *Elvis And The Memphis Mafia*

CHAPTER 7 TODAY, TOMORROW AND FOREVER

238 "The last year of his life was rough" Ritz, *Elvis By The Presleys*

239 "I've Seen Elvis In The Flesh"/"Expert's Advice" *Weekly World News*, June 28 1988

239 "Excessive, imprudent, unfair" All quotes from the court documents O'Neal, *Elvis Inc.*

240 "Had I realized that the Colonel" Soocher *They Fought The Law*

242 "Presley the singer emerges" Alan Light, *Rolling Stone*, August 6 1992

243 "You have to realize this is years" Author interview, 2003

244 "There have been so many 'edited' versions" Author interview, 2009

244 "I actually would have loved" Author interview, 2009

244 "When I saw Elvis Presley perform" Author interview, 2009

245 "Really spot-on for football" Augustin Sedgewick, 'JXL Exhumes Elvis, Scores X-Box,' _Rolling Stone online_, July 12 2002

246 "The Elvis fans wanted to meet" Author interview, 2008

246 "We got reviews" Author interview, 2008

247 "I'm surprised we're all still alive" Author interview, 2008

248 "We pretty much were not very enthused" All quotes from Ronnie Tutt, author interview, 2002

248 "I thought, there's no way" All quotes from Jerry Scheff, author interview, 2002

248 "It was very difficult to do" All quotes from Glen Hardin, author interview, 2002

249 "The Sweets could not get through it" Hopkins, _Elvis: The Biography_

Live Performances 1968-1970

1968

June 27   NBC Studios, Burbank, California (two shows)

June 29   NBC Studios, Burbank, California (two shows)

1969

July 31   Showroom Internationale, International Hotel, Las Vegas, Nevada

August 1   Showroom Internationale, International Hotel, Las Vegas, Nevada (two shows)

August 2   Showroom Internationale, International Hotel, Las Vegas, Nevada (two shows)

August 3   Showroom Internationale, International Hotel, Las Vegas, Nevada (two shows)

August 4   Showroom Internationale, International Hotel, Las Vegas, Nevada (two shows)

August 5   Showroom Internationale, International Hotel, Las Vegas, Nevada (two shows)

August 6   Showroom Internationale, International Hotel, Las Vegas, Nevada (two shows)

August 7   Showroom Internationale, International Hotel, Las Vegas, Nevada (two shows)

August 8   Showroom Internationale, International Hotel, Las Vegas, Nevada (two shows)

August 9   Showroom Internationale, International Hotel, Las Vegas, Nevada (two shows)

August 10   Showroom Internationale, International Hotel, Las Vegas, Nevada (two shows)

August 11   Showroom Internationale, International Hotel, Las Vegas, Nevada (two shows)

August 12   Showroom Internationale, International Hotel, Las Vegas, Nevada (two shows)

August 13   Showroom Internationale, International Hotel, Las Vegas, Nevada (two shows)

August 14   Showroom Internationale, International Hotel, Las Vegas, Nevada (two shows)

August 15   Showroom Internationale, International Hotel, Las Vegas, Nevada (two shows)

August 16   Showroom Internationale, International Hotel, Las Vegas, Nevada (two shows)

August 17   Showroom Internationale, International Hotel, Las Vegas, Nevada (two shows)

August 18   Showroom Internationale, International Hotel, Las Vegas, Nevada (two shows)

August 19   Showroom Internationale, International Hotel, Las Vegas, Nevada (two shows)

August 20   Showroom Internationale, International Hotel, Las Vegas, Nevada (two shows)

August 21   Showroom Internationale, International Hotel, Las Vegas, Nevada (two shows)

August 22   Showroom Internationale, International Hotel, Las Vegas, Nevada (two shows)

August 23   Showroom Internationale, International Hotel, Las Vegas, Nevada (two shows)

August 24   Showroom Internationale, International Hotel, Las Vegas, Nevada (two shows)

August 25   Showroom Internationale, International Hotel, Las Vegas, Nevada (two shows)

August 26   Showroom Internationale, International Hotel, Las Vegas, Nevada (two shows)

August 27   Showroom Internationale, International Hotel, Las Vegas, Nevada (two shows)

August 28   Showroom Internationale, International Hotel, Las Vegas, Nevada (two shows)

1970

January 16   Showroom Internationale, International Hotel, Las Vegas, Nevada

January 17 Showroom Internationale, International
Hotel, Las Vegas, Nevada (two shows)
January 18 Showroom Internationale, International
Hotel, Las Vegas, Nevada (two shows)
January 19 Showroom Internationale, International
Hotel, Las Vegas, Nevada (two shows)
January 20 Showroom Internationale, International
Hotel, Las Vegas, Nevada (two shows)
January 21 Showroom Internationale, International
Hotel, Las Vegas, Nevada (two shows)
January 22 Showroom Internationale, International
Hotel, Las Vegas, Nevada (two shows)
January 23 Showroom Internationale, International
Hotel, Las Vegas, Nevada (two shows)
January 24 Showroom Internationale, International
Hotel, Las Vegas, Nevada (two shows)
January 25 Showroom Internationale, International
Hotel, Las Vegas, Nevada (two shows)
January 26 Showroom Internationale, International
Hotel, Las Vegas, Nevada (two shows)
January 27 Showroom Internationale, International
Hotel, Las Vegas, Nevada (two shows)
January 28 Showroom Internationale, International
Hotel, Las Vegas, Nevada (two shows)
January 29 Showroom Internationale, International
Hotel, Las Vegas, Nevada (two shows)
January 30 Showroom Internationale, International
Hotel, Las Vegas, Nevada (two shows)
January 31 Showroom Internationale, International
Hotel, Las Vegas, Nevada (two shows)
February 1 Showroom Internationale, International
Hotel, Las Vegas, Nevada (two shows)
February 2 Showroom Internationale, International
Hotel, Las Vegas, Nevada (two shows)
February 3 Showroom Internationale, International
Hotel, Las Vegas, Nevada (two shows)
February 4 Showroom Internationale, International
Hotel, Las Vegas, Nevada (two shows)
February 5 Showroom Internationale, International
Hotel, Las Vegas, Nevada (two shows)
February 6 Showroom Internationale, International
Hotel, Las Vegas, Nevada (two shows)
February 7 Showroom Internationale, International
Hotel, Las Vegas, Nevada (two shows)
February 8 Showroom Internationale, International
Hotel, Las Vegas, Nevada (two shows)
February 9 Showroom Internationale, International
Hotel, Las Vegas, Nevada (two shows)
February 10 Showroom Internationale, International
Hotel, Las Vegas, Nevada (two shows)

February 11 Showroom Internationale, International
Hotel, Las Vegas, Nevada (two shows)
February 12 Showroom Internationale, International
Hotel, Las Vegas, Nevada (two shows)
February 13 Showroom Internationale, International
Hotel, Las Vegas, Nevada (two shows)
February 14 Showroom Internationale, International
Hotel, Las Vegas, Nevada (two shows)
February 15 Showroom Internationale, International
Hotel, Las Vegas, Nevada (two shows)
February 16 Showroom Internationale, International
Hotel, Las Vegas, Nevada (two shows)
February 17 Showroom Internationale, International
Hotel, Las Vegas, Nevada (two shows)
February 18 Showroom Internationale, International
Hotel, Las Vegas, Nevada (two shows)
February 19 Showroom Internationale, International
Hotel, Las Vegas, Nevada (two shows)
February 20 Showroom Internationale, International
Hotel, Las Vegas, Nevada (two shows)
February 21 Showroom Internationale, International
Hotel, Las Vegas, Nevada (two shows)
February 22 Showroom Internationale, International
Hotel, Las Vegas, Nevada (two shows)
February 23 Showroom Internationale, International
Hotel, Las Vegas, Nevada (two shows)
February 27 Houston Astrodome, Houston, Texas
(two shows)
February 28 Houston Astrodome, Houston, Texas
(two shows)
March 1 Houston Astrodome, Houston, Texas
(two shows)
August 10 Showroom Internationale, International
Hotel, Las Vegas, Nevada
August 11 Showroom Internationale, International
Hotel, Las Vegas, Nevada (two shows)
August 12 Showroom Internationale, International
Hotel, Las Vegas, Nevada (two shows)
August 13 Showroom Internationale, International
Hotel, Las Vegas, Nevada (two shows)
August 14 Showroom Internationale, International
Hotel, Las Vegas, Nevada (two shows)
August 15 Showroom Internationale, International
Hotel, Las Vegas, Nevada (two shows)
August 16 Showroom Internationale, International
Hotel, Las Vegas, Nevada (two shows)
August 17 Showroom Internationale, International
Hotel, Las Vegas, Nevada (two shows)
August 18 Showroom Internationale, International
Hotel, Las Vegas, Nevada (two shows)

August 19	Showroom Internationale, International Hotel, Las Vegas, Nevada (two shows)	September 3	Showroom Internationale, International Hotel, Las Vegas, Nevada (two shows)
August 20	Showroom Internationale, International Hotel, Las Vegas, Nevada (two shows)	September 4	Showroom Internationale, International Hotel, Las Vegas, Nevada (two shows)
August 21	Showroom Internationale, International Hotel, Las Vegas, Nevada (two shows)	September 5	Showroom Internationale, International Hotel, Las Vegas, Nevada (two shows)
August 22	Showroom Internationale, International Hotel, Las Vegas, Nevada (two shows)	September 6	Showroom Internationale, International Hotel, Las Vegas, Nevada (two shows)
August 23	Showroom Internationale, International Hotel, Las Vegas, Nevada (two shows)	September 7	Showroom Internationale, International Hotel, Las Vegas, Nevada (three shows)
August 24	Showroom Internationale, International Hotel, Las Vegas, Nevada (two shows)	September 9	Coliseum, Phoenix, Arizona
August 25	Showroom Internationale, International Hotel, Las Vegas, Nevada (two shows)	September 10	Kiel Auditorium, St. Louis, Missouri
		September 11	Olympia Arena, Detroit, Michigan
August 26	Showroom Internationale, International Hotel, Las Vegas, Nevada (two shows)	September 12	Miami Beach Convention Center, Miami Beach, Florida (two shows)
August 27	Showroom Internationale, International Hotel, Las Vegas, Nevada (two shows)	September 13	Curtis Hixon Convention Center, Tampa, Florida (two shows)
August 28	Showroom Internationale, International Hotel, Las Vegas, Nevada (two shows)	September 14	Municipal Auditorium, Mobile, Alabama
		November 10	Oakland Coliseum, Oakland, California
August 29	Showroom Internationale, International Hotel, Las Vegas, Nevada (two shows)	November 11	Memorial Coliseum, Portland, Oregon
		November 12	Coliseum, Seattle, Washington
August 30	Showroom Internationale, International Hotel, Las Vegas, Nevada (two shows)	November 13	Cow Palace, San Francisco, California
		November 14	The Forum, Inglewood, California (two shows)
August 31	Showroom Internationale, International Hotel, Las Vegas, Nevada (two shows)	November 15	International Sports Arena, San Diego, California
September 1	Showroom Internationale, International Hotel, Las Vegas, Nevada (two shows)	November 16	State Fair Grounds Arena, Oklahoma City, Oklahoma
September 2	Showroom Internationale, International Hotel, Las Vegas, Nevada (two shows)	November 17	Denver Coliseum, Denver, Colorado

Selected Discography
(All releases are RCA unless noted)

1967
SINGLES
'Indescribably Blue'/'Fools Fall In Love'
'Long Legged Girl'/'That's Someone You Never Forget'
'There's Always Me'/'Judy'
'Big Boss Man'/'You Don't Know Me'
EPS
Easy Come, Easy Go
ALBUMS
How Great Thou Art
Double Trouble
Clambake

1968
SINGLES
'Guitar Man'/'Hi Heel Sneakers'
'U.S. Male'/'Stay Away'
'You'll Never Walk Alone'/'We Call On Him'
'You Time Hasn't Come Yet, Baby'/'Let Yourself Go'
'A Little Less Conversation/'Almost In Love'
'If I Can Dream' /'Edge Of Reality'
ALBUMS
Speedway
Singer Presents Elvis Singing Flaming Star And Others
Elvis NBC-TV Special

1969
SINGLES
'Memories'/'Charro'
'His Hand In Mine'/'How Great Thou Art'
'In The Ghetto'/'Any Day Now'
'Clean Up Your Own Back Yard'/'The Fair Is Moving On'
'Suspicious Minds'/'You'll Think Of Me'
'Don't Cry Daddy'/'Rubberneckin''
ALBUMS
Elvis Sings Flaming Star
From Elvis In Memphis
From Memphis To Vegas/From Vegas To Memphis

1970
SINGLES
'Kentucky Rain'/'My Little Friend'
'The Wonder Of You'/'Mama Liked The Roses'
'I've Lost You'/'The Next Step Is Love'
'You Don't Have To Say You Love Me'/'Patch It Up'
'I Really Don't Want To Know'/'There Goes My Everything'
ALBUMS
Let's Be Friends
On Stage
Almost In Love
Elvis: That's The Way It Is

POSTHUMOUS RELEASES
BOX SETS
From Nashville To Memphis: The Essential 60s Masters I (RCA/BMG, 1993)
Walk A Mile In My Shoes: The Essential 70s Masters (RCA/BMG, 1995)
Live In Las Vegas (RCA/BMG, 2001)

1968 ELVIS COMEBACK SPECIAL
Let Yourself Go (Follow That Dream, 2006)
Out-takes from the *Elvis* special
The Complete '68 Comeback Special (RCA/Sony/BMG, 2008)
The original soundtrack, both sit-down and stand-up shows, and additional material
DVD: *'68 Comeback Special Deluxe Edition* (RCA/BMG, 2004)
The original special, both sit-down and stand-up shows, and additional material

1969 MEMPHIS SESSIONS
The Memphis Record (RCA/BMG, 1987)
Varying mixes of the Memphis 1969 sessions
Suspicious Minds: The Memphis 1969 Anthology

(RCA/BMG 1999)
Includes *From Elvis In Memphis*, *Back In Memphis*, and additional out-takes
Memphis Sessions (Follow That Dream, 2001)
Includes additional out-takes
From Elvis In Memphis (RCA/Legacy, 2009)
Includes *From Elvis In Memphis*, *Back In Memphis*, and the original singles in mono

1969 LAS VEGAS PERFORMANCES
Live In Las Vegas (RCA/BMG, 2001)
Elvis At The International (Follow That Dream, 2002)
All Shook Up (Follow That Dream, 2005)
Viva Las Vegas (RCA/Sony/BMG, two-disc edition, 2007)
Elvis In Person At The International Hotel (Follow That Dream, 2008)
All include a show from the 1969 Vegas run

1970 LAS VEGAS PERFORMANCES
Polk Salad Annie (Follow That Dream, 2004)
From the February 1970 Vegas engagement
One Night In Vegas (Follow That Dream, 2000)
The Wonder Of You (Follow That Dream, 2009)
Both from the August 1970 Vegas engagement
Elvis: That's The Way It Is Special Edition (RCA/BMG, 2000)
The original soundtrack, and additional performances
Elvis: That's The Way It Is (Follow That Dream, 2008)
Includes additional out-takes and live performances
DVD: *Elvis: That's The Way It Is Special Edition* (Warner Home Video, 2007)
Both original and special edition versions of the film

1970 NASHVILLE SESSIONS
Elvis Country (Follow That Dream, 2008)
Includes additional out-takes

Bibliography

Bartel, Pauline *Reel Elvis! The Ultimate Trivia Guide To The King's Movies* (Taylor Publishing Company 1994)

Bendewald, Judy Palmer *My Treasured Memories Of Elvis* (Memphis Explorations, 2009)

Braun, Eric *The Elvis Film Encyclopedia* (B.T. Batsford Ltd. 1997)

Brown, Peter and Pat Broeske *Down At The End Of Lonely Street: The Life And Death Of Elvis Presley* (Arrow Books Ltd. 1997)

Burk, Bill E. *Dot ... Dot ... Dot ... The Best Of Bill E. Burk* (Shelby House 1987)

Burke, Ken and Dan Griffin *The Blue Moon Boys: The Story Of Elvis Presley's Band* (Chicago Review Press 2006)

Carr, Roy and Mick Farren *Elvis: The Illustrated Record* (Harmony Books 1982)

Clayton, Rose and Dick Heard (ed.) *Elvis Up Close* (Turner 1994)

Collins, Ace *Untold Gold: The Stories Behind Elvis's #1 Hits* (Chicago Review Press 2005)

Cotten, Lee and Howard A. DeWitt *Jailhouse Rock: The Bootleg Records Of Elvis Presley 1970-1983* (The Pierian Press 1983)

Cotten, Lee *All Shook Up: Elvis Day-By-Day 1954-1977* (Popular Culture, Ink. 1985)

Dickerson, James L. *Mojo Triangle: Birthplace Of Country, Blues, Jazz And Rock'n'Roll* (Schirmer Trade Books 2005)

Esposito, Joe and Elena Oumano *Good Rockin' Tonight: Twenty Years On The Road And On The Town With Elvis* (Simon & Schuster 1994)

Evans, Mike *Elvis: A Celebration* (DK Publishing 2002)

Federal Bureau of Investigation *Elvis Presley: The FBI Files* (Filiquarian Publishing, 2007)

Flippo, Chet *Graceland: The Living Legacy Of Elvis Presley* (Collins Publishers San Francisco 1993)

Geller, Larry and Joel Spector with Patricia Romanowski *If I Can Dream: Elvis' Own Story* (Simon & Schuster 1989)

Glass, Bud (ed.) *Elvis: Behind The Image* (Praytome Publishing 2003)

Glass, Bud *Elvis Presley Paternity Suit Uncovered!* (Praytome Publishing 2006)

Goldman, Albert *Elvis* (Avon Books 1981)

Gordon, Robert *It Came From Memphis* (Pocket Books 1995)

Gordon, Robert *The King On The Road: Elvis Live On Tour 1954 To 1977* (St. Martin's Press 1997)

Gordon, Robert *The Elvis Treasures* (Villard Books 2002)

Gray, Michael and Roger Osborne *The Elvis Atlas: A Journey Through Elvis Presley's America* (Henry Holt 1996)

Guernsey's *Elvis: The Official Auction Catalogue* (Harry N. Abrams 1999)

Guralnick, Peter *Last Train To Memphis: The Rise Of Elvis Presley* (Back Bay Books 1994)

Guralnick, Peter and Ernst Jorgensen *Elvis Day By Day* (Ballantine Books 1999)

Guralnick, Peter *Lost Highway* (Back Bay Books 1999)

Guralnick, Peter *Sweet Soul Music* (Back Bay Books 1999)

Guralnick, Peter *Careless Love: The Unmaking Of Elvis Presley* (Back Bay Books 2000)

Hanna, Sherif and Ernst Mikael Jorgensen *Elvis Presley: That's The Way It Was* (FTD Books/Follow That Dream Records 2001)

Hopkins, Jerry *Elvis: The Biography* (Plexus Publishing 2007)

Jorgensen, Ernst, Erik Rasmussen, Johnny Mikkelsen *Reconsider Baby: The Definitive Elvis Sessionography 1954-1977* (The Pierian Press 1986)

Jorgensen, Ernst *Elvis Presley: A Life In Music* (St. Martin's Press 1998)

Klein, George with Chuck Crisafulli *Elvis: My Best Man* (Crown Publishing 2009)

Krogh, Egil 'Bud' *The Day Elvis Met Nixon* (Pajama Press 1994)

Love, Darlene with Rob Hoerburger *My Name Is Love: The Darlene Love Story* (William Morrow 1998)

Moore, Scotty with James Dickerson *That's Alright, Elvis* (Schirmer Trade Books 2005)

Moscheo, Joe *The Gospel Side Of Elvis* (Center Street 2007)

Mundy, Julie *Elvis Fashion From Memphis To Vegas* (Universe Publishing 2003)

Nash, Alanna *The Colonel: The Extraordinary Story Of Colonel Tom Parker And Elvis Presley* (Simon & Schuster 2003)

Nash, Alanna with Billy Smith, Marty Lacker, and Lamar Fike *Elvis And The Memphis Mafia* (Aurum Press 2005)

O'Neal, Sean *Elvis Inc.: The Fall And Rise Of The Presley Empire* (Prima Publishing 1996)

Osborne, Jerry (ed.) *Elvis Word For Word* (Osborne Enterprises Publishing 1999)

Osborne, Jerry *Presleyana VI: The Elvis Presley Record, CD, And Memorabilia Price Guide* (Osborn Enterprises Publishing 2007)

Pierce, Patricia Jobe *The Ultimate Elvis* (Simon & Schuster 1994)

Presley, Priscilla Beaulieu with Sandra Harmon *Elvis And Me* (Berkley 1986)

Ritz, David (ed.) *Elvis By The Presleys* (Crown 2005)

Schilling, Jerry with Chuck Crisafulli *Me And A Guy Named Elvis* (Gotham Books 2006)

Sharp, Ken *Writing For The King* (FTD Books/Follow That Dream Records 2006)

Sharp, Ken *Elvis: Vegas '69* (JetFighter 2009)

Simpson, Paul *The Rough Guide To Elvis* (Rough Guides 2004)

Soocher, Stan *They Fought The Law: Rock Music Goes To Court* (Schirmer Books 1999)

Stanley, David E. with Frank Coffey *The Elvis Encyclopedia* (General Publishing Group 1994)

Templeton, Steve *Elvis Presley: Silver Screen Icon* (The Overmountain Press, 2002)

Thompson II, Charles C. and James P. Cole *The Death Of Elvis* (Dell Publishing 1991)

Tunzi, Joseph A. *Elvis Number One: The Complete Chart History Of Elvis Presley* (JAT Productions 2000)

Tunzi, Joseph A. *Elvis Sessions III: The Recorded Music Of Elvis Aron Presley 1953-1977* (JAT Productions 2004)

Warwick, Neil, Jon Kutner, Tony Brown *The Complete Book Of The British Charts Third Edition* (Omnibus Press 2004)

West, Sonny with Marshall Terrill *Elvis: Still Taking Care Of Business* (Triumph Books 2007)

Whitburn, Joel *The Billboard Albums Sixth Edition* (Record Research Inc. 2006)

Whitburn, Joel *Top Pop Singles 1955-2006* (Record Research Inc. 2007)

Willis, Ellen *Beginning To See The Light: Pieces Of A Decade* (Alfred Knopf 1981)

Index

Acknowledgements

Thanks to Thomas Jerome Seabrook at Jawbone Press who got the ball rolling, John Morrish for his careful editing, and all at Jawbone Press. Many thanks to all my interviewees, especially for their patience with follow up questions, both for this project and others over the years: Chris Bearde, Bill Belew, Pete Bennett, Chuck Berghofer, Steve Binder, Allan Blye, Lenore Bond, Jerry Carrigan, Pamela Des Barres, Bobby Emmons, Larry Geller, Glen D. Hardin, Bones Howe, Wayne Jackson, Egil 'Bud' Krogh, Harvey Kubernik, Chris Landon, Mike Leech, Sandi Miller, Scotty Moore, Darice Murray-McKay, Julie Parrish, Norbert Putnam, Don Robertson, Jerry Scheff, Glen Spreen, Gordon Stoker, Ronnie Tutt, Reggie Young. Grateful thanks also to my transcribers, Ryann Donnelly, Natalie Walker, Gillian Gaar, Marti Jones. Gail Pollock was a big help in securing interviews, and deserves much praise for her efforts, and friendly conversations. Other people whose assistance on this book was very helpful, both with referrals and research: Mike Freeman, May Pang, Patsy Andersen, Anne Landon, Irene Robertson, Richie Unterberger, Joel Selvin, Brian Bell, Tanya Lemani, Barbara Leigh, Alanna Nash, Marty Lacker, Tom Kipp, Bill Kennedy, Jacob McMurray, Susan Graham, Bob Mehr. The books *Last Train To Memphis*, *Careless Love*, *Elvis Day By Day*, and *Elvis Sessions III* were especially useful, and I ended up breaking the spines on two copies of *Elvis Presley: A Life In Music*. Additional thanks to David Osgood, Carrie Stamper, Maurice Bisaillon. And mom.

This book is dedicated, with love and respect, to Scotty Moore, whose stinging guitar lines on 'Hound Dog' got me started on this journey.

Picture Credits